# Jiggs

*Lieutenant Colonel Cecil Harry Jaeger, OBE, Mus Bac, LRAM, ARCM, psm*

# Jiggs

A Biography of Lieutenant Colonel C. H. Jaeger,
OBE, Mus Bac, LRAM, ARCM, psm

by

## Colin Dean

Foreword by
Lieutenant Colonel (Retd) Frank Renton
Principal Director of Music (Army) and
Director of Music (1988–1992),
The Royal Military School of Music, Kneller Hall

In association with the International Military Music Society

Also published by Parapress:
*Sound the Trumpets, Beat the Drums: Military Music through the 20th Century,* Ed. Colin Dean and Gordon Turner

ISBN: 978-1-898594-89-5

First published in the UK by
PARAPRESS
9 Frant Road
Tunbridge Wells
Kent, UK TN2 5SD
www.parapress.co.uk

in association with the International Military Music Society

British Library Cataloguing in Publication Data
A catalogue record of this book is available from the British Library

Typeset in Palatino by Helm Information
amandahelm@helm-information.co.uk
www.helm-information.co.uk

Print management by Sutherland Eve Production
guyeve@theeves.fsnet.co.uk

Printed and bound in Great Britain by
Berforts Information Press Ltd

The cover painting is by Sean Bolan

# Contents

*Lt. Col. Jiggs Jaeger*

# FOREWORD

By Lieutenant Colonel (Retd) Frank Renton
Principal Director of Music (Army) and
Director of Music, The Royal Military School of Music,
Kneller Hall, 1988–1992

I must have first become aware of Jiggs in the early 1960s. I was a Musician in the Band of the Royal Horse Guards led by Major 'Tommy' Thirtle, an outstanding musician and a good, if idiosyncratic, conductor but never a confident showman in front of his audience. We were involved in a series of massed bands events with various other bands from the Household Brigade, and that included the Irish Guards. Their Director of Music, Major Jaeger, by comparison, was a flamboyant communicator who took our ability to play whatever he wanted completely for granted and concentrated on making sure everyone had a good time, and that included us as well as the audience.

It soon became obvious that, to Jiggs, everyone and everything was fair game in the business of entertaining the public, and that any one of us on stage with him, and that included the other Directors, could suffer his rather barbed wit if he thought it would get a laugh. "Build 'em up and knock 'em down" was at the core of his humour. Some couldn't take it and were unhappy; some tried to compete with him and all failed; he was a one-off. He was completely confident in his own ability to handle every situation and every audience, and sure that his approach to band entertainment was the right one, and who can say that he was wrong?

There are many reasons why bands of all stripes are not as popular now as they were in those days but one of them is the inability of so many conductors to communicate meaningfully with their audience. It was meat and drink to Jiggs.

In 1968 he came to Kneller Hall as the Director of Music; I was in my second year as a student bandmaster so Jiggs was now absolutely in charge of my future. He was brilliant. He had a clear understanding of what he was doing, he set Kneller Hall alight and if you could keep up with the pace he set, well then everything was fine. If you couldn't, it must have been very difficult.

Jiggs had an ongoing relationship with brass bands through his work with the Black Dyke Band and he knew that I was working with what had become one of the top bands in the south, so we had some common ground straight away and I got told to do all sorts of things that were above the previously perceived level of a humble student. I revelled in it, and in Jiggs's sense of musical adventure.

In 1969 I was posted to be Bandmaster of the Gordon Highlanders and I know he had a great deal to do with my being selected, even though I had come from a Household Division Band and so had little understanding of what life was like in the Infantry of the Line. When I arrived at the Regiment I discovered that the CO, Band President, Adjutant and RSM had all received a handwritten letter from Jiggs to the end that he was sending a good musician and conductor who had absolutely no experience of life in the real Army, or as a WO1 Bandmaster. Those letters were a lifesaver for me; I made enough mistakes in the first six months to have got the sack a dozen times but between a canny Band Sergeant, RSM and Officers who chose to teach me rather than chastise me, I survived and had seven very happy years with the regiment, and ultimately a long and enjoyable career in army music.

Seldom a day has passed between then and now that I haven't thought of or talked about Jiggs in some way. To so many people he was the catalyst of change in their lives. To me he was a shining light who guided in so many of the things I have done since knowing him.

His last words to me were, "Never forget, Frank Renton, as long as I am alive you will be nothing more than the poor man's Jiggs Jaeger: when I die you can take over." I took it as a compliment.

Frank Renton

# INTRODUCTION

Lieutenant Colonel Cecil Harry Jaeger was very rarely referred to by his Christian names. Indeed, some years ago a very senior Director of Music was interviewed on the wireless and referred to him as Colonel Charles Jaeger, adding that not many people knew his name was Charles – which is hardly surprising, as it wasn't! Colonel Jaeger was affectionately known to all as 'Jiggs' and, with no disrespect intended, this is the name that will be used throughout most of this book.

Jiggs was one of those men whom we refer to as a 'character'. As one highly respected military musician put it, "When Jiggs came into a room, everyone immediately knew he was there."

Many of the people I have spoken to refer to his being a rather complex individual: a man of great humour and personality, someone who could be very pompous at times yet with a friendly and informal demeanour rarely found in his contemporaries. On the other hand, he could sometimes be vindictive and would often react badly if he thought someone had got the better of him. He was a man who was extremely generous in devoting his time and experience to those who could benefit from it, sometimes, it must be said, at the expense of his own family who did not always see as much of him as they would have liked.

Where appropriate, I have reproduced the words of people who knew Jiggs. I have also included details of a number of his recordings and music programmes from concerts and parades to convey the type of repertoire that made him popular with so many people from all walks of life.

I never had the privilege of meeting Jiggs but I can, however, remember seeing him on parade with the Band of the Irish Guards for Guard Mounting and at the Queen's Birthday Parade. My main memory of seeing him in the flesh is from the first Military Musical Pageant at Wembley Stadium in 1969 when he conducted the Massed Bands and compered the Community Singing, while blissfully unaware that there was a thirteen-year-old schoolboy in the audience who would be his future biographer.

Also without his ever realising it, Jiggs played a big part in developing my reading ability, as I can remember, probably before I started primary school, the huge effort I made to read and understand the 'Note by C.H. Jaeger' on the back of an EP record sleeve, to try to learn more about the band pictured on the front cover.

I am very grateful to the many people who have made this book possible by sharing their memories of Jiggs, memories which all relate to events well over forty years ago. I am principally indebted to Maureen Everett and Chris Jaeger whose idea it was that I should write a biography of their father and who have provided invaluable help and encouragement throughout.

I am also especially grateful to Brian Sargent, without whom there would have been a glaring gap in the story during the wartime period. Also, to that great brass band legend, the late Dr Roy Newsome, who so kindly shared his memories of Jiggs's time with Black Dyke, just a few weeks before his own death on 10th October 2011, and to Lieutenant Colonel (Retd) Rodney Parker who sadly passed away on 1st July 2012.

Special thanks go to Lieutenant Colonel (Retd) Frank Renton for so kindly agreeing to write the Foreword.

## Acknowledgements:

John Ambler
Amanda Bain
John Barnett
Nigel Borlase
Brigadier Jonathan Bourne-May
Geoff Broom
Major John Carter
Colin Casson
David Cawdell
Denis Cleary MBE
Harry Copnall
Brian Culverhouse
John Curtis
Major Paddy Dunn
Malcolm Ellingworth
Gary Gibbs
Martin Grant
Paul Harvey
Terry Hissey
Mike Jeans

Dominic Kearney
Tim Lord
Colonel Sir William Mahon Bt, LVO
Mike Martin
Inge Millard
Martina Millard
Steve Misson
Dr Roy Newsome
Lt. Col. Rodney Parker
Brian Reynolds
Norman Rogerson MBE
Brian Sargent
Steve Sellwood
Major Philip Shannon MBE
George and Averil Skinner
Peter B. Smith MBE
Major Roger Swift
Lt. Col. Roger Tomlinson
Lt. Col. Malcolm Torrent
Major Gordon Turner MBE
John Weeks

Major General Peter Williams for granting permission to use material published in the Guards Magazine

The Commandant, The Royal Military School of Music, for permission to reproduce items from the School's Archives

Bill Grainger's History of the KOYLI Band

## The Author

Colin Dean was clearly destined for a life enjoying military music, since his parents met by the bandstand in Barking Park during the celebrations for VJ Night in 1945. He quickly inherited his father's interest in bands and ceremonial.

He worked for thirty years as a Chartered Insurer in the life assurance and financial planning industry before redundancy came along. This proved a real blessing, as since 2006 he has had the great privilege of working as Band Secretary of the Band of the Irish Guards.

Colin joined the International Military Music Society (IMMS) on its formation in 1977 and was to serve twenty years with the committee of the United Kingdom Branch, including seven years as its Chairman. He retired from the committee in 2010 but was asked to continue his involvement by joining the Society's Advisory Panel.

He has written numerous historical articles for the IMMS journals and other publications including Fanfare, the Guards Magazine and The Bearskin, and was the principal author (with a few friends) of *Sound the Trumpets, Beat the Drums*, published by Parapress in 2002, which covered the numerous events which military bands were involved in throughout the twentieth century. Colin has also compiled a book detailing the music programmes for Trooping the Colour each year since 1864 and this was the foundation for the Royal Heritage series of compact-discs recorded by the Band of the Coldstream Guards, three of which featured marches played at the parades spanning that period.

In December 2011 Colin was awarded a Commendation by the Director of the Corps of Army Music for his "exemplary service to Army Music".

Dedicated to the memory of my Dad, Bill Dean (1923–2009), who inspired and encouraged my interest in military music since before I can remember, and gave me the pocket money to buy my first record by the Band of the Irish Guards.

# CHAPTER 1

# EARLY DAYS

Cecil Harry Jaeger was born at 19 Bradstone Avenue, Folkestone in Kent on 29th April 1913 and named after the Cecil Hotel where his father worked at the time. The hotel was situated in London between the River Thames and the Strand on the site of a mansion, Cecil House, which had been occupied by the Cecil family since the 17th Century. The hotel was the largest in Europe with more than 800 beds and was later to become the first headquarters of the Royal Air Force after its formation in 1918. It was largely demolished in the autumn of 1930 although the facade on the Strand side remains as part of Shell-Mex House which replaced it. His second name, Harry, was the anglicised version of his father's name, Heinrich.

*The Cecil Hotel*

Heinrich Jaeger was born in 1879 and came to England from the town of Kassel in Germany to work as an interpreter, waiter and wine-expert at a number of the larger hotels including, of course, the Cecil in the Strand. Some documents show his occupation as a teacher, which probably indicates that he spent time teaching the various languages in which he was fluent and these linguistic skills would clearly have made him a valuable asset to the hotels.

He met his wife, Mina Pickering, while she was working as a waitress in London. Mina hailed from Scarborough in Yorkshire and was one of a family of fourteen children. She worked for a while in the restaurant at the local Victoria Hotel which was owned by Robert and Eliza Laughton, and Mina frequently encountered their son, the actor Charles Laughton, in his younger days. Although not having benefited from a particularly good education, Mina was a keen reader of novels. Her favourite author was Hall Caine and she had an avid interest in Edna Ferber and her novel *So Big*.

Mina moved to London with one of her sisters, Eva, and they shared a room and worked together as waitresses in various hotels and in the House of Commons. She was later to become a 'Nippy', serving at Lyon's open-air restaurant in Regent's Park.

Heinrich had the conviction that good food and good service should not be the preserve of the upper classes and would often take Mina to the classy restaurants for dinner. Much of their courting took place at the music halls and Mina could sing most of the popular songs of the day, while it seems that Heinrich developed a fascination for the way that the English language lent itself to the double-entendre in a way that his native German could not. He was particularly amused by a comedian who had a variation on 'Mary had a little lamb' substituting a bear for the lamb such that "Everywhere that Mary went you'd see her bear behind"! (How he would have loved the Carry-On films!).

The 1911 Census records their details as:

Jaeger   Harry;   Male;     Birth Year: 1879;   Age in 1911: 32;   District: Chelsea
Jaeger   Mina;    Female;   Birth Year: 1885;   Age in 1911: 26;   District: Chelsea

They had three children together, the first being Irene (known as Queenie), then George Edward, born shortly after George V had succeeded Edward VII as King, hence the names, while Cecil Harry followed in 1913. The family was living at Folkestone in Kent at the outbreak of the Kaiser's War on 4th August 1914. If Heinrich had had the foresight to realise what was on the horizon and become naturalised British, a good many lives would have taken a totally different course.

In the event, the war put an end to any hopes of what we would regard as a normal family life when Cecil was just fifteen months old, as Heinrich, being a

German national, was soon arrested as an enemy alien and interned in a prison camp on the Isle of Man. This deprived the family of its breadwinner and Mina became practically destitute, being required to report to the police at regular intervals.

After internment, Heinrich heard nothing from Mina for a whole year and was frantic with worry. When he eventually managed to make contact he found that she was living with another man and already had a child with him called Leslie (but generally known as Bob). The new man, known as 'Uncle Ern' to Mina's children, was a pastry cook and later a general cook at an army base and it seems that she was not very well treated by him.

George was later to write that it was 'Uncle Ern' who made him and Cecil virtually wards of the state, as for most of the war years they were brought up in charity homes, ironically for part of the time with a German widow, Mrs Danzfuss, as a foster parent. However, she made a point of proclaiming her patriotic love of England and her front room prominently displayed portraits of the Prince of Wales and the poet, Rupert Brooke.

Mrs Danzfuss lived in Tottenham in North London, which was conveniently close to Alexandra Palace when Heinrich and other prisoners were transferred there in 1918, so George and Cecil were able to visit him on two occasions. The prisoners treated the boys well and made them some excellent toys including a working windmill and model aeroplane.

Heinrich returned to Germany at the end of 1918 in the first exchange of prisoners between the opposing powers and he was given a small war pension on account of a partial paralysis affecting one side of his face which had occurred before the end of the war. He obtained a divorce from Mina and married again in Germany, fathering five more children, which meant that during the Second World War he was in the strange position of having sons in both of the opposing armies.

In 1923 George and Cecil were moved to the Newport Market Army Training School in Greencoat Place, Westminster. The school was named after the Newport Meat Market in Soho which had become a home for destitute boys during the latter half of the nineteenth century, the name coming from the nearby town house of the Earl of Newport.

The school was run very much on military lines with uniforms, dummy rifles for drill and strict discipline which included the boys scrubbing the place out from top to bottom several times a week on their knees, not to mention darning their own socks each week. There were certainly redeeming features among some of the staff who were quite charming to them but the course of Cecil's life was set when he was taught to play the cornet in the school band.

There were about a hundred boys at the school and there would be regular parades and route marches around the Westminster area, often led by the band.

Their uniforms were blue except on Sundays and special occasions when they would wear bright red jackets with brass buttons which they spent a good deal of time polishing with the aid of button-sticks to protect the cloth.

During the day the boys attended St Matthew's Church School in Great Peter Street, marching there and back, with Church Parades on Sundays at St Matthew's Church. One of the teachers at the day school who particularly influenced the boys was a lady who called herself Mrs Williams but whose real name was Mrs Skeffington. Her son, Arthur Skeffington, was later to become chairman of the Labour Party. After school she ran a drama club, teaching the boys to recite scenes from Shakespeare by heart and acting them out in costume in the nearby Trevelyan Hall. They also did scenes from Dickens as well as

*The Band of the Newport Market Army Training School. Boy Jaeger can be seen second from the left playing cornet and looking at the camera – something that became a lifelong habit!*

performing comic plays written by the headmaster, Mr Mitchell. All this gave the boys confidence in public speaking, which was to be of great benefit to them both later in life. Another big influence on young Cecil was Father Taylor, who trained the choir and taught the boys a good deal about church music, harmony, antiphony, Gregorian Chant etc.

Evenings were often spent doing physical training and there were annual treats which included visits to the Royal Tournament at Olympia, Christmas pantomimes at London theatres and visits to Twyford School in Hampshire to make use of the swimming pool, cricket pitch and other facilities. Summer holidays were spent at Ramsgate in Kent where they stayed in buildings owned by the Egyptologist Sir Arthur Weigall and his family, engaging in early morning swim parades whatever the weather.

Although George and Cecil did not technically fit the description, they were brought up more or less as orphans and that was the assumption made by the other boys at the school, particularly as they never had any visitors. However, one of the boys, George Saville, was later to recall that he had often wondered if the Jaegers did have family somewhere as they would occasionally go off for a while.

The School's annual prize-giving held on 11th January 1927 was attended by Admiral of the Fleet Earl Jellicoe GCB, GCVO, OM, who had commanded the Grand Fleet at the Battle of Jutland in 1916 and later became the First Sea Lord. It must have been a tremendous thrill for thirteen-year-old Cecil to receive a prize for musical excellence from the Earl, one of Britain's great national heroes.

*Boy Jaeger is presented with the School Prize for Musical Excellence by Admiral of the Fleet Earl Jellicoe GCB, GCVO, OM, on 11th January 1927.*

Early in 1927 the school moved to Orpington in Kent, close to the site now occupied by The Princess Royal Hospital. It was taken over by Shaftesbury Homes and this brought a big improvement in the conditions, including the addition of a dietician to the staff. Boys at the school normally joined the army once they reached the age of 14 but henceforth it was to become the Newport Market Army Bands School with the specific purpose to train them as army bandsmen, a move that was to set Cecil on the road to such great success.

Cecil and brother George had been very close, almost like twins, and they had become quite dependent on each other's company, as they were for many years each other's only family. George failed the War Office medical test and was unable to follow most of the boys into the army but, instead, was found a job as office boy to a firm of solicitors in King's Bench Walk, Temple, London, at fifteen shillings a week. He paid part of this to St Andrew's Home and Club, another charitable institution where he boarded not far from the school in Great Peter Street.

However, when the time came for Cecil to leave the school he was accepted into the Army and he was to dedicate the rest of his life to the service of King, Queen and Country.

# Chapter 2

# THE KING'S OWN YORKSHIRE LIGHT INFANTRY

Jiggs joined the army on 6th October 1927 as 4686532, a fourteen-year-old band boy in the Band of 1st Battalion The King's Own Yorkshire Light Infantry (1 KOYLI). His attestation papers recorded him as being 4 feet 9½ inches tall and weighing just 5 stone 9 pounds, with a 29–inch girth, fresh complexion, blue eyes and brown hair. He was pronounced 'fit' following a medical examination at the Central London Recruiting Depot in Great Scotland Yard.

The regiment was one of six English regiments designated Light Infantry, taking their customs and traditions from their role as skirmishers which required the soldiers to act in a more independent role and move swiftly into action, as opposed to the heavy infantry who went into battle in massed formations. As a result they adopted the bugle as a means of passing orders in the field as it could be heard at a far greater distance and was much easier to carry than the cumbersome drums, and they marched at 140 paces to the minute rather than the 120 (or thereabouts) for the remainder.

The sound and spectacle of Light Infantry bands, headed by their buglers and often marching considerably faster than the regulation '140', were always something extra special that attracted great affection from the general public.

The regiment was first raised in the West Riding of Yorkshire in 1755 as the 53rd Foot, becoming the 51st in 1757, the 2nd Yorkshire West Riding Regiment in 1782 and converting to a light infantry role in 1809, being re-named The King's Own Light Infantry in 1821. The Cardwell reforms of 1881 saw the regiment paired with the 105th Foot (Madras Light Infantry) to become the King's Own Light Infantry (South Yorkshire Regiment), the title changing to The King's Own (Yorkshire Light Infantry) in 1887. The brackets were dropped in 1920.

The 51st was one of the six celebrated 'Minden' regiments that fought so gallantly at the Battle of Minden in 1759 during the Seven Years War. It is said that the soldiers picked roses after the battle and the custom continued that soldiers wore roses in their headdress (white, of course, for a Yorkshire regiment) each year on 1st August, the anniversary of the battle. The *Minden March* was to become part of their regimental music.

The Regimental March was *With Jockey to the Fair*, an 18th-century folk song much used by Morris Dancers, and Regimental Sergeant Major Murray persuaded the Commanding Officer to adopt it as a regimental march when the 1st Battalion was in India in 1873. The Bandmaster, Mr Green, was the RSM's brother-in-law and he adapted the tune as a march, which became the authorised quickstep in 1882, introduced by a spectacular flourish from the regiment's buglers.

> 'Twas on the morn of sweet May-day,
> When nature painted all things gay,
> Taught birds to sing and lambs to play,
> And gild the meadows fair;
> Young Jockey, early in the dawn,
> Arose and tripped it o'er the lawn;
> His Sunday clothes the youth put on,
> For Jenny had vowed away to run
> With Jockey to the fair.

In later years, Jiggs was to suggest that the reason for his being sent to the regiment was the Yorkshire connection with his mother's maiden name being Pickering and the fact that she was born in Pickering. However, perhaps a more likely explanation could be that the KOYLI's Bandmaster had worked hard to establish contacts with a number of military schools and orphanages as many, if not most, band boys at that time were recruited from these institutions. The battalion was stationed in Dover Castle in Kent between 1925 and 1927 and the band included a number of boys whom the Bandmaster had recruited from the nearby Duke of York's Royal Military School so, despite its being a Yorkshire regiment, most of the bandsmen at that time came from southern based schools.

The Bandmaster in question was Mr Charles Edwin Raison, ARCM, known to the band as 'Crash' (due to his fondness for loud cymbal crashes) and he was to have a great effect on Jiggs's development and his future. He had served as a bandsman in 2nd Battalion The Royal Fusiliers (City of London Regiment) having joined them on 30th April 1914, and developed as a fine oboe player. He was appointed Bandmaster of 1 KOYLI on 10th December 1926 after having won the conducting prize at Kneller Hall, and was to remain with the battalion for almost twenty years, being appointed MBE and eventually leaving the army to become Director of Music of the Barbados Police until 1963. Jiggs later paid great tribute to Mr Raison, who helped and encouraged him considerably when he was a boy.

*Dover Castle*

*The East Casemates of Dover Castle which, along with the Spur Casemates, once
provided the barracks for the private soldiers.*

*Mr Charles Raison, the bandmaster who was to have such an influence on Jiggs's life*

The battalion had been stationed in Dover Castle since June 1925 and on 19th October 1927, a mere thirteen days after acquiring Boy Jaeger, it moved to its new station at Dettingen Barracks, Blackdown in Surrey as part of 6th Infantry Brigade in the Aldershot Command.

Life as a band boy in those days would have been very difficult, although for Boy Jaeger it was probably a natural progression from the conditions he had been accustomed to at his school. Being very slightly built, it was inevitable that he was sometimes bullied and he once told of an occasion when one of the perpetrators stole his sausage by spearing it off the plate with a fork. Boy Jaeger stuck his own fork into the boy's backside with all the force he could muster and, although he was disciplined, he was never bullied again.

The marches in the band's repertoire in 1927 included: *Bunch of Roses, El*

*Abanico, Punjaub (Old 51st Light Infantry Regimental March), Hoch Habsburg, Distant Greeting, Sons of the Brave, Preciosa Gipsy Chorus (Old 51st March), Under the Double Eagle, Wellington, Colonel Bogey, El Capitan* and *Light of Foot*.

In addition, Boy Jaeger would have begun to learn the combined band and bugles marches which so characterised the Light Infantry and Rifle regiments. In 1927 those in use in the battalion were: *Old Monmouthshire, Aldershot, 56th Brigade, Marching Through Georgia, Brussels En Fête, Paris Belfort, The Little Bugler, Respect Au Drapeau, Sambre et Meuse, Speakers, 140th Regiment, Grenadier Du Caucase, St Cyrienne, Les Allobroges, Brabant, Soldat De La Garde* and *Grenoble*.

As well as these there were a number of marches played just by the battalion's buglers: *The Major, Jimmy Kelly, Tuam, Cede Nullis, Death or Glory, Qui Vive, Valkyrie, Caesar's Camp, Vivat Rex, Quetta, The Workhouse, Les Clarions, Nippon, The Huntsman, Forerunner, Stormont, To Arms* and *The Sentry*.

The Battalion also had its own unique 1st and 2nd Officers' Mess Dinner Calls, written in three-part harmony for cornets rather than bugles.

The Battalion soon settled at Blackdown and on 15th December 1927 it hosted the first visit of the regiment's newly appointed Colonel-in-Chief, HRH The Duchess of York. This marked the beginning of an association which was to last for 75 years, for Her Majesty Queen Elizabeth, The Queen Mother, as she became, retained the appointment with The Light Infantry after the amalgamation in 1968. Buglers from the regiment sounded *Last Post* at her funeral in Westminster Abbey in 2002.

The band took part in the Aldershot Searchlight Tattoo during the following June but would Jiggs, at fifteen, have been too young to be included? Probably, although, like most of the band boys, he had learned to play the cornet and march on parade at school, and the transition to the disciplines of another institutional type of life in the army would doubtless have been taken in his stride.

It was normal at that time for boys to be part of the marching band from around 16 years of age so it seems likely that Jiggs would have taken part in the Tattoo the following year. This was held in Rushmoor Arena from 18th to 22nd June 1929* and opened with 1 KOYLI joining the Bands and Bugles of 2nd Battalion The Duke of Cornwall's Light Infantry, 2nd Battalion The King's Shropshire Light Infantry and 1st Battalion The Royal Ulster Rifles in a display of 'Bugle Marches and Band Accompaniment' playing *The Little Bugler* (Duthoit), *Sambre et Meuse* (Planquette arr. Rauski) and *Marching Thro' Georgia* (arr. Miller).

Later in the evening he would have been part of the Massed Bands of the Aldershot Command, marching on from a position in front of the woods to

---

*The music from the Tattoo was recorded and issued on a number of 78 rpm records; that sound can still be experienced as the records were re-released on compact disc in 2007 by Eagle and Lyre on 'Chivalry' E&L 007.

the march *El Abanico* (Javeloyes), changing to the slow march *Les Huguenots* (Meyerbeer arr. Godfrey) and joining with the Massed Corps of Drums and Massed Bugles to play the march *Aldershot* (Clark). The bands returned to the arena at 11.25 pm for the Grand Finale, marching on to *The Vanished Army* (Alford) and finally playing *Abide with Me, Last Post* and the *National Anthem*.

It must have been a huge thrill to a sixteen-year-old boy to have been part of such an occasion amidst massed bands numbering several hundred bandsmen. Would it have crossed the mind of Boy Jaeger that forty or so years later he would be standing on the rostrum in that same arena conducting massed bands of a similar size? Hardly! It is far more likely that his mind was more concerned with an empty belly, for soldiers were poorly fed in those days. Then there was the prospect of marching perhaps three or four miles back to their barracks after the Tattoo, having already marched that distance to get there earlier in the day and then been hanging around for several hours.

The 1930 Tattoo saw the Massed Bands of eighteen Battalions with the Royal Army Medical Corps Band, marching on in slow time to *Mollendorf's Parade March*, breaking into quick time with *Swing Away* (Cheeseman) and Ord Hume's bugle march *Bab-el-Mandeb*.

Boy Jaeger was clearly making good progress within the band. His first report in September 1928, less than a year after his enlistment, read: *"A very good type of boy. Works hard and will make progress on the cornet. Bright and Intelligent"*.

The following year: *"Has done very well and shows a marked progress"*.

Jiggs spent much of his spare time studying harmony and all band boys were given intensive schooling up until the age of eighteen. In October 1929 twelve soldiers from 1 KOYLI, including Boy C.H. Jaeger, obtained their First Class Certificates of Education. This was noted on his report in May 1930: *"An intelligent and honest boy. Very clean and keen. First Class Certificate of Education."*

He was just seventeen when he began the Pupils' Course at The Royal Military School of Music, Kneller Hall, entering on 26th May 1930. He passed in after being examined by the Director of Music, who recorded that he thought Jiggs's scales were *"very fair"* but he put against tone (in green ink) *"like a gaspipe"*!

Jiggs would undoubtedly have taken part in the concerts held on the bandstand at Kneller Hall on Wednesday evenings throughout the summer months, as part of a band numbering in excess of two hundred musicians. One of these concerts during the 1930 season included Wagner's overture to *Tannhauser*, perhaps Pupil Jaeger's first acquaintance with this great work, which was later to feature so frequently in his own concerts.

Pupil Jaeger demonstrated his athletic prowess by coming first in the Boys' Boot Race and taking third place in the half-mile. He progressed to man service during the course, having attained the age of eighteen on 29th April 1931. On 24th September 1931 it was noted that, *"He made exceptionally good progress on*

*Pupils' Course Kneller Hall. Special Certificate for music. Plays cornet and piano."*

While he was at Kneller Hall, 1 KOYLI moved to Lucknow Barracks at Tidworth to form part of the 7th Infantry Brigade so it was there that he returned when his course ended on 10th October 1931. This station meant that the band was to form part of the Massed Bands for the annual Tidworth Tattoos, held on a slightly smaller scale than Aldershot but great spectacles nonetheless.

The 1932 event was held from 30th July until 6th August, with the Massed Bands grouped into Brigades, 1 KOYLI being part of 7th Infantry Brigade and joining with the Bands of 1st Battalion The Royal Welch Fusiliers and 2nd Battalion The King's Royal Rifle Corps, along with the Band of the Royal Tank Corps whose Bandmaster was Mr F.G. Moss, Charles Raison's predecessor with 1 KOYLI.

They marched into the arena playing *I Do Like to be Beside the Seaside* and *Alexander's Ragtime Band* and then combined with the Bands of the 8th and 9th Infantry Brigades, the 2nd Cavalry Brigade and Royal Artillery (Salisbury Plain) Band to play the great tone poem *Finlandia* by Sibelius, finally marching out of the arena to *Under the Double Eagle* by J.F. Wagner (not Richard Wagner as shown in the official programme!).

1931 saw the band giving concerts at Bognor Regis from 21st June to 4th July, followed by a week on the West Pier at Brighton with some good weather and large audiences. Band Serjeant Mutimer's renditions of the cornet solos *Because, Until* and *I Hear You Calling* were particularly popular and the Bandmaster was plied with many requests for them. Boy T. Davis delighted the crowds with xylophone and tubaphone solos, while Corporal Craven's vocal solos in *Songs of the Plantation* were equally popular. In November 1931 the Band was involved in a production of Gilbert and Sullivan's *Iolanthe* by the Elsie Graham Light Opera Company at Salisbury.

Jiggs had by now begun to make a name for himself due to his prowess on the post horn and he was also in great demand at officers' mess guest nights at Tidworth, particularly when substituting the post horn with the barrel of a .303 rifle. As well as his musical talents, he was an excellent sportsman and regularly won the battalion's cross-country run and on one occasion won the mile, 880 yards and 440 yards on the battalion sports day.

Having progressed to become Bandsman Jaeger on 18th May 1932, he became Lance Corporal (unpaid) on 26th October 1932, becoming paid for the rank on 5th April 1934. His reports continued to bode well for his future. On 17th September 1932: *"Intelligent and industrious of above the average. Honest and trustworthy. Continues to make progress;"* in 1933: *"Continues to make progress as a musician. Industrious, trustworthy and self reliant;"* and the following year: *"Will improve as an NCO with more experience."*

The band travelled to its recruiting area at Easter 1933 to give a Sunday evening concert in the Assembly Rooms at Pontefract, attended by the Mayor and Mayoress. The programme included *Fingal's Cave* (Mendelssohn), part of Haydn's *Farewell Symphony*, *Passing of the Regiments* (arr. Winter), *More Melodious Melodies* (Finck) and *Grand Military Tattoo* (Rogan). Amongst the most popular items were xylophone solos by Boy T. Davis, a trombone solo by Bandsman E. Faulkner and post horn and coach horn novelties by Serjeant H.L. Mutimer and Lance Corporal C.H. Jaeger.

The 1933 season for the band included playing for three weeks at Hove, with their concerts featuring the male voice choir. On Armistice Day 1934 the band played at Winchester where the concert included a breezy opening to the programme with a march *Yield to None* composed by Mr Raison and based on the regimental marches of the KOYLI. This was to be the band's last public function in this country before leaving with the battalion for a three-year posting in Gibraltar.

The Battalion left Tidworth on the morning of 11th January 1935 with the Band of the 9th Lancers playing *Auld Lang Syne* as the train steamed out of the station to take them to Southampton. They sailed on the troopship *Nevasa*, experiencing particularly rough seas and a dreadful storm en route, but arrived in their new barracks to find they had their first real practice room for many years.

Once they had settled in, the Band and Bugles were heavily involved in the ceremonial events in the colony, including the weekly Changing of the Guard which took place at Government House*, as well as the Ceremony of the Keys at Casement Barracks. The string orchestra was making steady progress and played in church every Sunday. The band gave Sunday afternoon concerts in Alameda Gardens once a fortnight as well as a series of weekly concerts on the barrack square which proved popular with all ranks. The regimental dance band, The Pom Poms, was in great demand and took the Rock by storm.

One of the major events was the King's Birthday Parade, involving the entire Garrison, along with a representation from the Spanish Army, which, in 1935, was led by none other than General Franco. The Armistice Day parade that year was held on the Alameda Parade Ground with the Bands of Royal Marines, KOYLI and The Gordon Highlanders, all conducted by Mr Raison.

It was at this time, according to Bill Grainger in his privately published history of the KOYLI Band, that Lance Corporal Jaeger acquired the nickname by which he was to be universally known for the rest of his life. Gibraltar was

*Known as the Convent from 1704 to 1903. The name was changed to Government House in 1903 as a result of strong local Protestant political pressure, In 1943, King George VI visited Gibraltar en route for North Africa (where *inter alia* he visited 1st Battalion Irish Guards) and decreed that the name should revert to the Convent, which it remains to this day.

*The KOYLI Dance Band, the Pom Poms, 1935–36*
*Rear: Bandsman Halle; Bandsman Davies; Mr Raison (Bandmaster)*
*Front: Bandsman Faulkner; Bandsman Taylor; Lance Corporal Jaeger; Band Serjeant*
*Thompson; Bandsman Hughes; Bandsman Richards; Bandsman Reeves*

home to a number of peddlers of somewhat doubtful postcards which included a series of cartoons of what was termed an "amusingly sexist nature", the male character being a Mr Jiggs who bore a remarkable resemblance to a certain Lance Corporal Jaeger in the band!

Amongst the other members was Bandsman Ben Simpson who in later years was to become Band Sergeant of the Coldstream Guards, and Bandmaster of the Honourable Artillery Company. Playing E flat bass was Bandsman 'Flat' Farrar who was to serve under Jiggs as a member of the Band of the Irish Guards.

For part of the time in Gibraltar the band was required, somewhat unwillingly, to provide working parties to assist the Royal Engineers in laying cables, largely due to the battalion being under strength. Time was also spent firing on the ranges, with a number of bandsmen becoming 'marksmen', largely thanks to some 'assistance' from those checking the scoring!

The outbreak of the Spanish Civil War in July 1936 had a major impact on life for the battalion. An attempted *coup d'état* against the government by a group of Spanish Army generals left Spain divided between supporters of the existing Republican government and the new Nationalist government.

This all happened without warning, and the band had spent the day in French Morocco on a trip to Tangier, arriving back after having a fine time there, to find that their passes for a bullfight at La Linea the next day had been cancelled. The first the bandsmen knew of the revolt was on hearing shots being fired on the Spanish side of the frontier around the time of reveille. The battalion was confined to the Rock and for a while they were living with sounds and sights of the civil war. The war eventually ended in 1939 with the victory of the Nationalists, which brought the aforementioned General Francisco Franco to power.

Jiggs, meanwhile, had been studying hard with much support and encouragement from Mr Raison. The 'Band Notes' in the December 1935 edition of the regimental magazine, *The Bugle*, recorded congratulations to Lance Corporal Jaeger for his extremely fine festival anthem *Rejoice in the Lord*.

His fine reports continued: 15th August 1935: *"An excellent musician who is developing into an NCO and has done much towards the success of the dance band. Keen, hardworking and a good sportsman."*

9th September 1936: *"A very promising Bandsman who is going to Kneller Hall for the Students Course. He is an excellent musician, very enthusiastic. He has very good manners, is intelligent, industrious and trustworthy. He is strictly sober. A good sportsman."*

As 1936 drew towards its close it was time for Jiggs to leave behind his friends and colleagues and return to England to prepare for the next stage of his life.

# CHAPTER 3

# KNELLER HALL – STUDENT

C hristmas 1936 saw the country in the wake of the abdication crisis that had rocked the nation, King George VI having acceded to the throne just a few days before, on 11th December. This was about the time Jiggs was saying his farewells to his KOYLI friends and it must have been with a certain sense of trepidation that he returned to Kneller Hall on 29th December 1936 as a student to study to become a bandmaster (the term 'Student Bandmaster' was not introduced until 1950). He was promoted to corporal the following day. His classmates, in what was to be named The Churchill Class, included:

**Thomas Clegg**, 1st Battalion The Buffs. He came top of the class and was appointed Bandmaster of 1st Battalion The Welch Regiment on 19th December 1941.

**George Craig**, 2nd Battalion The East Yorkshire Regiment. He received a wartime commission in the Royal Army Service Corps and served as a major, working as a staff officer during the war. At the cessation of hostilities he resigned his commission and returned to Kneller Hall as a senior student and was eventually posted as bandmaster of Jiggs's old band, 1st Battalion The King's Own Yorkshire Light Infantry on 1st February 1947, some seven years after qualifying. However, the appointment was short-lived as he retired a few months later, seemingly suffering from the trauma of the war.

**James Hempstead**, 1st Battalion The Devonshire Regiment. Appointed Bandmaster of the 17th/21st Lancers on 19th December 1941. He retired from the Army in 1950 and became Bandmaster of the Gold Coast Police, followed from 1961 with ten years as Director of Music of the Fiji Police Force.

**Leslie Morley**, The Royal Leicestershire Regiment. Appointed Bandmaster of 1st Battalion The King's Own Royal Regiment on 19th December 1941.

**Thomas Noble**, 1st Battalion The Durham Light Infantry. Appointed Bandmaster of 16th/5th The Queen's Royal Lancers on 19th December 1941. He became an MBE and his arrangement of the regimental quick march was used until amalgamation in 1993.

**Donald Seed**, 1st Battalion The Border Regiment. Appointed Bandmaster of 2nd Battalion The Duke of Wellington's Regiment (West Riding) on 16th February 1942. He was the battalion's last Bandmaster before its disbandment, when he transferred to the 1st Battalion.

**Richard Soars**, Royal Artillery Mounted Band. Appointed Bandmaster of 1st Battalion The Royal Ulster Rifles on 19th December 1941, later becoming MBE.

**Ernest Wragg**, 1st Battalion The Suffolk Regiment. Appointed Bandmaster of the 5th Royal Inniskilling Dragoon Guards on 27th March 1945. He later became the School Bandmaster at Kneller Hall and subsequently emigrated to become Director of Music of The Royal Canadian Artillery Band (Coastal), based at Halifax, Nova Scotia, in the rank of Captain.

The remaining Student in the class photograph, W. Bidgood, was not appointed as a bandmaster.

*Caricature of Students at Kneller Hall with Jiggs depicted in the bottom centre.*

The Director of Music was Major (later Lieutenant Colonel) Hector Adkins, who had reigned at Kneller Hall since 1921 and whom Jiggs would have remembered from the pupils' course with his 'gaspipe' description of his playing. Known to all as 'Adko', he was far from popular and ruled with a system of fining bandsmen for any inattention or error. However, he was without doubt one of the most influential musicians ever to have served in the army and it is perhaps a little unfair that history remembers him now chiefly for his court-martial.

*Student Bandmasters circa 1937 with 'Adko' in the centre. For some reason Jiggs was not in the picture. (Photo: RMSM)*

The Coronation of King George VI took place on 12th May 1937 when Jiggs was still in his probationary period at Kneller Hall and involved him becoming one of the original players of the fanfare trumpets that are now so very much a part of military music.

It can reasonably be assumed that trumpeters would have sounded fanfares at Coronations since way back in history but these would have been State Trumpeters playing E Flat Cavalry Trumpets. Indeed, the State Trumpeters at the Coronation of King Edward VII in 1902 were made up of a Professor and seven Students from Kneller Hall. These trumpets produce what is perhaps the most stirring sound in all of military music although they are somewhat limited in the notes available to them.

For the 1937 Coronation, a complete family of valved fanfare trumpets was designed by 'Adko'. By adding a loop to the tubing of Bach or Aida trumpets they were made better balanced and easier to hold, particularly when a banner was attached. In addition, tenor and bass trombones were developed to fit the same basic size and shape as the trumpets so that they could be used alongside and be perfectly compatible visually. They were, of course, much heavier!

To embellish these new fanfare trumpets, a banner was designed by Mr Kruger Gray, a heraldic designer who was better known for the design of some of the coinage including the florin and half-crown. The banners depict the crown of The Royal Military School of Music and the clarion (or organ stops), which allude to the musical training at the school.

For the Coronation Service, the Trumpeters of The Royal Military School of Music, Kneller Hall were positioned high up on the organ loft in Westminster Abbey and, as far as can be ascertained, this appears to be the first occasion that they were used. They were to become one of our national institutions over several decades, performing at so many great state occasions, and Jiggs was to conduct them just four hours before his death.

The Trumpeters at the Coronation were conducted by Major Adkins and sounded fanfares specially composed for the occasion by Sir Ernest Bullock,

*The Coronation Service in Westminster Abbey with the Kneller Hall Trumpeters on the organ loft*

*The Kneller Hall Band and Trumpeters who took part in the Coronation of King George VI in 1937*

Organist at Westminster Abbey, who shared the orchestral conducting with Sir Adrian Boult. They also joined the orchestra and chorus in Hubert Parry's great anthem *I Was Glad*. Outside the Abbey were more Trumpeters from Kneller Hall who sounded fanfares composed by 'Adko' as members of the Royal Family arrived.

Jiggs and his colleagues must surely have had one of the best of all views of the coronation service and it would have undoubtedly been a fantastic experience and musical treat to be amongst so many of the top musicians of the day, playing such magnificent music together including the first performance of William Walton's great coronation march, *Crown Imperial*. Jiggs was later to describe the Coronation as *"One of the great musical highlights of one's life,"* and we can be certain that this was a sentiment shared by everyone who was in the Abbey that day. All those from Kneller Hall who played in the Abbey received the Coronation Medal.

The team of sixteen trumpeters and six side drummers in the Abbey included two other future Directors of Music. Major George Stunell was to direct the Band of the Royal Military Academy, Sandhurst, and is particularly remembered as the arranger of the marches of a number of the Army's smaller corps. Major 'Billy' Williams MBE ended his Army career with the Royal Artillery Mounted Band and went on to achieve great popularity as Director of Music of the much missed Metropolitan Police Band.

The Wednesday evening concerts at Kneller Hall date back to at least the 1880s and serve the dual purpose of providing entertainment for the local population while giving the Students the valuable experience of conducting a large band, up to 250 strong, in front of an audience. Student Jaeger's debut as a conductor appears to have been just a week after the Coronation, on 19th May 1937, taking the band through *Hussarenritt* (Hussars Ride) by Spindler. Also on the rostrum that evening was Jiggs's future brother-in-law, Student Vic Webster, who conducted John Ansell's *Three Irish Dances*.

Most of the conducting at that time appears to have been undertaken by the more senior students but Jiggs had his turn again on 22nd June the following year, conducting *La Manola* (Eilenberg), Student Webster this time closing the concert with the *Scherzo and Finale* from Beethoven's *5th Symphony*. On 17th August Jiggs was conducting the fiendishly difficult (for the clarinets) *Tarentelle de Belphegor* by Roch Albert, actually one of many pen names used by Louis Jullien employing two of his numerous Christian names. The last concert in the month was always designated a Grand Concert and on 26th July 1939 this included Jiggs conducting a male voice chorus in two items, *Little Jack Horner* and *Come to the Fair*.

Jiggs's first annual report as a Student came from the Adjutant on 30th September 1939: *"An intelligent and reliable NCO. Good at games. Clean, smart. Has plenty of initiative."* The following year he was: *"Above average in initiative and intelligence. Self reliant and willing to help others. Always well turned out."*

*Students receiving tuition with a bespectacled Jiggs sucking his pencil.*

Jiggs obtained the diploma of Associate of the Royal College of Music (ARCM) in 1939, later recalling that during his preparation he had been tipped off by a friend that the appointed examiner happened to have just one weakness in the brass field – he knew very little about the euphonium. As a result Jiggs, who was competent on most brass instruments, opted to take his practical on – the euphonium! He obtained the Licentiate of the Royal Academy of Music (LRAM) in 1941.

The Grand Concert held on Wednesday 30th August 1939 opened with four fanfares played by what were described in the programme as the 'Kneller Hall Coronation Trumpeters under Doctor H.E. Adkins'. Two of these fanfares had been composed by 'Adko' for playing outside the Abbey as the processions arrived: *Fanfare for Royal Dukes* and *Fanfare for Their Majesties*. The remainder of the programme that night was:

| | | |
|---|---|---|
| March | **The Sphinx** | *Student W. J. Hickman* |
| | Conducted by the Composer | |
| Overture: | **William Tell** | *Rossini* |
| | Conductor: Student E. E. Snape ARCM | |
| Xylophone Solo: | **Skeleton Dance** | *Abbey* |
| | Soloist: Pupil R. A. D. Myatt | |
| | Conductor: Sergeant J. Parrott | |
| Suite: | **Neapolitan Scenes** | *Massenet* |
| | Conductor: Student C. A. Adams ARCM | |
| Organ Divertissement: | **Imitations** | *Hurst* |
| | Student R. Hurst ARCM at the Organ | |
| Valse | **Les Patineurs (The Skaters)** | *Waldteufel* |
| | Conductor: Student G. Townsend | |
| Male Voice Chorus: | **Let the Bullgine Run** | *Arr. Terry* |
| | **The Smuggler's Song** | *Edmunds* |
| | Conductor: Student W. T. Brown | |
| Excerpts from: | **The Gondoliers** | *Sullivan* |
| | Conductor: Student C. H. Jaeger ARCM | |
| Song: | **The Toreador's Song from** *Carmen* | *Bizet* |
| | Soloist: Douglas Taylor, Baritone | |
| | Conductor: Student L. E. Cox ARCM | |
| Overture: | **The Flying Dutchman** | *Wagner* |
| | Conducted by the Director of Music | |

**Evening Hymn**

**Rule Britannia**          **The Last Post**

**God Save the King**

This concert took place just four days before the declaration of war and was thus destined to be the last held at Kneller Hall until normality returned on 7th May 1947. In fact, the Commandant's mobilisation plans were put into effect on 2nd September with all pupils being returned to their units. Kneller Hall was very quickly taken over by the staff of the General Headquarters Home Forces and instructions were issued for the students to evacuate the buildings, taking all personal kit and bedding. Student Jaeger was one of 22 Students to be accommodated in the squash court, the remainder being allocated to the silent rooms. His final examination took place a week later.

A letter from the War Office on 28th September confirmed the intention to close the school and stated that the 60 Students, less eight retained at Kneller Hall by GHQ, were to be granted up to 48 hours' leave and then report to their Depot Training Regiments where they were to remain available for recall should it be found possible to reassemble the students' courses. Reassemble they did, on 5th December 1939 at Churchill House in Aldershot, where the School was to remain until 1946. 'Adko' was given the additional responsibilities as Commandant as well as being the Director of Music.

Jiggs's final report from the Adjutant, dated 30th September 1939, read: *"A well educated NCO who is much above average in all respects, combined with being a good instrumentalist he has abundant common sense."* He eventually graduated, winning first prize for arranging and coming second in the competition to compose an original quick march. Again, his athletic talents had come to the fore, having been part of A Company's team winning the challenge relay race, and being awarded his School Colours in Athletics on 31st October 1939.

This must have been a time of immense frustration for Jiggs as, after three years of intensive study, he had finally qualified at a time when the wartime provisions meant that serving bandmasters were not allowed to retire and accordingly there were no positions available for the newly qualified students. Jiggs and his colleagues were therefore returned to their original regiments; in the case of Jiggs it was back to The King's Own Yorkshire Light Infantry.

*The graduating Churchill (1940) Class, presumably at Churchill House at the time when most of the Students (but not Jiggs and the others shown as insets) were given their appointments. Photo: RMSM*

Insets: *Student Craig, Student Wragg, Student Jaeger, Student Bidgood*
Back Row: *Student Soars, Student Morley, Student Noble, Student Seed*
Front Row: *Band Sergeant Major Hempstead, RSM Martin MBE, Lt. Col. Adkins, Student Clegg*

# CHAPTER 4

# WARTIME – KOYLI AGAIN

The outbreak of war on 3rd September 1939 had meant that the Band of 1st Battalion The King's Own Yorkshire Light Infantry effectively ceased to exist, with the band members becoming medics or in some cases, transferring to the Battalion or Brigade Intelligence sections.

In 1940 orders were given for bands to be re-formed, and the twenty or so band boys who were too young for overseas service formed the nucleus of the new KOYLI Band. Along with a number of professional musicians who were being called up and a few pre-war members who had returned to England due to illness, Mr Raison managed to mould them into an effective unit. The Band was based at Strensall Camp, some six or seven miles north of York, as part of VIth Infantry Training Centre, which was then the training centre for The West Yorkshire Regiment, The Lancashire Fusiliers and the KOYLI. A KOYLI officer who was based at Strensall at that time was to recall that, despite training hard, they lived quite comfortably and enjoyed the weekly band night dinners when the depot band and bugles played on the lawn or in the hall.

Jiggs returned to the band as principal cornet and, in addition, he was granted the honorary appointment of Bugle Major by Brigadier Leslie Weiler, commanding the VIth ITC. One of the boys recruited at Strensall to play E flat bass was Ray Pinkney, later to become Major Pinkney, Director of Music of the Royal Artillery Alanbrooke Band.

In order to make good use of his time at Strensall, Jiggs took up studies with Sir Edward Bairstow, which eventually led to him attaining the degree of Bachelor of Music at Durham University in July 1949, something which was then a very rare achievement amongst military musicians. Dr Bairstow had been the organist at York Minster since 1913 and was to hold the post until his death in 1946, as well as being Professor of Music at Durham University where he had completed his doctorate in 1902. His own compositions were mostly for organ as well as a small amount of chamber music.

While a Student at Kneller Hall, Jiggs had met his future wife, Eileen Webster, who was frequently at the School to play tennis with her elder brother, fellow-Student Victor Webster. Jiggs was once quoted as saying that Eileen could hit

*Bugle Major Jaeger at the head of the Band and Bugles of The King's Own Yorkshire Light Infantry, marching through York in 1941.*

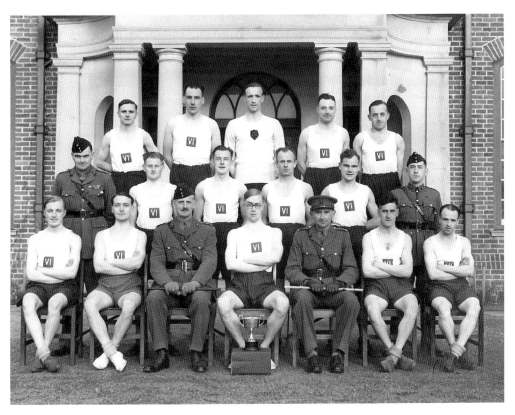

*Athletics Team – Strensall 1940–42.*
*Bugle Major Jaeger is second from left of picture, front row.*

a tennis ball like a man; whether this was intended as a compliment was never really established!

*Eileen Webster*

Victor Ernest Webster MBE ARCM was described as being "quite a card" and it seems that while a Student he liked nothing better than to rattle the cage and wind up 'Adko'. He was born in 1908 and had joined the Band of 1st Battalion The Suffolk Regiment in June 1924. He was two years ahead of Jiggs and took up his bandmaster appointment on Armistice Day 1938 with 2nd Battalion The Queen's Own Cameron Highlanders. After the outbreak of war he returned to that regiment's depot at Inverness to train band boys.

*Student Vic Webster*

He was to remain with the Camerons until December 1947 when he moved to Rhodesia to become Bandmaster of the 6th King's African Rifles, transferring again in 1952 to the Tanganyika Police and in 1964 to Zambia where he served until 1973. He continued to visit England each year and several times went on what the family described as "major benders" with Jiggs. He retired in Rhodesia but sadly got caught up in the excesses of Mugabe's thugs and died from a heart attack after being confronted by a gang threatening to take his house away from him.

Eileen Bertha Webster was born on 3rd September 1912 at Inniskilling where her father, Ernest Webster, was serving as Band Sergeant with The Royal Inniskilling Fusiliers. Ernest hailed from Manchester and continued to serve during the Great War in which he spent three years as a prisoner-of-war, with his family having no idea where he was or whether he was still alive. He was made to work in paper mills, where the prisoners did their level best to sabotage the machinery. He escaped twice and at the second attempt he lay low during the day and spent the nights travelling by crawling so as not to be spotted, eventually reaching Switzerland from where he was repatriated.

In the meantime, his wife and children had been helped by a relation to return to England, where they lived in Berkshire. Ernest eventually turned up and after the war he obtained work as a warder at Feltham Borstal; it seems that he got the job because they wanted someone to start a band there.

The family moved to a home on the site and this was where Eileen was brought up, the place being completely autonomous and self-sufficient with its own farm to provide meat and vegetables. Ernest's wife, Bertha, died from a heart condition when Eileen was 14; perhaps the birth of five children in six years proved too much for her. Eileen worked in London as a civil servant but was evacuated to Blackpool with her department during the war.

Jiggs and Eileen were married at All Saints' Church, Laleham in Middlesex on 14th September 1940, the day before what was to become known as Battle of Britain Day. Jiggs's address was shown as the Infantry Training Centre, KOYLI at Strensell. They got married from Eileen's sister's house in Staines, near Laleham. Jiggs had been careless over booking the hotel for their honeymoon so they had to return to the sister's late at night and knock on the window – not a good start to the marriage, as they had to spend their first night as a married couple sleeping on the floor.

*Eileen on her wedding day. No other photographs survived of the day.*

They lived in Strensell for their first year or two of marriage and it was at this time that Eileen suggested they use the more correct German form of pronouncing their surname – 'Yay-ger' rather than 'Jay-ger' as he had previously done.

During 1941 Jiggs became involved with the Choir of Monkgate Methodist Church in York. The Organist and Choirmaster, Mr 'Archie' Sargent, had built up a particularly fine choir which rather bucked the wartime trend by expanding steadily, giving numerous concerts in the locality despite the 'blackout' and petrol rationing.

As well as its essential contributions to the weekly services, the choir also gave many oratorio and cantata performances supporting various good causes, and achieved international fame at this time with its popular series of some 22 radio broadcasts which undoubtedly did much to help sustain national morale. Indeed, after each broadcast, Mr Sargent received sackfulls of mail expressing appreciation; he insisted on personally replying to each letter.

Jiggs had been listening to these broadcasts for some time and one Sunday morning in November 1941 he decided to apply to join; but it was by no means a snap decision as he was later to write: *"It had taken me a long time to make up my mind to go at all, for although I love singing in chorus, and even more in 'Messiah' choruses, I could not pluck up sufficient courage to go to Monkgate the previous year."* Jiggs's concern was that *"only the most experienced singers could be admitted to the chorus."*

*The Band and Bugles of the Infantry Training Centre, The King's Own Yorkshire Light Infantry, 22nd April 1941. Seated in the centre at the front is the Colonel of the Regiment, General Sir Charles Deeds, KCB, CMG, DSO. Bugle Major Jaeger is seen to his right (in the picture) holding his parade cane, with the Bandmaster, Mr Raison, to the General's left. Second from the left in that row is Band Serjeant Ben Simpson, later Bandmaster of the Honourable Artillery Company, while in the third row, third from the right (without the pouch belt) is Lance Corporal 'Flat' Farrar who later transferred to the Irish Guards and served for many years under Jiggs.*

Mr Sargent was rarely in a hurry to get away after a service and on this day, with the choir all gone, he was sitting on a bench changing his shoes, with his fourteen-year-old son, Brian. Jiggs appeared in the vestry presenting the image of a severe-looking man of decisive military bearing, immaculate in spruce and spotless uniform and rimless spectacles with a freshly printed visiting card at the ready and almost clicking his heels as he addressed the choirmaster.

*"Mr Sargent?"* he asked, *"My name is Jaeger; my card. I should deem it a privilege to be permitted to sing in your choir."* Jiggs's earlier fears were unfounded and to return to his own words: *"How little did I know of the spirit of fellowship that prevailed, and how unnecessary was this uneasiness."* That brief introduction led to a great friendship, not only on a musical level but also at a spiritual level since the Sargents were devout folk, out-going, warm-hearted and very hospitable. Jiggs later confessed that his apparent sternness that day arose from his nervousness.

Thereafter, whenever his military duties allowed, Jiggs would sing tenor in the choir, making the journey of six miles each way – not easy in wartime and the Sargents were never quite sure how he managed it. On some occasions Jiggs would take his trumpet to accompany Archie Sargent at the organ in services, concerts, cantatas and in *Messiah* (Handel); he played the *Trumpet Voluntary* (Clarke) on a number of occasions. When they first met at the church to rehearse together, the trumpet and organ could not be induced by any means known to sound at the same pitch. After trying vainly, Archie suggested that the organ should play in D flat and the trumpet in D, fortunately producing a perfect blend for the service that evening. The problem seems to have lain with the state of international confusion over the pitch of musical instruments, something since resolved.

This period was clearly a most fulfilling aspect of Jiggs's life as he was later to reflect on his introduction to the choir: *"I was very struck with the rehearsal – this was something different – this was something more than the singing of crotchets and quavers. It was ALIVE and REAL – there was sincerity and warmth and, above all, a purpose behind it. Was it that the rehearsal started with a prayer led by the choirmaster? Yes, indeed it was; of that I am certain, for never have I experienced such spontaneous expression as that which came from these ordinary folk."*

Jiggs composed an Introit, *Be Merciful Unto Me*, which he dedicated to Archie Sargent and the choir, and a *Reverie in F* for organ, dedicated to Mr Sargent. He was very diffident in offering the choral piece; he confessed to his lack of experience in the skill of choral writing.

A strong and deep friendship developed with the family that was to continue while Jiggs was at Strensall and, to an inevitably lesser degree, thereafter. He had a number of heart-to-heart talks with them when he described the injustice and misfortune of his early childhood. Brian Sargent was, at this time, attending grammar school where there was a strong tradition of playing chess, a particular forte of Jiggs. He would invariably enter their house with a call of *"Set 'em up, Brian!"* and then proceed with *"yet another ordeal of slaughter"* but eventually Brian's ability improved and he was able to beat him fair and square with no question of Jiggs playing below his full ability. Jiggs also helped Brian in his music studies with some elementary harmony.

Brian confessed that he never really understood the nature of Jiggs's duties at Strensall as he was able to spend quite a number of evenings, half-days and the occasional full day with them, sometimes staying at the house overnight. He spent time at York Minster studying for his degree and often had Eileen and friends visiting the camp. His transport to and from York was also something of a mystery, with Strensall railway station having been closed in 1930 and a shortage of buses during the rigours of wartime.

Mention must now be made of one of the most important ladies in Jiggs's life

*Jiggs's Introit*

– 'B Flat'. 'B Flat' was a black and tan Alsatian cross bitch named, it is thought, after the note she barked! She was more of an Alsatian than anything else, even allowing that her ears flopped forward when pricked, that she carried her tail higher than a thoroughbred and that there was much less grey – if any – in her coat than would be expected in an Alsatian.

She was described as, *"quite an exceptional animal, particularly in terms of sensitivity and affection and her capacity for tugging at the heartstrings was immense."* She showed no enthusiasm whatsoever for menial tasks and demeaning tricks such as fetching a newspaper or carrying a basket and, as for begging ... ! She

*Bugle Major Jaeger with Brian Sargent*

*B Flat*

had her dignity! Yet she would engage in rough-and-tumble with gusto and liked nothing better than to be taken on to the vast Monk Stray in York to have her attention drawn to distant feeding birds or rabbits which she would chase with boundless though futile optimism.

As for 'B Flat's' musical taste, she would often attend choir rehearsals at York and lie peacefully near the piano for hours at a stretch – but if the National Anthem was played she would immediately rise to her feet and stand in a dignified fashion and remain so until its conclusion!

At this stage, perhaps we should consider the question of Jiggs's name. As mentioned earlier, as far as is known, the names Cecil and Harry were never used but in the 1940s he had mysteriously acquired a third Christian name, 'Anthony', although it seems that he expressed a dislike of it. On Sunday 23rd November 1941 he visited the Sargents and the family diary records that he announced that he would like to be known as Michael. Although the 'whimsy' did not last long, the family diary for 1941 makes several references to *Michael Jaeger* visiting. Others recall that in later years when a Christian name was required he used the name Charles, which rather explains the error that was mentioned in the Introduction.

On 19th December 1941 the War Office issued a letter stating that promotion of qualified Students to Bandmaster could now be made within the limits of the peacetime establishment. Five members of the Churchill Class received their appointments on that day – but not Jiggs. The normal procedure is that Students are generally appointed in accordance with their position in their class, but nothing is ever 'normal' in wartime. No records can be found as to where Jiggs came in the class although he was later to recount that 'Adko' had a rather poor opinion of him. It is possible that a degree of compassion may have intervened as Eileen was by then heavily pregnant.

Jiggs and Eileen's first child, their daughter Maureen Isobel, was born on 6th January 1942 in a private nursing home at York; Jiggs was also in York at the time – to watch a football match. The nursing home is now a Vicarage and it seems that very little alteration had been made: it houses the same linen cupboard as when it was a maternity home.

Jiggs and a colleague called Clay teamed up and entertained in the locality with a very clever caricature of the Weston Brothers, comedians who simulated a pair of pseudo ex-public-school toffs, slickly dressed and equipped with monocles, one of whom sat at the piano, with the other draped over it. They alternately drawled stanzas of rhymed verse in a rapid but witty 'play the game, you cads' style, to a background of monologue-fashion chords on the piano. One of their performances was at the Monkgate Chapel after which Mrs Sargent's diary recorded *"Jiggs and Clay as the Weston Brothers were extraordinarily good."*

On 4th April 1942, after about 20 months back with the KOYLI, Jiggs informed

*The Band raising money for the Relief Fund with Jiggs dressed as Charlie Chaplin.*

the Sargents that he was to return to The Royal Military School of Music, still at Churchill House in Aldershot. This inevitably meant that his visits to the Sargents thereafter were generally brief and fleeting, often between trains at York Station, but it was a time of approaching fulfilment which signalled that he could at last look forward to his soon being appointed as a Bandmaster.

## CHAPTER 5

# THE 4TH QUEEN'S OWN HUSSARS

After a few months back at Churchill House, Jiggs was appointed Bandmaster of the 4th Queen's Own Hussars on 21st July 1942, although he did not actually take up the post until 19th October.

*Bandmaster Jaeger*

The 4th Hussars had a proud history, having been raised in 1685 as the Princess Anne of Denmark's Dragoons, being known as Berkeley's Dragoons after 1688. They won their first Battle Honour at Dettingen in 1743, fought throughout Wellington's Peninsular Campaign and in 1854 were part of the famous Charge of the Light Brigade at Balaclava in the Crimea. However, they will always be specially remembered as the regiment in which Winston Churchill served as a young subaltern. In 1958 the regiment was amalgamated to form The Queen's Royal Irish Hussars, with a further merger in 1993 to form the present day regiment, The Queen's Royal Hussars (The Queen's Own and Royal Irish).

The band, in common with most others, had effectively been disbanded on the outbreak of war with its kit handed in and stored with the rest of the regimental property. When the regiment moved to Market Weighton in the East Riding of Yorkshire, the boys and younger members of the band moved to Perham Down on Salisbury Plain where they remained with Bandmaster Reginald Ridewood. Mr Ridewood had been with the band since 1937 and was the composer of a particularly fine march entitled *The Queen's Own*, which really ought to be heard a lot more. He *may* also have composed the paso doble *Amparito Roca* but that is something destined to remain a mystery.

About three or four months later, the bands began to be re-formed but, despite efforts to reclaim former 4th Hussars band members, only personnel from training units were made available. By this time the Band had lost its individual identity, being obscured by other nomenclature such as the Band of the 57th Training Regiment, Royal Armoured Corps or No. 5 RAC Band. It moved with the 57th to Catterick in Yorkshire where it gained popularity and began to work on engagements including Savings Week Campaigns, broadcasts etc.

Mr Ridewood had died in June 1942 and the band was temporarily directed by Mr Alec O'Connor, Bandmaster of The Argyll and Sutherland Highlanders, until Jiggs arrived about three months later. Archie Sargent's diaries record how thrilled he was to be taking over the band. He led them on a tour in the Bristol area, after which they were sent to Italy. The timing was very unfortunate for Jiggs as he was about to sit for his Bachelor of Music examination but had to leave a few days before it took place. Jiggs had to appeal to the Sargents to look after his beloved companion B Flat in his absence, as quarantine regulations, let alone the impracticality, would naturally have forbidden her to accompany the band.

His appointment meant that the family had to move out of their quarters in Strensall and so Eileen and six-months-old Maureen moved down to the south coast to live in Manvers Road, Eastbourne with her father Ernest who had moved there with his second wife. It was certainly not a particularly good place to be, since the town was very badly hit by the bombing raids.

*Bandmaster Jaeger marching stiffly at the head of his band on a parade circa 1943, accompanied by an unruffled 'B Flat', looking for all the world as though she was out for an afternoon stroll. The location is not known but must be somewhere in this country as quarantine restrictions would have prevented B Flat going overseas with the band. B Flat came to be regarded as the 4th Hussars band mascot.*

*Bandmaster Jaeger with B Flat, 1944*

Jiggs was back at Catterick in 1943 with his band, and during the summer of 1944 they were attached to Western Command Headquarters and made an extensive tour of South Wales.

*Jiggs directing the 4th Hussars Dance Band at Bridgend, South Wales.*

Then came a short spell of embarkation leave during which Jiggs rang the Sargent family with the news that, being again under orders, he had to go to Italy with his band and appealed to them to look after B Flat in his absence. They rather felt that they had little alternative but to consent, and the rewards in terms of companionship from a large dog were great, despite the difficulties in meeting her needs for regular exercise at a time when they were heavily committed to much time-consuming musical activity.

In August 1944 the band sailed from Gourock on the Clyde in the *Orontes*, destined to reach Naples after ten days and playing twice a day during the voyage, greatly adding to the ship's entertainment. When they finally reached Naples the band was routed on a none-too-pleasant 23-hour train ride in open trucks to the Royal Armoured Corps Training Depot (RACTD) at Foggia. However, once they had arrived, the RACTD looked after them very well and the band showed its appreciation by providing much regular entertainment for them and the many troops passing through. After a brief period they faced another wearying three days' journey to Taranto where they remained in transit for six weeks, placed at the disposal of the local welfare officer.

The bandsmen found themselves giving two performances a day at venues long distances apart. Coupled with the very hot conditions and living under canvas, this soon weakened many of them, with Jiggs himself having to play on two occasions in order to keep the band going. To add to the many discomfitures, the transit camp was completely washed out by torrential rain on three or four occasions. Their music was, however, very much appreciated and the local Brigadier gave them £20 for the band fund as they departed to board HMCS *Prince Henry,* bound for Piraeus in the south of Greece.

*The Band on the quayside at Piraeus*

The first British soldiers arrived in Athens just eight days after the country was liberated from German occupation, and two days later the band was giving a series of concerts to the local population and enjoying a most friendly and overwhelming reception from the Greeks. Public performances brought forth tumultuous ovations and Jiggs invariably received bouquets. He wrote of the tremendous enthusiasm when they arrived: *"On a parade yesterday a lady rushed and kissed me whilst I was marching in front of the band. I always enjoy being kissed but it is somewhat distracting to have a band and a complete regiment marching behind you at the same time."*

However, this was not to last as three months later, in December 1944, the band was caught up in the uprisings that led to the civil war. Instruments were handed in and the bandsmen had to draw out rifles as combatant troops for six weeks, manning pillboxes, loading supplies of ammunition and coming under constant shelling and sniping, fortunately without sustaining any casualties.

*Christmas 1944 in Athens*

During the brighter days that followed, the Band was again in great demand and was despatched to every part of Greece including the Peloponnese, where every principal town was visited, and then flying on a Dakota to the Salonika area. The Colonel of the Regiment, Winston Churchill, made two visits while the Band was in Greece and on the second occasion he asked to hear them. Unfortunately Jiggs was not present, as he had been flown to Cairo to replenish the band stocks, leaving the Band Sergeant in charge.

*Athens, March 1945*

*Athens 1945*

On 21st January 1945 the band played at a parade church service for The 1st King's Dragoon Guards, held on the Areopagus, by the Acropolis, on the spot where Saint Paul preached to the men of Athens, and this formed *"a fitting tribute to those KDG who had died or been wounded, and a thanksgiving for those who had survived"*.

*Tripoli March 1945 – Jiggs is in the peaked cap*

Just a week later, while still in Athens, Jiggs was able to listen to the Monkgate Choir on the wireless and immediately wrote to Archie Sargent to tell him how, *"It was a great thrill to listen to the choir and organ last night – it was terrific – and I enjoyed every second of the broadcast ... in spite of the fact that afterwards I crept into bed in a strange, unsettled land, with a head filled with thoughts of home."*

*Leading his Band through Athens in 1945 at a parade to mark the end of the war*

The war in Europe finally ended and a note in the regiment's diaries records that on 27th May 1945 it came under command of CRA 78th Division and that its Commander, Major General R.K. Arbuthnot CBE DSO MC, took the salute at the Victory Thanksgiving Service with the regimental band under the direction of Bandmaster C.H. Jaeger in attendance.

*Jiggs (in the peaked cap) with his bandsmen at Salonica in Greece 1945*

When the band departed for Italy, a sign of the appreciation that was felt came in the form of a donation of £60 to the Band Fund with a personal letter from General Sir Ronald Scobie. The band travelled by sea but Jiggs had been flown on ahead, meeting the band at Riccione in Northern Italy, from where it was sent to Rome for a week's leave.

*Showing off! Rome 1945*

They then were attached to the 8th Army and moved to forward areas to entertain troops. This was at the time when hostilities had ceased and the band's entertainment was well attended and greatly appreciated, with concerts given in Forli, Ferrara and in San Marco Square in Venice. The band then moved to Austria and met the regiment at Paternion where they were given an excellent reception and stayed for two months visiting all regiments of the 78th Division, providing the music for Division's Victory Parade.

Next the band moved to Vienna where it remained for five months, being the only British Army band in the city, and received a visit from the Director of Music at Kneller Hall, Captain Meredith Roberts, who expressed his approval of the excellent results produced during the tour.

*The Band on parade at Schönbrunn Palace for General Mark Clark, US Army*

It was during this time that Jiggs was given the honour of conducting the Vienna Symphony Orchestra for a series of five concerts, a quite remarkable privilege for someone who had been a bandmaster for barely three years.

The Vienna Symphony Orchestra was formed in 1900 (the same year as the Irish Guards!) as the Wiener Concertverein (Vienna Concert Orchestra) and it acquired its present name in 1933. After the invasion of Austria in 1938 it was forced into use for propaganda purposes and lost many of its members who had to work in munitions factories, so it disbanded on 1st September 1944.

It re-formed after Austria's liberation and gave its first post-war concert on 16th September 1945, playing Mahler's 3rd Symphony under the baton of Josef Krips. Just twelve days later, it wished to give a concert at the Vienna Konzerthaus "as a mark of friendship and esteem for the Allied Forces in Vienna" to celebrate the end of the war. As the 4th Hussars were then stationed in Vienna, Jiggs was invited to conduct them.

It may seem a little difficult today, to take in how such a young and still very inexperienced bandmaster should be asked to conduct such a prestigious orchestra, not just in a few marches and 'lollipops' but in major works. Exactly how this invitation came about is not known but we do know that Jiggs had already made himself popular with the Viennese with Sunday concerts by the 4th Hussars in the grounds of Schönbrunn Palace so perhaps he got to know members of the orchestra and impressed them with his musical knowledge and ability?

If the orchestra wanted a conductor from the Allies then Jiggs was clearly the man in the right place at the right time, being someone who somehow musically personified the liberating armies. After all, very few of us today can truly appreciate the euphoria that must have been felt regarding the Allies at that time after years of Nazi occupation.

This is all now pure conjecture, but a look at the reports from the music critics of the local newspapers tells us that Jiggs created a great impression. His first concert with the orchestra was held at the Konzerthaus on 28th September 1945 and the programme was:

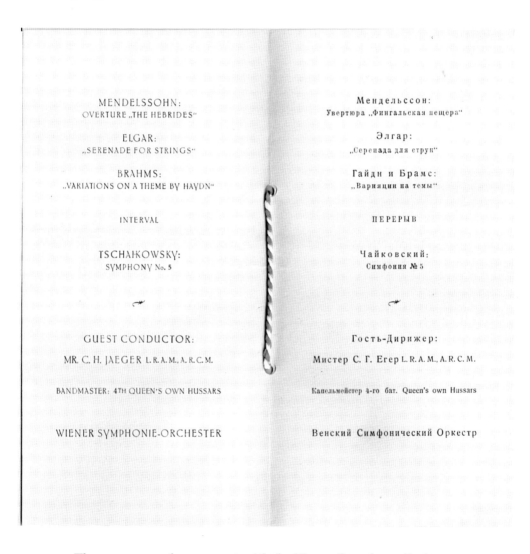

| | |
|---|---|
| MENDELSSOHN:<br>OVERTURE „THE HEBRIDES" | Мендельссон:<br>Увертюра „Фингальская пещера" |
| ELGAR:<br>„SERENADE FOR STRINGS" | Элгар:<br>„Серенада для струн" |
| BRAHMS:<br>„VARIATIONS ON A THEME BY HAYDN" | Гайдн и Брамс:<br>„Вариации на темы" |
| INTERVAL | ПЕРЕРЫВ |
| TSCHAIKOWSKY:<br>SYMPHONY No. 5 | Чайковский:<br>Симфония № 5 |
| GUEST CONDUCTOR: | Гость-Дирижер: |
| MR. C. H. JAEGER L. R. A. M., A. R. C. M. | Мистер С. Г. Егер L. R. A. M., A. R. C. M. |
| BANDMASTER: 4TH QUEEN'S OWN HUSSARS | Капельмейстер 4-го бат. Queen's own Hussars |
| WIENER SYMPHONIE-ORCHESTER | Венский Симфонический Оркестр |

*The programme for a concert with the Vienna Symphony Orchestra*

*Bandmaster Jaeger conducting the Vienna Symphony Orchestra*

*Das Kleine Volksblatt Wien* reported the concert as follows:

### ENGLISH GUEST CONDUCTS THE SYMPHONY

*At the Great Concert Hall the Vienna Symphony Orchestra held a concert in honour of the Allies and Bandmaster C. H. Jaeger (England) conducted. It was the first time in this season that a foreign conductor has led the Symphony Orchestra. The modest personality of the guest conductor, who studied at the Royal Military School of Music and conducted big concerts in England, gave the socially interesting concert a youthful and artistic peculiarity. Firmly, yet softly, he led the orchestra through a programme of the great classics.*

*The wonderful orchestral overture 'Hebrides' by Mendelssohn, led one into the realm of the romantic.*

*After Elgar's melodious Serenade, followed by Brahms' Variations on a Theme (St Anthony's Chorale) by Haydn, came the first symphonic work by Brahms, with its variety of melodiousness.*

*At the end of the enjoyable evening, the 5th Symphony by Tchaikowsky was heard, of which the fine interpretation demonstrated the ability of the orchestra to modulate. Of this, I think mainly of the soft stringed instruments and the delicate woodwinds under the slightly fast conducting of Mr Jaeger.*

*The spontaneous applause demonstrated to the guest conductor the deserved appreciation. The Vienna Symphony Orchestra spared no effort to give a good performance. Many of them played again after being in the K.Z. concentration camps or working behind armament machines in the past. They too deserve their old famous reputation.*

From the *Osetrreichische Volkstimme* – 2nd October 1945:

## VIENNA SYMPHONY CONCERT IN HONOUR OF THE FOREIGN ALLIES

*Friendly relations between the Austrian population and the Allied Forces were strengthened when a concert was given by the Vienna Symphony Orchestra under the direction of an English guest conductor.*

*High ranking officers of the Allied Nations and representatives of the Vienna Town Hall were present and, together with the large assembled audience, were most impressed with the orchestra's playing as in the best days of the past.*

*In Mr C.H. Jaeger, Bandmaster of the 4th Queen's Own Hussars, we made the acquaintance of a young and exceedingly talented conductor. His accurate reproduction of the separate works, plus his amazing spirit and temperament were a pleasant surprise. For a symphony concert such as this, it was a noticeable performance for so young a conductor.*

The concert was repeated on Sunday 21st October 1945 at the Grosser Konzerthaus-Saal and the *Weltpresse Wien* reported:

*This afternoon Mr Jaeger, the English Military bandmaster, conducted a Symphony Concert. Clearness of comprehension and precision in performance are his most charming qualities, with distinct reserve still emphasised.*

*The Haydn Variations by Brahms and the 5th Symphony by Tchaikowsky, the latter being in a certain measure melancholy transfigured, were produced with crystal clear and most amazing expressiveness.*

*The conductor was greatly applauded.*

From the *Neues Osterreich Wien*:

*This afternoon a concert given by this orchestra in the Concert Hall made a great impression. Here we made the acquaintance of Mr C.H. Jaeger, Bandmaster of the 4th Queen's Own Hussars, a thoroughly talented conductor, who made a good figure on the platform.*

*It was very interesting to watch this young Englishman leading the Vienna Symphony Orchestra, giving precise commands and that strictly performed rhythm which emphasises his origin from the military band. Besides Tchaikowsky's 5th Symphony he conducted a few smaller works and was well applauded from a well filled house.*

From *Das Kleine Volksblatt Wien*:

*The English Bandmaster, Mr Jaeger, whom at a previous concert we have come to know as a talented conductor, led the Vienna Symphony Orchestra in a well chosen programme in the great Concert Hall yesterday afternoon.*

*Mendelssohn's Hebrides Overture, Elgar's String Serenade and Brahms's Symphonic Variations on a Theme by Haydn, as well as Tchaikowsky's 5th Symphony, gave the young guest conductor renewed opportunities to prove his splendid conductorship.*

A further concert took place at the Grosser Konzerthaus-Saal on Sunday 10th February 1946 with the programme being:

| | |
|---|---|
| Mozart: | Symphony No. 40 |
| Grieg: | Piano Concerto |
| *Interval* | |
| Brahms: | Symphony No. 3 |
| | |
| Piano: Professor August Gollner | |

Again, we can look at the music critics' views on the concert, firstly from the *Wiener Kurier Wien*:

*This time the conductor was Bandmaster Jaeger. The attractive young conductor, whom we had already met, successfully leading the Vienna Symphony Orchestra last summer, introduced two symphonies: Mozart's G Minor and Brahms' Third with great ambition and fine musicianship.*

*Grieg's Pianoforte Concerto, played by Professor A. Gollner, linked the symphonies. Like a north-country symphony the work, rich of bitter-sweet ballad charms, is melodically and rhythmically sensitive. Soloist and conductor shared the success.*

From *Das Kleine Volksblatt Wien*:

*In the Sunday Afternoon Concerts of the Great Concert Hall, Mr C. H. Jaeger was heard again after a long interval. Mozart's G Minor Symphony and*

*Brahms' impressive Third were linked by Grieg's Piano Concerto, played by the Symphony Orchestra with professor August Gollner as soloist.*

Jiggs conducted the Vienna Symphony Orchestra in five concerts altogether but the programmes for the remaining two could not be found. Later in 1946 the orchestra was to acquire another guest conductor – Herbert von Karajan!

*Bandmaster Jaeger enjoying a cup of tea at the reception following one of the concerts with the Vienna Symphony Orchestra*

In later years Jiggs was to tell people that he learnt a great deal from conducting the Vienna Symphony Orchestra, as he sensed that its professional musicians were expecting the conductor to be able to interpret the music: much more so than when he studied at Kneller Hall when he felt he mainly learnt to beat time, quite a different thing.

In November 1945 Jiggs returned to England and, with eight other bandmasters, sat for the psm (passed school of music, the army's advanced musical certificate). They were examined at Kneller Hall by Sir Stanley Marchant, one time Organist and Master of Choristers at St Paul's Cathedral, Lieutenant Alf Young from the Royal Engineers Band, and the Commandant.

Jiggs managed to find time during this brief period back home to visit Monkgate one weekend with Eileen and Maureen for the Choir's performance of *Messiah* on 25th November 1945, which was given as Archie Sargent's thanksgiving undertaking to mark the end of the war. It was around this time that B Flat became over-excited and over heated in a countryside romp with an Alsatian and plunged into a local beck; she became thoroughly drenched and contracted a severe attack of what was virtually rheumatic fever, which was to return to haunt her during her final days.

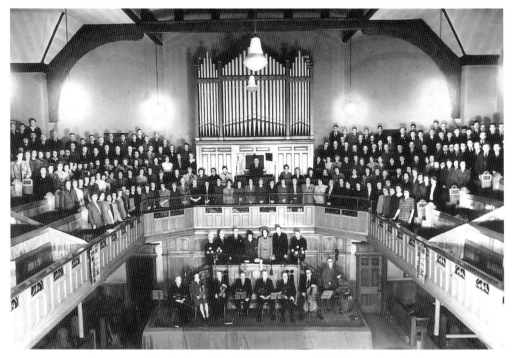

*Monkgate Methodist Messiah Chorus, York, November 1945*

Jiggs was back serving in Central Mediterranean Forces (CMF) in Caserta, Italy, the following January when he received notification of his psm results as follows:

> *Bandmaster Jaeger C, 4th Hussars, RAC, at present serving in CMF was successful in passing in all subjects for the recent examination for the Advanced Certificate held here last month.*
> *His detailed marks are:*
> *Harmony 84; Aural 77; Viva Voce 77; Instrumentation 80; Conducting 76; Remarks: Pass*
> *I shall be glad if you will convey to him the news of his success and my congratulations on passing the examination at his first attempt, which is a very rare achievement.*

> *(Sd) A. T. B. BIGNOLD-de-COLOGAN*
> *Lt. Col.*
> *Commandant*
> *Royal Military School of Music*

The results were forwarded to Jiggs along with his own Commanding Officer's sincere congratulations and compliments as he was, indeed, only the third bandmaster ever to obtain pass marks in every subject at the first attempt. At about the same time, Jiggs passed the second part of his Bachelor of Music examinations.

By now, many of the bandsmen had begun to return to the UK to be discharged to civilian life with their age and service groups, and by 1st January 1946 only twelve men remained of the band that had left Britain eighteen months before. This left them virtually unable to perform on their own, a situation remedied by combining with the Band of The Royal Norfolk Regiment, something that proved most successful.

In March 1946 Jiggs received a signal: *"The Band of the 4th Queen's Own Hussars, consisting of one Warrant Officer and ten other ranks, with three tons of kit, will be despatched to Calais by 1st April."* They duly returned and were sent to the 57th Training Regiment RAC at Catterick where they tried to build on the depleted numbers, hoping that former 4th Hussars bandsmen still serving would re-join the band.

Jiggs wasted no time in visiting his good friends, the Sargents, as he was back with them on 2nd April 1946 and twice more within the following two months. The Monkgate Choir's 1946 performance of *Messiah* took place on 24th November with a chorus of 150 voices and Jiggs as the solo trumpeter. Five days later, five buses conveyed the full company for a repeat performance at Trinity Methodist Church in Pocklington, about twelve miles to the east of York. According to a contemporary press report, *"It was a grand performance, which was fully appreciated by the crowded congregation."*

The choir's journal in 1946 tells that, *"Be Merciful unto Me, a beautiful miniature written by Bandmaster C.H. Jaeger and dedicated to A.W. Sargent and the Monkgate Choir, was sung for the first time"* (see pages 32–3).

In July 1946 a competition was held at Kneller Hall to choose a bugle march for the Army Cadet Force. Jiggs's submission was awarded the first prize of ten guineas by the adjudicators, Captain Alf Young and Bandmaster Henry Pipe of 2nd Battalion The Oxfordshire and Buckinghamshire Light Infantry. A letter published in *The Cadet Journal* described it as *"one of the best marches I have heard played by a bugle band"* and wrote of how well it sounded with first and second parts. The correspondent went on to say that he felt that the march did great credit to the ACF and stressed that, although it was a difficult march to play, the hard work required really paid off.

In recognition of his war service, Jiggs was awarded the 1939/45 Star, Italy Star, Defence Medal and War Medal. He already held the Coronation Medal (1937) and was also to receive the Long Service and Good Conduct Medal (1946) Coronation Medal (1953) and the OBE (1968).

With the band now back at Catterick, Eileen and Maureen had to wait until mid-1947 before they could get a quarter there and were to experience one of the severest winters ever with just paraffin heaters for warmth. They remained at Catterick until Jiggs was posted to Sandhurst in 1948. The Sargents continued to look after B Flat whenever Jiggs was away overseas with his band and on 11th October 1946 she produced what Jiggs described as *"a perfect scale, plus one dead"*. A further eight pups arrived on 11th October 1949, in Brian Sargent's bedroom!

Jiggs worked hard to build up the strength of the band once again, and in September 1947 they were able to take a public engagement at Kirbymoorside in Yorkshire. His efforts were clearly very much appreciated, with the regimental journal recording that *"Every inch of progress was won through untiring effort and if in need of inspiration, we never require to look further than to the Bandmaster."*

During this time when he was based at Catterick Camp, Jiggs conducted the Darlington Orchestra whenever he could, as well as conducting the Richmond Male Voice Choir and teaching at Richmond High School.

*The Band in Darlington*

*Conducting the Orchestra at Richmond High School in 1947*

*Richmond Male Voice Choir in 1947 with Jiggs holding up the ears of B Flat*

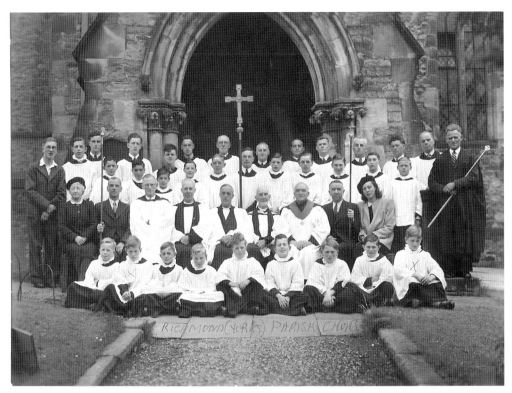

*Richmond Parish Choir, Jiggs in the rear row on the right side of the archway*

In mid-November, the band's six years' sojourn at the 57th Training Regiment RAC finally ended and they were reunited with their regiment which had just arrived at Cavalry Barracks in Colchester, Essex. Prior to leaving Catterick they gave a farewell concert attended by the GOC, Major General T. Cary DSO, who thanked them for their hard work and singled out the Bandmaster to credit him for its excellent playing and turnout.

The band establishment at this time, as fixed by the War Office, was 1 Bandmaster, 1 Sergeant, 2 Corporals, 3 Lance Corporals, with men and boys up to a total of 41. The actual strength was 34 including 8 boys which shows the progress that had been made since the return from overseas.

At Colchester the NAAFI Club was the venue for the band's first concert but Jiggs was destined to stay there for just a few months, as the time came for him to move on to the next stage of his career, having been selected for a commission. The 4th Hussars recorded that they were *"Sorry to see Mr Jaeger depart. He had done us well through all the difficult war years since 1942."*

Difficult years indeed, as he had gone to them as a newly qualified bandmaster and taken them through the hardships and deprivation of the war, to rebuild them again almost from scratch, as emphasised by his Commanding Officer's testimonial:

*The Band under the guise of the 57th Training Regiment, Royal Armoured Corps. Jiggs is in the centre of the three seated figures, seen to the left of the bass drum.*

*"I have only known Bandmaster Jaeger for a very short time but he impressed me most favourably. The Band which the Regiment had not seen for many years arrived in first class condition due entirely to Jaeger's hard work. He is I believe a first class musician and is spoken of very highly by the Military School of Music. He has tact, is quiet and has a strong sense of discipline. He is in my opinion a man who should go a long way as a Conductor of music. I am delighted he has obtained a commission as Director of Music at the RMA and I am sure he will do well."*

The 4th Queen's Own Hussars had no regimental quick march at that time as, historically, cavalry regiments had no real need for them. They traditionally paraded on horseback, so had an officially approved Regimental Slow March as well as Regimental Trot and Canter tunes. Mechanisation had changed all this, so Jiggs was ordered to write a quick march for them. 'Berkeley's Dragoons' was the result, taking its title from the Honourable John Berkeley, the first Colonel of the Regiment when it was raised in 1685. The march was written in the 1940s and published in 1952, later being incorporated into the new regimental march of The Queen's Royal Irish Hussars on amalgamation in 1958.

# CHAPTER 6

# THE ROYAL MILITARY ACADEMY, SANDHURST

Jiggs was commissioned as a Lieutenant on 6th March 1948 and appointed Director of Music of the Royal Military Academy Sandhurst Band.

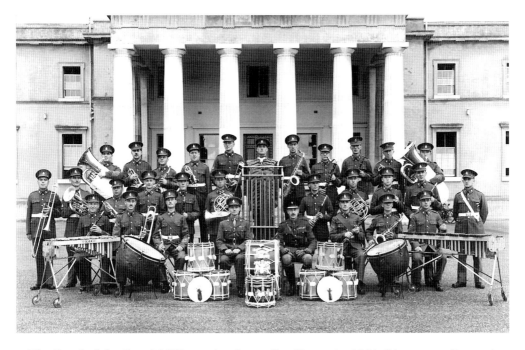

*The Band of the Royal Military Academy, Sandhurst in 1948. Lieutenant Jaeger is pictured to the left of the bass drum.*

The Royal Military Academy, Sandhurst, had been formed the previous year by merging the Royal Military Academy based at Woolwich with the Royal Military College that was already at Sandhurst, near Camberley in Surrey. The Sandhurst Band dated from 1813, the first recorded bandmaster having been Thomas Sullivan who served with them from 1845 until 1856, when he left to become a professor of brass instruments at the newly created Military Music Class which was due to open at Kneller Hall. No doubt the time at Sandhurst and the sound of the military band had something of an influence on his son, who was to become Sir Arthur Sullivan.

In August 1947 the band, along with a number of Royal Artillery and Corps bands, was upgraded to become a Staff Band to be led by a commissioned officer as Director of Music. The first incumbent was Lieutenant Leslie Statham but within a few months he transferred to the Welsh Guards, thus creating the vacancy for Jiggs.

Many years later, Jiggs told how his appointment came about. In the early 1940s 'Adko' was filling the dual appointments of Commandant and Director of Music at The Royal Military School of Music at Churchill House, and faced a court-martial based on what, in hindsight, appear rather trivial irregularities for which there was little evidence.

A number of the Students were called as witnesses for the prosecution, including Jiggs. Despite 'Adko' being thoroughly hated by most of the Students, Jiggs, perhaps sensing that he was being unfairly 'got at', steadfastly refused to say a word against him and declined to recall any of the events under scrutiny, simply saying that he was not at the School at the time. This led the officer in charge of the court martial board to describe Jiggs as being a 'hostile witness' who had not told everything he knew, with a promise to remember this in the future.

Imagine Jiggs's dismay, when many years later, this same officer appeared on the panel to select a bandmaster to be commissioned into the Sandhurst Band, particularly when he looked at Jiggs and remarked that he recalled they had met before. Far from the feared outcome, the officer instead praised Jiggs for the great loyalty he had shown to 'Adko' – and he got the job!

Most of the band's work at that time was confined to the College and included passing out parades, Royal and VIP visits, church parades, dinner nights and concerts. It was during his time at Sandhurst that Jiggs once again took up playing the *Post Horn Galop* on a .303 rifle.

On 14th July 1948, barely three months into the job, Jiggs directed the band at the first Passing Out Parade of the Royal Military Academy, Sandhurst, taken by His Majesty King George VI. The parade marched on to the sound of *Old Comrades* (Teike) and *Sons of the Brave* (Bidgood) and the King was received with a Royal Salute, after which he inspected the parade to *May Blossom* (Weir), *Les Huguenots* (Meyerbeer) and *Pageantry* (Stanley). The parade marched past in slow time to *Scipio* (Handel), *Coburg* and the *Royal Artillery Slow March*, and in quick time to *The British Grenadiers, Wings* and *The Yorkshire Lass*. After the parade the King decreed that these occasions should in future be known as the Sovereign's Parade and these continue to this day.

*Jiggs and Eileen with their daughter Maureen (aged about 6) and Brian Sargent,
with B flat paying no attention whatsoever, in the garden at the Sargents' home
in Hempland Lane, York. It was probably taken in April 1948 shortly after Jiggs's
commission and appointment to Sandhurst.*

Jiggs's appointment gave the family the opportunity for a much more settled existence, moving from Catterick to live in officers' quarters at Sandhurst where they were able to enjoy the splendidly spacious grounds of the Academy. Particularly enjoying this was B Flat who had the time of her life chasing the officer cadets on their bicycles! She looked rather fearsome (like an Alsatian) and sometimes rather frightened them. She also greatly enjoyed the most delicious-looking food that Jiggs's orderly somehow managed to acquire for her from the officers' mess.

However, Jiggs was only to stay at Sandhurst for a year, and he was later to suggest that he was moved because he caught too many trout in the lake!

In 1948, Jiggs's brother George set about trying to trace their father and his second family in Germany. He knew that they had been living in Kassel but they had had no correspondence since the 1920s and he had lost any form of contact with him because the city had been destroyed by bombing.

With the assistance of the International Red Cross, George managed to trace them to the small village of Lendorf, some miles out of Kassel. This was in the American-occupied zone and severe restrictions were in place as to who could travel in that area. George sought help from his Member of Parliament, Harold Wilson, and with help from his secretary the American authorities eventually agreed that he could visit if a doctor's certificate was obtained to say that Heinrich was in poor health and unlikely to live much longer. The certificate was duly obtained and the visa granted.

George flew to Frankfurt and took the train to Singlis where Heinrich met him with a horse and trap borrowed from a local farmer, piled his bags aboard and drove him to meet his new wife and family. Heinrich was, in fact, in the best of health but who could say that a separation of thirty years did not justify his little deception?

*Heinrich Jaeger and his second wife (known simply as 'Mutti' [mother]) at the back of the group with their five children: middle row: Heinz, Ernst and Roland, with Irene and Hans in the front.*

Heinrich had acted as an interpreter to the American Forces when they first arrived in the area and had joined the Mormons as a lay speaker. He and 'Mutti' had five children altogether, three of whom had been compelled to fight in the German army.

One son, Heinz, had been posted missing in Norway and was never seen again. Roland deserted from the German Army in the nick of time, having had the foresight to apply for leave as soon as allied forces crossed the Rhine and burned his uniform long before they arrived. Ernst was captured by the Americans and worked on a prison farm in the middle west of the United States and had recently returned when George visited. Hans had been too young to have been called up during the war, while their young daughter, Irene, bore the same name as Heinrich's English daughter.

# CHAPTER 7

# IRISH GUARDS – LIEUTENANT JAEGER

O n 8th April 1949 Jiggs was appointed as the fourth Director of Music of the Irish Guards at the age of only thirty-five and, as he once put it, with no qualification whatsoever in terms of being indigenous to that country. It was not until 2008 that a Director of Music with that particular qualification was appointed to the band.

*An early portrait of Lieutenant Jaeger with the Irish Guards*

The Irish Guards was still a very young regiment, having been formed in 1900 at the wish of Queen Victoria to commemorate the bravery of Irish soldiers in the South African Wars. The band began to function in the spring of 1901 and in its 49 years' existence had had just three Directors of Music: Captain Charles Hassell OBE, RVM, Captain James Hurd and Major George Willcocks MVO, MBE.

Major Willcocks, generally known as 'Polly' Willcocks (he was very partial to a nice cup of tea so was always putting the kettle on), was appointed Senior Director of Music of the Brigade of Guards in March 1948 and conducted the Massed Bands at the Opening Ceremony of the Olympic Games, held that year at Wembley Stadium. However, he had missed out on his one opportunity to direct the Massed Bands at the King's Birthday Parade because the parade that year was cancelled due to rain in the early morning. Needless to say, the weather cleared up in good time for the parade and there were huge numbers of disappointed spectators but it was too late to reverse the cancellation order.

He wrote some very fine marches including *Guards Armoured Division* and *Sarafand*, both of which are still regularly played by the Foot Guards bands. There were also a number of fine marches for brass band such as *The Champions* which is regarded as something of a classic and which has recently (2012) been scored for the Irish Guards Band by Musician Nick Walkley.

Major Willcocks was born in London on 23rd February 1899 and thus had the potential to serve through to his sixtieth birthday in 1959. Had this been the case, Jiggs would have had another ten years to wait until there was a vacancy in the Brigade of Guards. Looking back, it seems likely that he would have been appointed to the Royal Artillery (Woolwich) Band following the death of Lieutenant Colonel Owen Geary in 1955, in which event we can be sure that he would have relished having control of the fine orchestra that the regiment then possessed.

However, Major Willcocks's poor health led to him retiring early, in April 1949, and the following month he sailed with his family from Southampton on the *Athlone Castle* to start a new life in Southern Rhodesia. He later returned to England and became the Musical Director of the Ford Motor Works Band which he soon built up to become one of the finest civilian military bands in Britain. He was also highly successful in the brass band world and took the Fairey Aviation Band to victory in the Open Championship in 1956. He was the professional conductor of the Black Dyke Mills Band from 1957 to 1961 and won the National Championships with them in 1959 and 1961, and the Open in 1957, as well as taking third place in 1958 and 1960.

It must have been a rather turbulent time for the band when Jiggs took over the baton, as they had just lost a much respected conductor ten years earlier than expected. In addition, the band had spent the first three months of the previous year, 1948, on active service in Palestine in support of the Guards

Brigade stationed there during the troubles. During that time one of the cornet players, Lance Corporal Ted Jones, had been killed by a sniper when the band was ambushed on the return journey after making a sightseeing tour of Jerusalem and Bethlehem.

It was also at about this time that there was a change of Band Sergeant, Sergeant J. Field retiring to be replaced in the appointment by Sergeant 'Nobby' Clarke, better known throughout the Brigade of Guards as 'Clap-hands Charlie'. The strength of the Band was just 50, some 15 musicians short of its establishment.

However, on a brighter note, life in post-war London was returning to a state of comparative normality, something epitomised by the sight of the Guards once again wearing full dress uniform after many years in wartime khaki. One aspect of the uniforms that did not survive the war was the gold lace on the musicians'

*Lieutenant Jaeger wearing the frock coat of the Irish Guards. Drum Major M. Ward is seen here wearing, unusually, a plain tunic without the gold lace normally worn in that appointment. Full dress was only reintroduced to the Foot Guards in 1948 and it inevitably took time before everyone had the correct pattern uniform. On the left of the picture is Johnny Parker, the band librarian, who went on to become the librarian at Covent Garden Opera House.*

tunics, similar to the pattern still worn by drum majors. With the austerity measures then in place the Band was wearing rank and file guardsmen's tunics; it was 1965 before a compromise was found for the musicians with the addition of shoulder wings to the uniform.

Jiggs took over a band with a tremendous reputation, as evidenced by a remark by the Kneller Hall Inspectorate while reporting on the Band of the Welsh Guards in November 1948. The latter band received an excellent report and the top grading, but the comment was made that they were *"Musically perhaps not quite up to the Irish and Scots, but nevertheless they well deserve an unqualified classification as Outstanding"*.

The appointment to the Irish Guards on 8th April 1949 came less than seven years after Jiggs's first appointment as a bandmaster and just eleven months after he was commissioned. Looking from today's perspective it may seem strange for someone to reach the Foot Guards after less than a year as an officer but, in fact, the opposite was true as he was only the third Guards director of music to be appointed while already commissioned.

To explain the context of Jiggs's appointment, perhaps we should break to look back at how the post of Director of Music developed. Bandmasters in the early days held the rank of sergeant until the introduction of warrant officer rank on 1st July 1881. The elevation to commissioned rank came following the personal intervention of Queen Victoria, firstly by awarding an honorary commission to Dan Godfrey of the Grenadier Guards, as part of her Jubilee honours in 1887.

In 1899 the Queen's Private Secretary wrote to the War Office expressing Her Majesty's concerns that bandmasters could not receive commissions and her reasoning as to why she felt this to be unjust. The result, needless to say, was that over the next few years a number of bandmasters were commissioned, all seemingly on personal recommendations from the sovereign; the title of Director of Music was introduced in 1914 to differentiate the officers from warrant officers.

The concept of personal commissions was not ideal and it was decided that from 1st March 1919 the bands of the Household Cavalry, Royal Artillery, Royal Engineers and The Brigade of Guards were all to be led by commissioned officers as Directors of Music. There was a total of eleven such appointments (including Kneller Hall which was primarily a teaching post), reduced to ten in 1922 following the amalgamation of the 1st and 2nd Life Guards. The first Director of Music to move between appointments was Lieutenant (later Lieutenant Colonel) George Miller, who transferred from the 1st Life Guards to the Grenadier Guards in 1921.

An additional nine Director of Music posts were created on 11th August 1947, and when the Directorship of the Welsh Guards became vacant in March 1948 the appointment went to one of these newly commissioned officers, Lieutenant Leslie Statham, rather than to a bandmaster. This set the precedent for the future, the one exception in the Foot Guards being Major James Howe who was appointed to the Band of the Scots Guards in 1959 directly from being a Bandmaster in The Argyll and Sutherland Highlanders.

Returning to our story, Jiggs at least had the experience of eleven months as an officer when he arrived at the Irish Guards. He found himself in illustrious company amongst some of the great names that are so prominent in the history of military music: Fred Harris with the Grenadiers, Douglas Pope with the Coldstreamers and Sam Rhodes with the Scots Guards, the latter being Major Willcocks's successor as Senior Director of Music. With the Welsh Guards was Lieutenant Leslie Statham, whose appointment the previous year had created the vacancy for Jiggs to take over the Sandhurst Band. A highly respected musician, Leslie Statham composed a great number of marches and a good deal of light music under the pen name of Arnold Steck, which rate amongst some of the finest compositions of that era.

Life with The Micks, as the regiment is widely known, meant a great deal needed to be learned very quickly about the intricacies of providing the music at a whole range of military and state occasions such as Guard Mounting, Guards of Honour, Investitures, State Banquets and much more besides.

After just over three months in the job, Jiggs had one of his first tastes of the big occasion on 27th July 1949 when 1st Battalion Irish Guards received new Colours from His Majesty King George VI, Colonel-in-Chief Irish Guards, in the grounds of Buckingham Palace. This was before his own characteristic marches and arrangements filled the repertoire but the music, nevertheless, took on a distinctive Irish character (*see overleaf*).

Amongst the other engagements undertaken by the band in 1949 were the Chester Tattoo, and a ten-day visit to Northern Ireland with the Pipes and Drums and a Drill Demonstration Squad of the 1st Battalion Irish Guards for a ceremony of Beating Retreat, at which the General Officer Commanding Northern Ireland was present. The band also played at a service in Belfast Cathedral and they visited a number of important centres and played to huge crowds on almost every occasion. That summer, Jiggs returned to Kneller Hall as guest conductor at one of the Wednesday evening concerts.

Jiggs's move to the Irish Guards meant that the family had to move out of Sandhurst so they initially went to stay with Walter Ambrose and his wife at the Staff College at nearby Minley Manor. Eileen used to take Maureen into Camberley to school riding on the handlebars of her bicycle. They were unable to get a quarter in London for a while so went to live in Laleham in Middlesex (near Staines) and had a hiring (a home rented by the army) in the road where Eileen's sister lived.

**PRESENTATION OF COLOURS TO THE FIRST BATTALION**
**By HIS MAJESTY KING GEORGE VI**
**Colonel-in-Chief of the Regiment**

**BUCKINGHAM PALACE: 27th July 1949**

| | | |
|---|---|---|
| 1. Battalion entering Buckingham Palace Grounds | St Patrick's March | *Bidgood* |
| 2. Royal Salute | National Anthem | |
| 3. Trooping of the Old Colours | | |
|     Slow March | Erinalia | *arr. Somers* |
|     Quick March | Wearing o' the Green | *Trad* |
|     Escort for the Colours | The British Grenadiers | |
|     Present Arms | National Anthem | |
|     Escort for the Colour | The Grenadiers March | |
| 4. Old Colours marched to the front and off parade | Auld Lang Syne | *Trad* |
| 5. Royal Salute | National Anthem | |
| 6. Inspection of the Battalion by His Majesty | Eileen Alanagh | *Trad* |
| 7. General Salute when Colours are unfurled | Scipio | *Handel* |
| 8. Colours marched in Slow Time to Line | National Anthem | |
| 9. Advance in Review Order | The British Grenadiers | |
| 10. Royal Salute | National Anthem | |
| 11. March Past in Quick Time | St Patrick's Day | |
| 12. Marching out of Buckingham Palace | Killaloe | *Morrelli* |

| | |
|---|---|
| Director of Music: | Lieutenant C.H. Jaeger |
| Drum Major: | Drum Major M. Ward |
| Pipe Major: | Pipe Major A. Phair |

*Graduating as a Bachelor of Music in 1949.*

UNIVERSITY OF DURHAM.

*Cecil Harry Jaeger*

HAVING COMPLIED WITH ALL THE CONDITIONS
REQUIRED BY THE UNIVERSITY, HAS BEEN
ADMITTED TO THE DEGREE OF *Bachelor of Music.*

*Vice*-CHANCELLOR.

REGISTRAR.

DATE *1st July 1949.*

After some time at another hiring in Kingston, they eventually got into married quarters at Wellington Barracks towards the end of 1950, in a corner behind what remained of the Guards Chapel. Their son, Christopher, was born in Chiswick Hospital on 25th April 1950, on a Tuesday, the same weekday as his parents and sister. He lived with them at the barracks until he was three years old, being very much weaned on military music.

Maureen recalls how she used to play amongst the ruins of the old chapel, destroyed by a V1 flying bomb in 1944: *"The altar was miraculously left intact and in the interim a temporary Nissan hut-type structure was constructed as a seating area. The resident barracks children, including me, used to climb into the gap and play in the 'secret garden' running up and down the weed-covered crumbling pulpit – so much for health and safety!*

*I also travelled alone to convent school, aged ten, walking to St James's Park station – thence to Sloane Square, skirting around past Peter Jones and on to Draycott Avenue. Riding my bicycle unaccompanied around Victoria, Buckingham Palace and Hyde Park Corner, and skating on the lake in St James's Park during a prolonged icy spell are among other vivid memories."*

Amongst Maureen's other early memories was an occasion when she had invited a friend for tea and Jiggs caught her unawares with a joke which made her choke, with orange squash coming down her nose! Also, as a teenager, refusing to let him give a talk at her school (playing tunes on a golf club, length of hosepipe etc.) due to the potential embarrassment he might have caused her, as he could be something of a loose cannon and she would never know quite what he would say (she now realises in hindsight what a breath of fresh air he would have been with his quirkiness being much appreciated by the staff). Eileen was a far better bet, always turning up at Speech Day wearing the right hat and saying the right things and NEVER making 'inappropriate' comments!

Jiggs absolutely loved animals and had a really magical way with them, always making a big fuss of the Irish wolfhound. He came to enjoy horse riding and used to ride out some mornings very early with the Household Cavalry on a horse borrowed from Combermere Barracks, having been granted a riding permit by the Crown Estate Commissioners.

Maureen recalls an amusing episode from these days when Jiggs was crossing St James's Park from Wellington Barracks en route for a parade at Horse Guards, in full dress accompanied by his orderly, Whiteside: *"To set the scene, our budgie Peter (aka Houdini) had made yet another bid for freedom a couple of days earlier. Suddenly Jiggs spied Peter in the shrubbery and, having despatched Whiteside to fetch his cage, crossed the railings, ignoring the 'Please keep off the Grass' sign. After some coaxing, the budgie flew down and perched on his bearskin. The bearskin was whipped off and Peter posted into his cage, at which a cheer went up from the crowd of sightseers who had gathered to watch the drama unfold. Bearskin reinstated, Director of Music and orderly proceeded in a dignified fashion to Horse Guards Parade."*

In 1954 the family moved out of London into married quarters in Ninehams Road in Caterham, Surrey, home of the Guards Depot. Chris won a scholarship to Caterham School and had a very happy childhood with frequent trips with his Dad to various functions.

Jiggs did not drive at this time but cleverly solved the problem of returning home after late night engagements in a novel and very practical manner by booking a Caterham based coach company for the jobs. David Cawdell recalled a day during his initial training at the Guards Depot when he was allowed out to accompany the band to a concert in Northampton for the Fire Services Benevolent Fund.

On the journey home most of the band members were dropped off at Chelsea Barracks and only Jiggs and David were left on the coach as it returned to its base so Jiggs suggested that he sat with him for the remainder of the journey back to Caterham. *"It was a very kind thing to do and an honour for me to sit beside the great man for a cosy and informal chat about how I was getting on etc. I was knackered really and very tired and fell asleep on his shoulder. Many Guards officers would have brushed me aside or bellowed at me but Jiggs, in his fatherly fashion, allowed this very raw recruit to sleep peacefully and only woke me with a gentle shake when we arrived back at those Gates of Hell."*

For concerts at Eastbourne the band generally used what is best described as a 1½ decker, which departed with them at an early hour in order to make a detour to collect Jiggs at Caterham. On one occasion the band was returning from Eastbourne and Jiggs was duly dropped off at Caterham before the remainder continued to Chelsea Barracks. However, the coach barely got any further before breaking down, with the result that the musicians returned to the Jaeger residence to await a replacement vehicle and very much enjoyed the home-made cake which Eileen kindly supplied for them.

The band had a very full schedule of concerts in the various parks and seaside bandstands, and it featured regularly in broadcasts for the BBC. The band's broadcasts at this time averaged about once a fortnight, one of the more notable being a special programme on 2nd April 1950 when they played the Regimental Marches of those Irish Regiments whose bravery led to the formation of the Irish Guards in 1900.

In the early 1950s Jiggs paid a visit to the Duke of York's Royal Military School at Dover, doubtless recalling his short time stationed in the castle nearby for his early days with the KOYLI, and the number of his fellow band boys who had been recruited from the school. The visit certainly made an impression on one of the boys who played in the school's band as Roger Tomlinson recalls:

*"He arrived alone, but with all his trappings – trumpet, fanfare trumpet, cornet, piccolo cornet, miniature cornet, post horn, coach horn, jaegerhorn, French horn,*

*soprano, alto and tenor trombones, various members of the saxhorn and tuba families, a sundry collection of tubing and pipes, a kettle, a tubular chair, a .303 rifle and so on, and for the best part of an hour regaled us with a quite unique and fascinating one-man presentation on the history of brass instruments.*

*Afterwards Alf Singer (the school's bandmaster) introduced me to the great man and I found myself telling him, much to my surprise, for I hadn't realised it at that time, how it had always been my ambition to join an Army band when I eventually left school."*

Roger was left clutching Jiggs's card with an open invitation to join the Band of the Irish Guards when the time was right. In fact, he was eventually to join the Band of the Royal Corps of Signals but Jiggs's visit was certainly the great inspiration and something which bore considerable fruit for Army music in general as Lieutenant Colonel Tomlinson was eventually to become Director of Music of The Blues and Royals and later Principal Director of Music (Army).

In May 1951 the Band of the Irish Guards had the honour of playing at Queen Mary's 84th birthday luncheon party, after which members of the Royal Family spoke to the Band which, according to the regimental magazine, *"was at one time virtually under the command of Prince Charles who conducted the music with great enthusiasm, almost unable to control his animation. This gave great delight to the more august personages present, and to the band in particular."*

This was the year of the Festival of Britain: the closing setting of the National Anthem and Fanfare played by the Massed Bands on the last day had been arranged by Jiggs.

In 1951 Jiggs attended a dinner at Kneller Hall to mark the retirement of the Commandant, Colonel E.H. Collins, and the Adjutant, Lieutenant Colonel A. Bent. Other than Douglas Pope of the Coldstream Guards, all the Directors of Music holding senior appointments were present, Jiggs being very much the new boy amongst them. The photograph taken before the dinner represents a gathering of men who have since passed very much into legends in the military music world. They are listed opposite with their eventual ranks:

*The Dinner at Kneller Hall in 1951*

*Left of picture:*   Lieutenant Colonel Sam Rhodes, Director of Music, Scots Guards

*Left of table:*   Lieutenant Colonel David McBain, Director of Music, Royal Horse
Guards (The Blues)
Major (Retd) Tommy Chandler, retired Director of Music, Welsh Guards
Major (Retd) George Willcocks, retired Director of Music, Irish Guards
Major Leslie Statham, Director of Music, Welsh Guards
Wing Commander 'George' Sims, Organising Director of Music, Royal
Air Force

*Right of table:*   L.G. Waite, Boosey and Hawkes
Major Alf Young, Director of Music, Royal Engineers (Chatham)
Lieutenant Colonel 'Jiggs' Jaeger, Director of Music, Irish Guards
Lieutenant Colonel F.V. (Sir Vivian) Dunn, later Principal Director of
Music, Royal Marines
Lieutenant Colonel Fred Harris, Director of Music, Grenadier Guards

*Top table from left of picture:*
Lieutenant Colonel Albert Lemoine, Director of Music, The Life Guards
Lieutenant Colonel A.G. Bent, Retiring Adjutant
Colonel E.H. Collins, Retiring Commandant
Lieutenant Colonel Owen Geary, Director of Music, Royal Artillery
Colonel D.C. Campbell Miles, Incoming Commandant
Lieutenant Colonel W.H. Mabbot, Incoming Adjutant
Lieutenant Colonel Meredith Roberts, Director of Music, Kneller Hall

In December 1951 the Band of the Irish Guards combined with the Luton
Girls Choir under Jiggs's baton to make a recording on the Parlophone label
(R.3483), produced by George Martin:

|  |  |
|---|---|
| Princess Elizabeth of England | *Haydn Wood* |
| Britain Sing (Trumpet Voluntary) | *Henry Purcell* |

The 6th February 1952 saw the death of King George VI and the Band of the
Irish Guards was positioned in Chancery Lane for the proclamation of Queen
Elizabeth II two days later. It took part in the State Funeral on 15th February
when it was paired with the Band of the Coldstream Guards, with the two bands
playing alternately on the very long march in slow time from Westminster
Hall to Paddington Station. The marches played in the procession by the Irish
Guards were those taken from the Piano Sonatas of Beethoven and Chopin, and
the Dead March from Handel's *Saul*.

On Saturday 1st March 1952 the band again joined forces with the Luton
Girls Choir, along with the Luton Choral Society (both directed by Arthur E.
Davies) for *Blue Rhapsody*, a concert at the Royal Festival Hall in aid of the
National Children's Home, a cause clearly close to Jiggs's heart. The concert,

*The Band of the Irish Guards with Lieutenant Jaeger, in Fleet Street by the junction with Chancery Lane, waiting to play the National Anthem following the reading of the Proclamation of the Accession of Queen Elizabeth II on 8th February 1952. The drums are draped in black in mourning for King George VI.*

compered by the BBC's McDonald Hobley, came less than a month after the death of the King and the band began the second half by playing *Solemn Melody* by Sir Henry Walford Davies in his memory, followed by joining the choirs in *Song of Loyalty* by Eric Coates as a salute to the new Queen.

Amongst the other pieces by the full ensemble were the *Easter Hymn* (Mascagni) and a selection from *Merrie England* (Edward German), while the band items included a selection from *La Traviata* (Verdi), *Orpheus in the Underworld* (Offenbach), *Dance of the Tumblers* (Rimsky Korsakov) and *Post Horn Galop*. The soloist in the latter was Lance Corporal Robert Oades, for whom the band's liaison with the choir proved particularly fruitful, as the following year he married one of the girls, Marion Large.

1st Battalion Irish Guards was stationed at Llanelly Barracks in Hubbelrath as part of the British Army of the Rhine (BAOR) and provided the Escort for the Colour and Number 2 Guard at the Queen's Birthday Parade in Germany, the salute being taken by the British High Commissioner*. The Massed Bands were drawn from the Cavalry and Infantry regiments based in BAOR, including The

King's Own Yorkshire Light Infantry, and Jiggs flew out to Germany to put them through their paces for the parade.

Court Mourning for the late King came to an end with the Queen's Birthday Parade in June and the band paid a two week visit to Scotland soon after, which gave Jiggs ample opportunity to catch a good few unsuspecting trout as well as playing on some of the better golf courses. Golf was a game he played for its enjoyment, if not as an expert, after having overcome something of a detestation developed when he was a Student at Kneller Hall and 'elected' to caddy for 'Adko', the Director of Music.

---

*Despite Germany not being a Commonwealth country, he was then not the British Ambassador. The British High Commissioner, H.E. Sir Ivone Kirkpatrick, was the United Kingdom representative in the Control Commission Germany. The appointment lapsed in May 1955 when the West German Government was fully established.

# CHAPTER 8

# CAPTAIN JAEGER

## Promotion to Captain came on 24th July 1952

Throughout Jiggs's time with the band they were regular performers on the bandstand at Eastbourne, one of the concerts in 1952 being broadcast on the BBC Light Programme. The announcer for the broadcast was Philip Slessor, very well known in his day from such programmes as the comedy show 'Much Binding in the Marsh' and as the first announcer for 'Friday Night is Music Night'. To the immense amusement of the audience, said to number about five thousand, he was duly checked for his 'haircut' by Jiggs when he came on stage!

The bandstand at Eastbourne is surely the finest in the country, having large wooden screens with glass windows on both sides which keep out the wind, mounted on rails so that they can be pushed around to the back of the bandstand out of the way in fine weather when they are not needed. Jiggs preferred this latter position, as he could see his reflection in the glass panels which meant that the musicians frequently had to endure the inevitable problems of keeping their music in place in the face of a strong sea breeze so that Jiggs could admire his own conducting expertise.

His infectious personality and humorous style of presenting concerts were as much the reasons for their success as his skill in selecting programmes and the high quality of his musicians. Many of his quips have more or less passed into folklore: *"Thank you for your support; I shall always wear it;"* *"How nice to see you all sitting there looking so browned off. It must be the sun, it can't be the daughter."* A little short in stature, Jiggs would explain this by telling his audience that he was once six feet tall but he had done so much marching as a youngster that his legs wore down. When not in uniform and introduced to someone he would take his bowler hat through ninety degrees and say, *"My name's Jaeger; I expect you know yours!"* Corny stuff now, perhaps, but his audiences loved it – as they say, it was the way he told them!

*Jiggs relaxing on the front at Eastbourne*

Despite his jovial demeanour, Jiggs was hot on discipline within the band. He always knew those who were trying to 'swing it' and it upset him to think that his kindness and compassion were sometimes mistaken for signs of weakness. He wanted his band not only to sound great but to look good as well, always expecting his men to be smartly attired, and woe betide anyone spotted with the wrong coloured socks or dirty fingernails. He had a disconcerting habit whereby, if he got his teeth into any musician, he would 'hound' him for exactly three years and then behave towards him as if nothing had been amiss.

The cockney euphonium player 'Pincher' Martin was probably the closest band member to Jiggs and the only one who would call him 'guvnor' rather than 'sir'. They would often have a lunchtime drink together at Eastbourne and turn up for the afternoon concert with just minutes to spare before the opening march. Jiggs's orderly would be ready with his uniform and Pincher would quickly change into his. *"Come on Pincher,"* Jiggs would say. Having sunk four or five pints Pincher was seen to reply, *"Just a minute Guvnor,"* and make for the Gents. *"You haven't got time for that – we are on in a minute,"* so poor old Pincher would have to endure a 1¾ hour concert with a very full bladder. He was seen coming off the bandstand some days almost bent double!

*'Pincher' Martin quenching his thirst*

Colin Bradbury was with the band for his National Service and went on to be principal clarinet of the BBC Symphony Orchestra for thirty years, but was perhaps not the smartest of soldiers. Despite his outstanding talent with the clarinet, Jiggs once sent him back to the Depot due to his shoes not being polished to the correct standard when the band played at a cricket match at Burton's Court, adjacent to The Royal Hospital, Chelsea.

Another National Serviceman who served with the band was John Barnett: *"Jiggs probably saved my life. An exaggeration? Well, you judge. I was posted to the Royal Artillery at Oswestry where the food was unspeakable, thence to Rhyll in North Wales where the lieutenant in charge, realizing that I was already an acknowledged oboist, with consummate logic posted me to the Royal Artillery Band at Woolwich, where the food was excellent as it was the home of a cooking school. The Director of Music said to me, "Barnett, we've no room for you here so you'll have to go to Korea to fight," and thus I was put on a draft of 21 days leave.*

*I then went and played to Jiggs. He listened to me and said: "Barnett, I give you carte blanche." Jiggs loved using words which I suspect he did not always completely comprehend. No matter, he had a warm heart; he went to Whitehall and got me off the draft for Korea. My next posting, after signing on for five years, was to Caterham, a place as near to a concentration camp as I ever wish to roam, thence to Wellington Barracks for twelve weeks after which, together with bandsman Tony Jennings (who was destined to become the bass clarinet in the BBC Symphony Orchestra), we shared a freezing top floor room in Vincent Square, a stone's throw from our band practice rooms in Horseferry Road.*

*A normal day would as often as not consist of guard mounting or band practice in the morning, maybe trying out one of Jiggs's excellent arrangements, then afternoon lessons at the Royal College of Music and possible amorosity in Hyde Park (so many young students seemed to be attractive girls) and as like as not followed in the evenings by playing with one or other of innumerable amateur orchestras. Life was good. Jiggs was fun. I bought myself out for the princely sum of eighty pounds and toddled off to the Royal Opera House for thirty-two years as solo oboe. All thanks in no small measure to Jiggs."*

Jiggs was very much for the regiment and popular with the officers. He would always provide a band when they wanted one, particularly while the 1st Battalion was stationed at Chelsea Barracks when they would play during boxing matches in the gym. His confidential report for 1952 included: *"Under this officer's direction the Band has thrived during the past year. He is a great enthusiast and throws himself wholeheartedly into his work. He maintains good supervision over the band in all aspects of administration. Lieut. Jaeger sets himself a high standard of smartness and turnout and sees that the band do likewise. He is a good disciplinarian. He is very keen on his regiment, he is a first class musician and undoubtedly produces excellent results."*

1952 came to an end with the annual band reunion at Victoria, with many past members attending, including two who were in the original band when the regiment was formed.

Jiggs's willingness to help those in trouble came to the fore following the disastrous floods which hit large areas of Norfolk, particularly King's Lynn, at the end of January 1953. Just two days later, the Wisbech Male Choral Society secured the use of the local Empire Theatre to present a concert to raise money for the Distress Fund set up in support and the services of the Band of the Irish Guards were readily offered free. The concert took place on 1st March and the programme included the overture, *The Italian Girl in Algiers* (Rossini), *Pineapple Poll* (Mackerras) and *Belle of the Ball* (Leroy Anderson), along with items by the choir and soloists, all ending with the combined forces in the *Soldiers' Chorus from Faust* (Gounod).

10, Downing Street,
Whitehall.

June 9, 1953.

Dear Captain Jaeger,

The Prime Minister and Lady Churchill have asked me to express their thanks to you for conducting the orchestra of the Irish Guards to such admirable effect during the Foreign Office Banquet at Lancaster House on June 5. The orchestra's contribution to the success of the evening was very noticeable and the Prime Minister hopes that you will tell all its members what pleasure their performance gave to him and to his guests.

Yours Sincerely
J.R. Colville

Captain C.H. Jaeger.

*A letter expressing Sir Winston Churchill's appreciation*

The Band of the Irish Guards had been the very first military band to broadcast, back in 1923 on the 2LO station, and in early 1953 it achieved what was considered something of a landmark by giving the first broadcast performance of the *Symphony in B Flat for Wind* by the German composer, Paul Hindemith, written two years earlier for the United States Army Band (Pershing's Own), based in Washington.

This went out at six o'clock in the evening of 8th May 1953 on the BBC's Third Programme, but all was not as it should have been. The symphony had been recorded by the band, augmented to ensure the full instrumentation was available, on 30th March in the studio in Maida Vale for a fee totalling £189. On the day of the broadcast, the engineer misunderstood the labelling of the records, which had become somewhat confusing owing to the number of re-takes which had to be made and, as a result, the symphony went out on the air with the movements in the wrong order. A clearly embarrassed BBC producer immediately wrote to Jiggs to apologise, with a promise to transmit it again in its correct form and an undertaking personally to ensure there would be no further mistakes.

March 1953 had seen the death of Queen Mary, with the Massed Bands of the Brigade of Guards in the procession taking her coffin from St James's Palace to Westminster Hall. However, more joyous occasions loomed and on 29th May Her Majesty The Queen attended a Ball at Hampton Court Palace given by the officers of the Household Brigade, with music from the Micks' dance orchestra, alternating with the Band of The Life Guards.

The band then moved into Earl's Court to prepare for the Coronation on 2nd June. When the great day arrived, detachments from all ten battalions of Foot Guards took part in the outward procession from Buckingham Palace to Westminster Abbey for the crowning. In the centre of the Foot Guards column marched the Band of the Welsh Guards, immediately followed by the Band of the Irish Guards and then the Massed Corps of Drums of 1st Battalion Irish Guards and 1st Battalion Welsh Guards, the three elements playing alternately.

In the afternoon they formed part of the considerably larger procession for the return journey to the palace over a much longer route, which did so much to brighten a nation still recovering from the effects of the war, as well as probably being the greatest ever stimulus for the sale of the newfangled invention called the television. Marching around the streets of London with his band on that cold and very wet day must undoubtedly have been a source of great pride to Jiggs, and we can be sure that he would have cast his mind back to 1937 and been wistfully reflecting on his role at the heart of the previous coronation.

The following week saw the Queen's Birthday Parade in London, after which the band began to prepare in earnest for the Queen's visit to Northern Ireland. The province was familiar territory in those days before the political situation made things difficult, and the first week of the tour saw the band in its familiar public relations role of drumming up potential recruits for the regiment. Sunday 29th June 1953 was a particularly busy day, with a broadcast from the

BBC Studios in Belfast and then a quick dash to St Anne's Cathedral to take part in Evensong.

As a prelude to the Royal Visit, all the participating Bands and Pipes and Drums took part in Beating Retreat at the Headquarters, Northern Ireland District, Lisburn, before His Excellency the Governor in a wonderfully colourful ceremony set against a background of trees.

The Queen arrived in Belfast on 1st July for the three-day visit, which began with a State Banquet at Government House, Hillsborough on the first evening, followed the next day with a Civic Luncheon at the City Hall, both with the Orchestra of the Irish Guards in attendance.

After another dash through several miles of traffic-choked roads, the band arrived at Stormont to support a Guard of Honour found by 1st Battalion Irish Guards for the Queen's visit to Parliament. The available space reduced the size of the Guard of Honour to 80 instead of the customary 100 and meant that the band was very unusually positioned opposite them, with Jiggs standing barely six feet behind Her Majesty. However, the setting in Stormont's grounds on a hill overlooking the city of Belfast, along with the perfect summer weather, made this an incomparable spectacle. Commanding the Guard of Honour that day was Major James Chichester-Clark, who was later to become particularly familiar with Stormont as Prime Minister of Northern Ireland from 1969 to 1971.

*A Royal Salute as the Queen arrives at Stormont. Jiggs can be seen standing about six feet behind Her Majesty*

A Garden Party followed, and after the band had been entertained to tea it left to take part in the first performance of the Balmoral Tattoo, arranged to celebrate the Coronation. Although it was not possible for the Queen herself to attend the Tattoo, the Governor and the Colonel of the Irish Guards were among the distinguished guests to see the Massed Bands under Jiggs's direction. The remainder of the tour was far less hectic, with the fishing rods and golf clubs being put to good use.

The Hindemith broadcast earlier in the year did not pass unnoticed by John Weeks, who was due to be auditioned by Jiggs shortly afterwards and so he thought he would try to impress him by playing part of Hindemith's *Clarinet Concerto* which he had discovered while at the Royal College of Music the previous year. John was accepted into the band and about six weeks into his training he was sent for by Jiggs and had his first outing with the band for the Belfast visit, where he played at two of the indoor engagements but was deemed "too raw" to be allowed to march.

When he was eventually allowed to march, he lost his name by being caught out of step and was hauled up and put on extra drill at Chelsea Barracks. This was not the best way to start his army career so he decided that a way to impress Jiggs would be to compose a large overture for the band, very much in the Hindemith style. *"I worked away at it at Westminster Central Library and proudly presented it to him. I think he was quite impressed, pencilling 10/10 at the end. Then, in his facetious way he changed it to 10/1000!"* The overture, entitled *Ceremonies*, existed in piano score for 30 or more years and John eventually decided to score it for military band and send it to the band with the dedication: 'A Gift to the Irish Guards Band in memory of Lieutenant Colonel Jaeger'.

John Weeks also recalls a rather embarrassing situation when the band travelled to Pirbright from Waterloo station for a morning parade. *"I, along with my friend Robert Gittings, just missed the train which entailed a half hour wait for the next one. While we were hanging around, who should turn up but Jiggs, who had also missed the train. He was quite affable and we eventually travelled down to Pirbright together. On arrival at the station there was a staff car waiting for him. He said to us, 'You'll need to get a taxi.' This we did, arriving (in convoy) on the square at Pirbright just as the Band was beginning to form up (we had to pay the taxi fare!). Normally we would have been in big trouble for arriving late, but since we arrived simultaneously with Jiggs there was nothing anyone could say so we didn't get punished."*

John was one of a good number of the musicians in the Guards at this time who were music students from the colleges who had opted to serve an additional year of their National Service, three in total, to get into a band. Many of these went on to reach the top of their profession as principals with the country's leading orchestras and a good number look back at their time with the Irish Guards as having set them on the right path by instilling the discipline and musicality required.

One such man was Paul Harvey, now very much one of the great names of the clarinet world, who joined the band in 1953 and who recalled his early impressions of Jiggs: *"It was taken for granted that one measured up to the musical standard – otherwise one would not have been there – but even more demanding was the high standard of humorous repartee expected from even the lowliest members and gauging the narrow dividing line between this and military indiscretion.*

*On one of my first Guard Mountings I stood quivering on the square as Jiggs progressed through the ranks, chatting amicably or otherwise with members of the band. Upon confronting me, he prodded my (then) skeletal chest with his baton and demanded in tones of mock severity: 'Where are your medals, Harvey?'*

*Knowing by now what was expected, I did my best: 'Gone to be cleaned, sir!' Jiggs shook his head sadly and moved on.*

*On the next guard the question was repeated. 'The weight was pulling my tunic out of shape, sir.' So it went on at every guard for weeks: 'Lent them to the Band Colour Sergeant, sir,' 'On loan to the Imperial War Museum, sir,' and finally 'I haven't earned any yet, sir, but I shall continue to do my duty in the hope of eventual recognition.'*

*The last elicited his habitual response – 'Steady, now!' which meant he conceded my repartee was gaining some degree of polish. On the next guard, I heard him asking a new recruit, 'Where are your medals, Bloggs?'*

Paul also recalls getting lost during the spin wheel at his first 'Trooping', eventually finding his way back to his position. *"Swivelling my eyes to the right, I saw it was Jiggs. He swivelled his to the left and we eyed each other under our bearskin fringes. 'Welcome home, Paul Harvey,' he said!"*

Another of Paul's memories is, *"Whenever I play Mozart's 'Marriage of Figaro' overture I remember frosty Guard Mountings, shivering in the palace forecourt with an icicle hanging off my clarinet bell. Jiggs would say 'Put out Figaro to get the clarinets' fingers warmed up!' and then conduct it one in a bar!"*

Paul spoke volumes in writing of a day when he overheard a remark by *"a morose Grenadier to a bored Coldstreamer as all five bands were standing about at Wellington Barracks one pay day. 'How is it,' he grunted, 'that whenever you see the Irish they're always laughing at something?'*

In May 1954 the band received an invitation to go to Toronto in August to make its fourth appearance at the Canadian National Exhibition. The original visit had been made in 1905 under Mr Charles Hassell, just four years after the band's formation and its performances clearly made a big impact, judging from the glowing press reports which are framed and still displayed on the wall outside the current band office. Return visits were made in 1913, again with Mr Hassell, and in 1935 under Captain James Hurd.

As a result of this invitation a Mr Lester MacArthur of Boston, Massachusetts visited London with a view to extending the tour to the United States. He was met at London Airport by Jiggs, along with Sergeant Laurie Ward, at some unearthly hour of the morning and driven to the barracks.

Once they had all recovered from the early start, Mr MacArthur sat in the rehearsal room as the band played through a selection of carefully chosen pieces. After this he jumped up on the rostrum and exclaimed something along the lines of, *"Jeepers fellers, we kinda sorta gut some swell bands back in the States but I reckon you'se guys gut 'em all licked, and brother, that sayin' sumpin'!"* Roughly translated into English, this meant that he was impressed and so negotiations soon got under way for the tour, which would last for two months.

The impending tour was big news and shortly before the band was due to depart the press descended in force on Wellington Barracks, amply sustained by the copious quantities of sherry that were on offer. The BBC was there as well with a number of musicians being interviewed by Mr Godfrey Talbot and much press coverage ensued, including a full page of photographs in the *Sphere* on 28th August 1954. The *Daily Telegraph* reported that the Governor of Boston, Massachusetts, where there was a big Irish community, had issued a proclamation naming 13th September 'Irish Guards Day', the day the band was to give its first concert in the United States. Jiggs was quoted as saying that the repertoire would vary from Gilbert and Sullivan selections to an arrangement of music at the Trooping the Colour ceremony and arrangements of standard classics.

Amongst the scores being taken was Hindemith's *Symphony in B flat for Wind*. Jiggs told the *Telegraph* that, *"We shall be more concerned with showing the musical traditions of British military bands than with playing music familiar to Americans. The Hindemith score will go with us because it may be asked for at a number of educational and discussion group engagements we have undertaken. We are hoping that our own tour will serve to whet American appetites for the Scots Guards Band who will follow us. They started to make their own arrangements before us."* Jiggs also took the opportunity to show off to the media a silver salver bearing a facsimile signature of Field Marshal Earl Alexander of Tunis, Colonel of the Irish Guards, which was to be presented to the Irish Regiment of Canada.

On Monday 23rd August just after four o'clock in the afternoon, the Band set off from London Airport in a Super Constellation of Trans-Canada Airlines. This was John Weeks's first ever flight and he recalls that Jiggs and some of the senior members of the band were in the First Class section. *"When we had been airborne for about half an hour a message came back from Jiggs, inviting anyone who felt so inclined to go and play him at chess. My knowledge of chess was very rudimentary, but I thought I'd have a go. It was probably one of the shortest games on record, as I was checkmated even before we reached the Irish Coast! During the game I remember Nobby Clarke looking out of the window and seeing a large island. 'Cor!' he said, 'you can see the whole of Ireland at once.' It was actually the Isle of Man!"*

They landed at Montreal for refuelling but, on taking off again were beset with technical problems which caused a delay of nine hours; they eventually reached Toronto in 85 degrees of blazing sunshine. The officer accompanying the band on this tour was Major the Honourable James Chichester-Clark who was well acquainted with life in Canada, having served there from 1947 to 1949 as Aide-de-Camp to the Governor-General, Field Marshal Earl Alexander of Tunis.

The band had the honour of playing before Her Royal Highness The Duchess of Kent (mother of the present Duke of Kent) when she opened the Exhibition on 27th August 1954; the programme for the band's first concert on 27th August was:

| | | |
|---|---|---|
| Regimental Quick March: | St Patrick's Day | |
| March: | Toronto City | *Jaeger* |
| Overture: | The Barber of Seville | *Rossini* |
| Selection: | Patience | *Sullivan* |
| Waltz: | Voices of Spring | *Strauss* |
| Selection: | Cavalleria Rusticana | *Mascagni* |
| Two Pieces: | a) Swedish Polka | *Hartley* |
| | b) Amparita Roca | *Texidor* |
| Valsette: | Septembre | *Godin* |
| Selection: | Bric-A-Brac | *Monckton* |
| | *Daily 'Special Request' Item* | |
| Finale: | The Wedding of Louis Alonzo | *Giminez* |
| Regimental Slow March: | Let Erin Remember | |
| | God Save the Queen | |

The opening march, *Toronto City* very cleverly incorporated well-loved Canadian melodies and was later renamed *Canada on the March*, perhaps as Jiggs realised that the Canadian composer Robert Farnon had already composed a march with that same title. This was the first of a total of 28 concerts in the Band Shell in the afternoons and evenings every day excluding Sundays, with the final concert culminating with *1812* and a reflective *Nightfall in Camp*. The band was received with tremendous enthusiasm from audiences which numbered 20,000 and more each day (including Jiggs's brother, George, who was living in Canada at that time) and they shared the billing with a number of Canadian bands and the Leslie Bell Singers. Among many pleasant experiences in Toronto, the Band visited Niagara Falls as guests of the Irish Regiment of Canada, and the silver salver was duly presented.

*The Band, Pipes and Drums in the Band Shell at the Canadian National Exhibition in 1954*

The Band left Toronto by train on 12th September and travelled to Boston in the United States to start the second part of the tour. However, this is when things started to go very wrong. They arrived at 1.00 pm after an 18-hour journey, four hours late due to the effects of Hurricane Edna which was then causing a great deal of damage and was responsible for twenty deaths. The band had witnessed the wreckage of a freight train that had fallen victim the previous day and they arrived to find no electricity or telephone network, and flooded streets.

The musicians stopped at the YMCA, changed straight into Guard Order and went to the City Hall to play some marches on the steps before returning for tea. The opening concert commenced at 8.00 pm in the Symphony Hall but the effects of the weather, combined with a boycott by the Irish element of the population, inevitably caused a much reduced audience. However, the lack of numbers did not stifle the enthusiasm and the Boston Herald reported: *"The Band of the Irish Guards made its debut in the United States last night and at once added a new and glorious dimension in the art of the Brass Band. The essence of this famous British military organization lies in the richly glowing textures it reveals in everything it does; if it was a treat to the ear, it was meanwhile a treat to the eye".*

The next performance was in Providence, Rhode Island where the aftermath of 'Edna' included several thousand dollars' worth of damage to the roof of the concert hall, and a downpour just before the first concert made some of the band wonder whether they should cape-up. Fortunately only a few drops got through and the audience more than doubled itself on each of the remaining two nights.

Next stop was Philadelphia where: *"The Redcoats from England were here last night and conquered Philadelphia. At least those several thousand Philadelphians at the Arena were conquered and captivated by the red-coated Band of the Irish Guards in their first visit to the City."*

The band went on to play at a number of other venues, experiencing generous American hospitality, albeit with something of a shortage of sleep. They visited a proper American 'Rodeo' and the Empire State Building, along with the shops on Fifth Avenue, the lights on Broadway, a magnificent drive through the Adirondack Mountains from Burlington to Hamilton and, lastly, a very entertaining night in Detroit.

This is when it became apparent that things had gone badly wrong, with the MacArthur organisation in serious financial difficulties, such that it could no longer pay for the luxurious American Greyhound coaches in which the musicians had been travelling in Boston. However, the band was not stranded because these coaches took the musicians to Ambassador's Bridge over the Detroit River at the Canadian border, where they changed onto the somewhat basic Canadian Army transport. The Canadian Army more or less took them over from then on and accommodated them in barracks for the final week of the tour.

They arrived at the Oxford Street Barracks in London, Ontario, in the mid-afternoon, drew their bedding and were just settling in when Jiggs told them that they were to move on to spend that night in the Mayfair Hotel in Kitchener, Ontario (a city once known as Berlin) and on their arrival the Band marched through the town behind the local band for a reception at the town hall. After the evening show they returned to London (Ontario) where the news was confirmed that MacArthur's organisation had finally gone bankrupt and that they would not get more than $15 out of the $40–$50 still owing to each of them. Jiggs later found himself involved with a press conference as news of the collapse of the tour spread.

The band had a paid engagement at Strathroy where a former Irish Guards officer lived. The Mayor entertained them at the Parish Hall and they then marched through the town, totally deserted when they had arrived but now packed with just about every one of 3–4,000 inhabitants. The concert, the last official one of the tour, had an audience of 2,000, which must have been the largest ever in relation to the size of the local population.

Things took another turn for the worse when the band travelled to Kingston for a concert and a tyre burst on the second of the two Army buses. It took three hours for it to be replaced although the musicians managed to stay inside for most of the time, away from the bitter wind. Laurie Ward mischievously announced that there was a cafe a quarter of a mile along the highway and five thirsty musicians set off to find it. By the time they realised they had been 'had' the heavens had opened and they eventually returned cold, thoroughly drenched, bedraggled – and still thirsty!

The concert had been due to start at 8.00pm and Jiggs and those on the first coach had no idea what had happened to the second coach. Ever the showman, and desperate not to let people down, Jiggs with two or three assistants managed to keep the audience entertained until the rest of the band finally arrived.

The second coach (or rather the first, which had returned to collect the musicians after a further breakdown caused by a stuck gear lever) finally arrived at Kingston at about 10.00 pm and Jiggs's announcement that they were to change straight into uniform to play a 30-minute programme was received in a deathly silence. They were cold, wet and hungry and there was great discontent amongst the band that night, one member describing it as "the blackest day of all".

Despite everything, the tour was a great success, although financially it was very disappointing. Jiggs was quoted in the press saying, *"An act of God in the form of the hurricanes Carol and Edna forced the band to cut short the U.S. tour. Naturally enough, the people of those fair cities [Boston, Massachusetts and Providence, Rhode Island] were more interested in bailing 15 feet of water out of their basements than in hearing the Irish Guards Band."*

He remarked of the Canadian itinerary, *"In a way we have been singing for our supper,"* as they had been playing in Army camps across Canada in return for their food and lodging. The band was forever grateful for being rescued and looked after by the Canadian Army.

Before they arrived home, Eileen had received a letter from a Toronto resident (signature unclear) telling of how much enjoyment the band had brought to them in Canada. Part of the letter read: *" .... may I tell you that Captain Jaeger endeared himself to many people in many different walks of life. His ability to bring the finest music not only to those who understand and appreciate it but also to music lovers who could never express their appreciation in musical terms was wonderful. This was evident in his introductions of his selections and was enhanced considerably by the whimsy he used which endeared him to the listeners. What I am trying to say is – old and young, men and women – all derived so much pleasure from his band and his priceless personality.*

*Many of us who had the privilege of meeting the Captain personally found him charming, easy of manner, with an amazing ability to make friends and also a desire to share his friends. I would like to say Mrs Jaeger that I feel you are not an entire stranger. At the drop of a hat, the Captain would haul out his wallet, pat it lovingly, open it to its picture compartment – 'my son, our daughter' and – the pièce de resistance – 'my wife', with such a love light in his eyes that we felt his family had become part of us."*

He had certainly made an impact!

In 1954, perhaps without ever realising it, Jiggs came very close to ending his time with the Irish Guards Band after just five years, when the appointment of Director of Music at Kneller Hall became vacant. Again, we will briefly break from Jiggs's life here to give some background to this appointment.

The Military Music Class opened at Kneller Hall in 1857 with a civilian, Henry Schallen, as its first Musical Director. Mr Schallen had served as Bandmaster of the 17th Lancers when the school's founder, the Duke of Cambridge, had been the regiment's commanding officer so this connection seems likely to have been the reason for his appointment.

The position of Director of Music at the school was occupied by civilians until the first soldier, Samuel Griffiths, was commissioned into the post on 24th December 1890 as Honorary Lieutenant. Griffiths died on 24th March 1896 while still serving, and was succeeded by Arthur Stretton, followed in 1921 by Hector Adkins ('Adko'), both of whom were appointed as Lieutenants and eventually promoted to Lieutenant Colonel. 'Adko's' court-martial in 1942 led to him being reprimanded over just three of the twenty-one very minor charges brought against him. Although he was not dismissed from the service his position inevitably became untenable and he resigned later that year.

The question then arose as to who should be appointed to succeed him. A letter from the War Office dated 8th May 1943 offered the appointment to Captain Joseph Thornburrow, Director of Music of the Royal Horse Guards (The Blues) although this was withdrawn on 31st May, amidst much speculation that this was because it became known that Thornburrow was a nephew of 'Adko'. However, War Office papers from 1954 held in the National Archives rather imply that Captain Thornburrow declined to accept the appointment as: "*In 1942 ... the post was offered to and rejected by every Director of Music in the Army.*"

The post eventually went to Bandmaster (Warrant Officer Class One) Meredith Roberts from the Royal Artillery Portsmouth Band, who was commissioned on 30th August 1943 with eventual promotion to Major and Local Lieutenant Colonel. Roberts conducted the Kneller Hall Trumpeters in Westminster Abbey at the Coronation in 1953 but ill health forced him to retire later that year, which left the War Office once again wrestling with the thorny question of a successor much earlier than had been expected, as well as the matter of whether the incumbent should be granted the local rank of Lieutenant Colonel.

A list of possible candidates was submitted to the Director of Personal Services (DPS) at the War Office by the Commandant at Kneller Hall, along with comments as to their suitability. Although the files are now in the public domain, as these officers are still very much household names within the military band world, it would be a little unfair here to name names.

However, it was noted that one candidate "*Temperamentally may not be too well suited to the appointment"* whereas another was considered *"Highly qualified musically"* but *"May lack personality and character to deal with the man management side".* A third candidate *"Failed psm on three occasions in two subjects – conducting and aural. Director of Music RMSM is solely responsible for teaching these two subjects", "Has an 'outstanding' band"* but *"Has considerable business acumen which might not be in order at RMSM."*

The remaining candidates were Captain David McBain of the Royal Horse Guards (The Blues): *"Failed psm in one out of five subjects; Well qualified musically; temperament and experience suitable for appointment"* and Captain Jaeger of the Irish Guards. Of the latter, the Commandant wrote: *"Has had a meteoric career; Young; May lack experience; Very much alive."*

All these officers were interviewed by the Director of Personal Services and all *"were of remarkably high standard"* and he felt that the choice should lie between Captain McBain and Captain Jaeger. In setting out his reasoning to the Adjutant General he noted that, *"In addition to his duties as Chief Instructor at Kneller Hall, the officer holding the appointment has to accompany the Commandant in his capacity of Inspector of Army Bands on the periodic inspections and is responsible for reporting the musical efficiency of the band being inspected. Too junior a Director of Music might not find it easy to do this when a band directed by an officer many years his senior was being inspected.*

*I formed the opinion during the interviews that Captain Jaeger was unquestionably the outstanding candidate from nearly every point of view and was certain to have a profound influence on Army bands and military music if given the appointment. The only drawback is his seniority. He is only 40 years of age and still has 20 years to serve.*

*Captain McBain, on the other hand, is considerably more senior, has 7½ years to serve and would be a suitable candidate for the post, though he has not got the same breadth of vision and personality as Jaeger. He is due for promotion to substantive Major in the middle of January 1954.*

*The choice between these is simply a case of deciding whether it would be better for the future efficiency and prestige of Army bands, to appoint an outstandingly well-qualified man to Kneller Hall with the prospect of his serving there for 20 years, or whether a more senior and more experienced Director of Music who will within the next month be promoted to substantive Major would not be a more suitable choice. I am sure that both would fill this post efficiently.*

*On balance I recommend that Captain McBain should be selected for the appointment now and that Captain Jaeger should remain where he is for the present and be considered again when the appointment falls vacant which, if McBain gets it, will be in about 7½ years. If you would like to interview these two officers before making the final decision I will arrange it."*

The hand-written reply from the Adjutant General confirmed: *"I agree to upgrading to local rank. My selection is McBain, recognising that Jaeger may follow him in time."* Captain McBain was appointed from 11th November 1954 with temporary rank of Lieutenant Colonel and held the post with distinction, particularly through the celebrations for Kneller Hall's centenary in 1957.

The Adjutant General's comment about 'local rank' opened a can of worms and the outcome was relevant for Jiggs later in his career so, again, some explanation of what happened is called for. Directors of Music were commissioned on the same basis as Quartermasters, in other words, promoted from the ranks rather than by direct entry to Sandhurst. A Quartermaster officer's post could not be designated for a particular rank, as this was something granted to individual officers and not related to his appointment.

The quota for Lieutenant Colonel Quartermasters at that time was calculated as a percentage over the whole Army (4%). Therefore, with 24 Directors of Music, only one could be a substantive Lieutenant Colonel although there was also a general pool of vacancies, one of which could go to a Director of Music depending on his respective seniority with other Quartermasters. In practice, Directors of Music would normally succeed to a 'pool' vacancy as they tended to be amongst the most senior Quartermasters, but this was not automatic. When the substantive Lieutenant Colonel retired, the 'pool' officer took the substantive vacancy and the 'pool' vacancy then went to the next suitable candidate on the Quartermaster roll.

Although it was initially suggested that Captain McBain should be granted the rank of Local Lieutenant Colonel, the War Office was reluctant to grant local rank when the responsibilities appeared to warrant the rank of Lieutenant Colonel. However, there were already two Lieutenant Colonels: Owen Geary at the Royal Artillery (Woolwich) Band (substantive) and Albert Lemoine with The Life Guards ('pool'). In addition, Sam Rhodes had been granted Local Lieutenant Colonel rank in July 1953 at the request of the Major General in recognition of his extra responsibilities as Senior Director of Music, Brigade of Guards.

The War Office felt it would be unfair to other Quartermaster officers if the quota for Directors of Music was increased, so faced something of a dilemma. The Adjutant General (AG) wrote to the Military Secretary on 28th February 1954: *"Since receiving your minute I have gone into the question of rank for the Director of Music at Kneller Hall once again and am more than ever convinced that this must be recognised as the Senior Director of Music appointment in the Army and the incumbent must be of Lieutenant Colonel rank.*

*In 1942 when we were looking for a Director of Music for Kneller Hall, the post was offered to and rejected by every Director of Music in the Army. It eventually went to Bandmaster (WO1) Roberts who was promoted into this important post. The reason for this was that the appointment carried no extra rank or prestige and Directors of Music of staff bands were not prepared to forego their share of profits from paid engagements which acceptance of the post involved.*

*I purposely did not offer it to all and sundry (this time) as I did not wish to repeat the lamentable experience of 1942. My choice was Captain McBain of the Royal Horse Guards and I consider that he should hold rank equal to the Senior Director of Music in the Army. This will not only compensate him to some extent for the financial loss he must suffer but will enhance the prestige of the appointment and military music in general."*

The solution came from the Director of Personal Services on 29th June 1954 when, *"I have investigated the possibility of changing the designation of the appointment from 'Director of Music' to a title such as 'Chief Instructor and Technical Adviser to the Inspector of Army Bands', thus making it a Regimental appointment. This would enable us, subject to the Establishment Committee agreement, to designate it as a Lieutenant Colonel's appointment. There would be no objection to filling it with a Director of Music and McBain could continue in the appointment with a temporary rank of Lieutenant Colonel. He would become what the Military Secretary's branch designates a Director of Music, misemployed."*

With the agreement of the Adjutant General it was thus agreed: *"To take establishment action to alter the appointment at Kneller Hall from 'Director of Music' to 'Chief Instructor and Adviser to the Inspector of Army Bands' with the rank of Lieutenant Colonel and to reach agreement that there will continue to be 25 Directors of Music in the Army in spite of the fact there will be only 24 Director of Music appointments when the change has been effected."*

Everyone seemed happy with this arrangement except a financier who wrote quibbling that the occupant would draw regimental rates of pay of £3 1s 6d a day as compared with Lieutenant Colonel (Director of Music) rate of £2 17s 0d. It was a delight to see him firmly put in his place by DPS: *"Thank you for bringing to my notice the implication regarding rates of pay. I must confess that it had escaped me up to now. However, I welcome it as an added inducement to prospective Directors of Music to attain the high musical qualification required for selection for this appointment, and because it underlines the AG's policy that the appointment shall be the senior and most important in the Army open to Directors of Music.*

*May I take it you will raise no objection to the proposal?"*

The financier very grudgingly agreed!!

Two questions arise here: firstly, with such a strong recommendation why was Jiggs not given the appointment when it next became vacant in 1961? The post went to Lieutenant Colonel Basil Brown from the Royal Engineers, a very ironic appointment if the suppositions about Major Thornburrow being rejected in 1942 were correct, as Brown was also a nephew of Hector Adkins!

The other question, which can only ever be a matter of conjecture, is how army music might have developed had Jiggs been appointed in 1954 with the potential for almost twenty years at its head? Perhaps a parallel can be drawn here with Lieutenant Colonel F. Vivian Dunn, who had been appointed Principal Director of Music of the Royal Marines a year earlier, in 1953. He was to occupy this position for fifteen years and thus had a long period in which he was able to set in place a structure and training programme that proved highly successful and exert an influence that is still felt to this day.

Jiggs had first met the then Major Dunn shortly after his appointment to the Irish Guards. Lieutenant Colonel Sir Vivian Dunn, as he became, was later to recount, *"It was immediately evident that we both spoke the same language and a keen sense of rapport developed that lasted throughout his life."* Sir Vivian went on to describe how their conversations invariably centred on the full range of the classical repertoire and of Jiggs being extremely well read, enterprising, stimulating and liking nothing better than a lively argument on any subject at all!

With his classical background and training at the Royal Academy of Music, Sir Vivian's circle of close friends covered a large slice of the music world and he tended not to mix with his military music colleagues socially. Jiggs was a notable exception and it is true to say that of all Sir Vivian's really close friends, he held Jiggs in particularly high regard; indeed his son Paddy went so far as to say that they were 'special buddies' in the broadest sense of the description.

It seems reasonable to suppose that, had they headed their respective organisations in tandem for nearly a decade and a half, there would have been a good deal more cross-pollination of ideas between the bands of their respective services – but it was not to be.

Meanwhile, B Flat had been living with the Sargent household for some while but, as time went on, they were no longer able to exercise her adequately and so in January 1950 Jiggs had transferred ownership to some close family friends,

*Maureen and Christopher at Wellington Barracks in the mid-1950s. The remains of the Guards Chapel, destroyed by a flying bomb on 18th June 1944, can be seen behind them to the right of the picture. The buildings to the left have long since been demolished.*

a Methodist minister and his wife in Swindon, who were keen to have her. She settled happily with them but, sadly, had to be put to sleep on 23rd March 1955 having succumbed to arthritis in the rear quarters which caused her much distress and made it very difficult for her to move about the house.

*Christopher supplementing the band's percussion section at Wellington Barracks; Band Colour Sergeant 'Nobby' Clarke, at 6 feet 7 inches, towers over him.*

*Christopher at Wellington Barracks, watched by Band Sergeant George Prior. The instrument he is playing is a bugle horn, which appears to be engraved and was perhaps something that Jiggs acquired from his days as Bugle Major in the KOYLI.*

In 1954, the music publishers Boosey and Hawkes organised an international competition for a new march, a straightforward 'marching' march, with a prize of 100 guineas. A total of 605 entries was received and a panel of experts was assembled to adjudicate, with the winning entry being played as part of a grand concert at the Royal Albert Hall on 14th April 1955 by the Massed Bands of the Brigade of Guards, along with the Kneller Hall Trumpeters. The conducting was shared among the five Directors of Music and the panel of judges, with Jiggs conducting the first item, *Sigurd Jorsalfar* by Edvard Grieg. The winning march, *Ad Astra*, composed by Willi Loffler, was never to attain the popularity hoped for by the publishers.

*A gathering of Directors of Music at the International March Competition: Left to right of picture: Major Ille Gustafsson (Royal Swedish Army), Captain Jaeger, Captain Rocus Van Yperen (Royal Dutch Forces), Lieutenant Colonel Sam Rhodes (Scots Guards), Captain Francois-Julien Brun (Garde Republicaine), Lieutenant Colonel David McBain (Kneller Hall), Herr Otto Zurmuhle (Municipal Band, Lucerne) and Major Fred Harris (Grenadier Guards).*

On 3rd August 1955 the Band flew to Germany to take part in an International Festival programme organised by Volkswagen to celebrate the production of its millionth car since the war. Also taking part were the Band of the Swedish Life Guards, bands from Belgium, France, Holland and the American Army, along with the Vienna Ballet Company, Negro dancers from the Gold Coast and, attracting particular interest from the band, the Moulin Rouge Can-Can dancers from Paris.

The band was quartered in four excellent hotels in Braueschweig, some distance from the Volkswagen town of Wolfsburg, but was bussed in for rehearsals at the specially erected wooden open-air arena with the stage backed by an enormous wide stairway rising about 60 feet, painted bright yellow. On the Festival Day itself, Saturday 6th August there was an audience approaching 200,000 with a line of 40 new cars which were to be raffled to Volkswagen workers between the items in the programme.

*(Also overleaf) The International Festival in Germany to celebrate the production of Volkswagen's millionth Beetle car.*

For some reason that no-one can remember, the band wore forage caps rather than bearskins, led by Jiggs wearing his frock coat. They appeared sixth in the programme and marched on playing *The Queen's Guard* (Keith) to an enormous roar, which entirely drowned the music, a reception which the musicians would not easily forget. The Micks naturally stole the show, with the enthusiastic Germans clapping and stamping in time as they finally marched off playing *Old Comrades* (Teike).

The hospitality received by the band was most generous and Jiggs hit on the idea that, while the performers were all relaxing with refreshments during the evening, the band should express their appreciation by going along to the table where Volkswagen's top man, Dr Nordhoff, was dining to play some of his favourite marches, including *Old Comrades*. Dr Nordhoff rounded off the evening with a speech in which he made a point of praising how well the band played the marches and promised them all a watch. True to his word, in due course a consignment of 60 watches arrived at Chelsea Barracks, each one inscribed with the name of the musician for whom it was intended.

While the band was in Germany, Jiggs took the opportunity to visit his father and his German family. This was to be his only visit but the family were overjoyed to see him and made him very welcome. His sister, Irene, also made the trip with her second husband to see her father so he had the satisfaction of meeting all three of his English children again. Heinrich Jaeger died in September 1958.

Jiggs's methods of recruiting for the band did not always follow conventional lines. Early in August 1955 the band was marching out of Buckingham Palace to lead the Old Guard back to Wellington Barracks when the time-beater, Band Colour Sergeant 'Nobby' Clarke burst the skin on the bass drum. Jiggs immediately sensed the problem and hurried back to the Corps of Drums to order their bass drummer to start playing with the band. The Corps of Drums was from 1st Battalion Scots Guards and the young man in question, Boy Harry Copnall, had only enlisted on 3rd January that year, fresh from a mining village and with no training in music. Harry was to recall later that *"for a lad of 16 years of age to be told to play with the all-hallowed Micks band was unbelievable"*.

Boy Copnall had clearly done a good job, as that afternoon he was summoned from Wellington Barracks to report to Jiggs at Chelsea Barracks and asked if he would like to join the Irish Guards Band as the time-beater to replace Nobby Clarke, who was soon to retire. Harry explained his very meagre musical knowledge but Jiggs was not put off easily and insisted that he have an audition that, bizarrely, consisted of Harry marching around the practice room playing the Regimental Slow and Quick Marches on the bass drum. He passed!

Despite the promise of proper percussion lessons never really materialising, Harry Copnall progressed through the ranks, eventually to become the Band Sergeant Major, finally retiring in 1986 as one of the band's great characters.

*The Band posing for a photograph on the square of the old Chelsea Barracks. The buildings to the left of the picture were along Chelsea Bridge Road.*

Early in 1955 the Band of the Royal Marines School of Music under Lieutenant Colonel F. Vivian Dunn recorded a long-playing record at EMI's Abbey Road Studio No. 1 which, incidentally, had been opened by Sir Edward Elgar in 1931.

The producer was Brian Culverhouse, a man to whom military band enthusiasts owe a large debt as he was to produce a great number of LPs of a quality which has stood the test of time and which shines through today, since many have been re-released on compact disc.

With Brian's agreement, Jiggs had been allowed to attend the sessions and, in the course of their conversations, he invited Brian to Chelsea Barracks to hear the Irish Guards. As a result, Brian decided to produce a recording with the band and was later to recall, *"The quality of the playing of the Band made me decide not to record an entirely military programme but some orchestral works arranged for concert band."*

Although Jiggs had made a number of 78 rpm records with the band, this was to be his first long-playing record and the recording took place at Abbey Road on 5th and 6th October 1955. The record was issued in 1956 on the EMI label, CLP 1076, and proved a big success, with subsequent reissues:

## THE BAND OF THE IRISH GUARDS

*Side 1:*
St Patrick's Day *(Trad arr. Kappey)*
Let Erin Remember *(Trad arr. Jaeger)*
Shepherd's Hey *(Trad arr. Hartley-Grainger)*
Pitter Pat Parade *(Llavalle-Ventre)*
Andalucia *(Lecuona arr. Beeler)*
Dance of the Tumblers (from Snow Maiden Act 3) *(Rimsky-Korsakov arr. O'Donnell)*;
Fandango *(Bradford-Perkins arr. Werle)*
Jigger's Corn *(Jaeger)*

*Side 2:*
Marche Lorraine *(Ganne)*
Perpetuum Moblie Op. 257 *(J. Strauss arr. Winter)*
Diabolero *(Spurgin)*
Irish Washerwoman *(Trad arr. Hartley trans Winter)*
La Sorella *(Gallini arr. Lang)*
Wood Nymphs *(Coates arr. Godfrey)*
El Caballero *(Olivadoti)*

This LP was directly responsible for providing the band with at least one new recruit, in the form of oboist Mike Jeans. He had the option of joining either the Grenadiers or the Irish but after hearing this recording and the style of music included, his mind was made up in favour of the Irish, a decision he was never to regret. Listening to the record again in 2011 he wrote, *"Even with a more critical ear and better equipment than I had in 1956 the recording stands up remarkably well and Jiggs's personality and input are palpable in the verve and spirit of the playing; considering how much standards have risen over the profession as a whole over the last fifty years, there is some excellent playing."*

An extended-play (45rpm) record was issued with *St Patrick's Day, Let Erin Remember, Marche Lorraine, Andalucia* and *Diabolero*, the latter composed by Anthony Spurgin who composed a good deal of light music for orchestras and military bands which was frequently played by the Irish Guards.

During the Easter holiday in 1956 Jiggs went up to Cromer in Norfolk to be the guest conductor for a week's tuition course and concert by the National Youth Brass Band of Great Britain, an example of the time and interest he devoted to helping young people. The band had been formed by Dr Denis Wright and was made up from around a hundred hand-picked players from all over the UK, including David Cawdell who was fortunate enough to have been chosen for several years and ended up in the principal euphonium seat.

By the time of the 1956 course he had already been accepted to join the Band of the Irish Guards, and so had the pleasure of Jiggs's company and the experience of playing under his baton all week. *"He, of course, knew that I had been accepted for the Micks and I remember clearly him saying to me, 'David, I do not need to audition you, I've heard enough already.' Commendation or criticism? You decide. Thus began three of the happiest years of my life."*

*Captain Jaeger receiving a basket of shamrock from HRH The Princess Royal for distributing to members of the Regimental Band on St Patrick's Day 1957 at Wellington Barracks*

1957 marked the centenary of The Royal Military School of Music and a series of concerts was held on the bandstand at Kneller Hall to mark the occasion, including performances by Massed Bands from the Royal Marines and from the Royal Air Force. On Monday 10th June 1957 it was the turn of the Massed Bands of the Household Brigade, under the Senior Director of Music, Lieutenant Colonel Albert Lemoine, The Life Guards, a rare example of a Household Cavalryman being shown with that title. Each of the Directors of Music took his turn to conduct a major work and a lighter number, with Jiggs taking the baton for *Invitation to the Waltz* by Weber and the *Dance of the Tumblers* from *Snow Maiden* by Rimsky-Korsakov.

*Signed photograph presented to Jiggs by Percy Grainger inscribed: "To Captain C.H. Jaeger in boundless admiration of his conducting genius & with warm thanks for his superb interpretation of my music, from Percy Grainger, June 1957."*

The Band of the Irish Guards was involved with two films in 1957, principally when the orchestra, conducted by Jiggs, took part in the ballroom scene in *The Prince and the Showgirl* at Pinewood Studios. They also recorded the music for the coronation procession scene and it was said that Jiggs wrote a special arrangement of *The British Grenadiers* in 'wiggle' time for Marilyn Monroe, who starred in the film alongside Laurence Olivier. The second film was *Island in the Sun* for which the band played the background music for scenes set at Government House in the West Indies. However, the main event for Jiggs in 1957 was leading the band on a world tour which lasted for some 3½ months during which time the band visited Canada, the United States of America, Australia, Rome and Singapore. Forty-one musicians and 15 Pipers and Drummers took part with Major J.G.F. Head, Irish Guards as the Administrative Officer.

They departed from London in two parties on 19th and 20th August and eventually arrived in Toronto to take part once again in the Canadian National Exhibition, an engagement entailing programmes during the afternoons and evenings, with a free day on Sundays. The band, needless to say, attracted high praise from all quarters with its playing and fine displays of piping and dancing complemented by the superb lighting and sound amplification in the band shell. The Household Brigade Old Comrades Association in Toronto gave the Band a party which lasted well into the night with a good deal of drinking and reminiscing.

*Jiggs in Toronto sitting at the table paying out subsistence to his musicians: left to right: George Munton, Nobby Clarke, Bob Horton, Jim Gladen and Chris Hyde-Smith.*

On 8th September the Band flew via New York to Los Angeles with perfect visibility over the 300 miles of the Grand Canyon Ranges. They stayed in Los

Angeles over four days, giving two concerts at the Shrine Auditorium which was packed to its capacity of 10,000 on both occasions, with the band being given a tremendous reception and attracting wonderful Press comments. They managed to visit Warner Brothers' Studios in Hollywood where they met a number of famous film stars and then moved on to Disneyland.

*Major Head and Jiggs with the conductor of the Disneyland Band.*

Nearly 19 hours' flying, with brief stops at Fiji and the Canton Islands (about 1,850 miles south of Hawaii), took the band to Sydney and thence to Melbourne, arriving there on 16th September. The Band travelled on a chartered Qantas Super Constellation and it was a very long journey. Major Head decreed that everyone must shave before they got off the plane – not a popular decision in view of only cold water being available.

At Melbourne, the band played in the Olympic Swimming Stadium from 17th to 29th September with the imagination of the audience a little stretched as they were asked to imagine that the tiled floor of the Olympic pool was the gravelled surface of Horse Guards Parade! *"Ladies and gentlemen, presenting – from Buckingham Palace, London – The Band, Drums and Pipes of the Irish Guards".* The sixty musicians marched down a wooden ramp into the shallow end of the pool (fortunately drained of water!) to present a version of the Trooping the Colour ceremony and, since the deep end was ten feet below seating level, most of the band could not be seen until marching back to the shallow end during the slow troop.

| | | |
|---|---|---|
| March On: | **With Sword and Lance** | *Starke* |
| Royal Salute: | **National Anthem** | *Arr. Jaeger* |
| Inspection Music: | **Erinalia** | *Somers* |
| | **The Red Cloak** | *Mansfield* |
| Troop Music: | **Les Huguenots** | *Meyerbeer* |
| | **St Patrick's March** | *Bidgood* |
| Music for the Escort: | **British Grenadiers** | *Trad* |
| | **Grenadiers Slow March** | *Arr. Harris* |
| Slow March Past: | **Eileen Allanah** | *Arr. Jaeger* |
| | **Let Erin Remember** | *Arr. Jaeger* |
| | **Scipio** | *Handel* |
| | **Men of Harlech** | *Trad* |
| | **Garb of Old Gaul** | *Reid* |
| Quick March Past: | **Old Comrades** | *Teike* |
| | **St Patrick's Day (Pipes)** | *Trad* |
| | **British Grenadiers** | *Trad* |
| | **Rising of the Lark** | *Trad* |
| | **Hielan' Laddie (Pipes)** | *Trad* |
| | **Sons of the Brave** | *Bidgood* |
| March Down the Mall | **The Champion** | *Graham* |

After one of the performances Jiggs was approached by Archie Burt who had attended the Newport Market Army Band School, albeit two or three years after Jiggs, and produced the photograph of Boy Jaeger receiving his prize – see Chapter 1.

Some of the concerts were broadcast as far afield as Brisbane, Sydney, Adelaide and Perth and they clearly generated a good deal of interest, as a crowd of about 2,000 people greeted the band on arrival in Adelaide where they took part in a wreath-laying ceremony, being inspected by His Excellency The Governor, Sir Robert George, prior to marching around the city cheered by countless thousands of people. The Governor and Lady George were extremely kind to the band, attending many of its concerts and inviting them to cocktails in Government House. As in Canada, the local Household Brigade Old Comrades Association also gave the band a wonderful party, presenting Jiggs and other senior members with suitably inscribed silver tankards.

From Adelaide the band visited Port Augusta and Port Pirie before giving an open-air concert in the Wayville Oval back in Adelaide with an audience of 33,000 people. The tour continued with the band eventually reaching Sydney where it gave 20 concerts in the Tivoli Theatre, two of which were attended by

*Australia 1957. HE The Governor of South Australia, Air Vice Marshal Sir Robert George, inspects the Band in the grounds of Government House at Adelaide, with Jiggs and Major Head in attendance.*

the Governor-General, Field Marshal Sir William Slim, who was most generous in his appreciation of the band.

Back in Sydney, the band's last open-air ceremonial parade took place in a temperature of 101 degrees in the shade. They then flew to Adelaide over hundreds of square miles of forest fires, the sight of which had to be seen to be believed, and later to Perth for yet another outstanding reception.

Jiggs's arrangement of *Waltzing Matilda* proved particularly popular during the tour and he was, of course, fully enjoying being the centre of attention and very much in demand. Harry Copnall, tall, smart and the youngest on the tour, was also attracting a good deal of interest from the media, so much so that on one occasion Jiggs sidled up to him and warned him to stop pinching his publicity!

A champagne and chicken party for the band finally marked the end of the tour. A lot of things went on during those five months but one of the funniest came as they were leaving to fly home from Perth when Percy Martin was late getting to the airport. After it had taken off for the three-day flight home, he was duly marched in on 'Orders' (into the aircraft loo) and given 'three days confined to plane'. As it turned out the band arrived back two days late. After the very hot temperatures to which they had been accustomed, the fog at London Airport was so dense that they had to stop over for a night in Rome and another in Frankfurt, before finally returning to dear old Blighty.

By the time they reached London it was estimated that they had given 140 concerts and travelled more than 35,000 miles, encircling the world by Qantas and BOAC. The Australian stretch alone had covered 4,000 miles in ten weeks, playing in 25 cities and provincial centres. Jiggs's summary of the tour was that *"it was generously thought to have been the greatest boost to Commonwealth relationships since the recent Royal Tour"*.

On April 29th 1958 the hit show *My Fair Lady* opened in London and David Cawdell recalls the following morning: *"On April 30th the Micks were on duty at Guard Mounting at Buckingham Palace and were entertaining the crowds as the Micks always do. Jiggs handed round some manuscript parts and when we looked it was a complete selection from* My Fair Lady *which we sight-read and played perfectly. I cannot think that Jiggs had been sitting up all night writing out the parts but he probably had had a sneak preview of the orchestral parts beforehand. I also don't know how he got round the copyright laws, but play it we did."*

*Irish Guards Band Reunion in the 1950s. Jiggs is holding the silver cup which was presented to the band in thanks for their tour of Canada in 1905.*

CHAPTER 9

# MAJOR JAEGER

**Jiggs was promoted to Major on 24th July 1958**

The band's next long-playing record, EMI CLP 1240, followed on from the success of the 1956 recording:

## THE BAND OF THE IRISH GUARDS

*Side 1:*
Overture: Ruy Blas *(Mendelssohn arr. Retford)*
Ouvre Ton Coeur *(Bizet arr. Lang)*
Trumpets Wild *(Walters)*
Concetta *(Dexter)*
Broadcast from Brazil *(Bennett)*
Blue Plume *(Jaeger)*

*Side 2:*
Overture: The Marriage of Figaro *(Mozart arr. Duthoit)*
Sunset Strip Polka *(Palange)*
Guards Armoured Division *(Willcocks)*
Parade of the Pomegranates *(Roger arr. Richardson)*
Thunder and Lightning *(Strauss arr. Carey)*
Dance in the Twilight (from *Springtime*) *(Coates)*
Allegro Deciso (from *Water Music*) *(Handel arr. Harty and Duthoit)*

Jiggs had a close association with the National Association of Boys' Clubs over many years right up until his death. No one is too sure quite how he got involved initially but he was extremely active in helping them wherever he could, serving for ten years as chairman of the Arts Advisory Committee.

Chris recalls: *"My father had been an indefatigable worker for the Boys' Club movement for many years, perhaps something inspired by memories of his own difficult upbringing? He travelled many thousands of miles visiting clubs where there was an interest in making music and was a prolific speaker at many conferences and meetings where his talks and demonstrations were a great source of inspiration to the boys. Sometimes, it seems, he was not overly impressed with the type of music he heard while visiting the clubs but generally he was able to encourage and advise the boys in order to motivate them to pursue their musical interests."*

*Jiggs passing on some good advice at the Southend Boys' Club*

As an example of this, in October 1963 he was the guest conductor of the Aspley Boys' Club Symphony Orchestra in a concert at Nottingham's Albert Hall. Another visit to the Nottinghamshire Association came in 1966 when he travelled to the Ollerton Residential Centre to visit and give a talk on the "Instruments of the Military Band" as part of their Senior Boys' Training Course.

In 1957 the Association's National Committee had decided to stage a Grand Boys' Club Show at the Royal Festival Hall to mark the launch of their annual

Club Week. Teddy Wagg, the Honorary Treasurer, came up with the name *Clubs Are Trumps* and the mainstay of the show from the beginning was the great entertainer, Frankie Vaughan, perhaps best remembered for his trademark hit song '*Give Me the Moonlight, Give Me the Girl*'. A whole host of stars took part over the years, including Vera Lynn, Billy Dainty, Des O'Connor, Bill Owen, Benny Hill, Jimmy Tarbuck, Norman Vaughan and many more.

The Band of the Irish Guards first took part in the show's second year, 1958, and *Clubs Are Trumps* thereafter became an annual engagement, with the band generally marching in from the back of the hall and playing a few pieces, as well as providing background music and accompanying the various artistes and the musical acts by boys from all over the country, often with very little notice of what was expected of them. Frankie Vaughan became a close friend to Jiggs, as did a number of other show business personalities, particularly Kenneth Horne who visited their house with his wife, and Leslie Crowther.

Clubs Are Trumps. *Jiggs with Frankie Vaughan, Earl Mountbatten, Norman Collier, Viscount Althorp (later the 8th Earl Spencer) and an unidentified gentleman in the foreground*

Jiggs's interests in supporting good causes also extended to the Variety Club of Great Britain. He had a long association with the Royal Academy of Music,

*Jiggs shaking hands with the Duke of Gloucester. The Duke was the President and a very active supporter of the Boys' Clubs and Clubs are Trumps throughout his life.*

the Royal College of Music and the Trinity and Guildhall Colleges of Music as an examiner on the boards of their bandmastership diploma examinations. Jiggs had that great gift to get on with just about everyone, although he disliked anyone pompous or self-important with no sense of humour – and he most certainly did not like bossy women!

Another visit to Northern Ireland came on 10th May 1958 to add musical support to the Review by HM Queen Elizabeth, the Queen Mother to mark the Golden Jubilee of the Territorial Army at the Royal Naval Air Station, Sydenham. The Band of the Irish Guards played before the parade with:

| | |
|---|---|
| The Red Cloak | *Mansfield* |
| Paso-Doble – Gallito | *Gomez* |
| Irish Airs – Erinalia | *Somers* |
| The Queen's Guard | *Keith* |
| Golden Spurs | *Rhodes* |
| Eileen Allanah | *arr. Jaeger* |
| With Sword and Lance | *Starke* |

The Massed Pipes and Drums of the Territorial Army, Northern Ireland, gave their display and played for the inspection of the parade, after which the band took over to play for the march past of the corps and regiments on parade, ending with Carl Teike's famous march, *Old Comrades*. The Band of the Royal Warwickshire Regiment under Bandmaster R.F. Hilling played in the Royal Enclosure before the parade.

On the following day, Sunday 11th May 1958, the band played at a service at St Anne's Cathedral, Belfast, preceding the service with *Nimrod* (Elgar), *Mortify Us By Thy Grace* (Bach) and *Where'er You Walk* (Handel), with Walton's *Crown Imperial* as the outgoing voluntary.

The following month the band again supported the TA's Jubilee, this time at a Service of Thanksgiving at Westminster Abbey on Saturday 21st June 1958, playing a similar programme as well as a fanfare composed by Jiggs which preceded the National Anthem.

*The Band of the Irish Guards playing at Stormont in Belfast*

The band was back in Belfast in September 1958 for a Grand Concert at the Ulster Hall with the Faulet Girls' Pipe Band, with the proceeds going to the Welfare Funds of the Irish Guards Association (Ulster Branch). The concert opened with the regimental marches and included the Overture to *William Tell* (Rossini), *Toccata and Fugue* (Bach) and *Hibernia*, a selection of well-known Irish airs arranged by Charrosin. The second half featured 'Soloists' Galore' and the concert ended with *Nightfall in Camp* (Pope).

*The Band of the Irish Guards playing at Stormont in Belfast.*
*Band Sergeant Jim Gladen is the soloist*

Jiggs was back at Kneller Hall on 28th May 1958 as a guest conductor for one of the Wednesday evening concerts, taking the band through the Fantasia on Irish Melodies entitled *Let Erin Remember* arranged by Fritz Brase.

The band's accommodation at this time was in the old Chelsea Barracks, which dated from the 1860s, and comprised a couple of small offices and a practice room above the guardroom at the back entrance in Ebury Bridge Road. There were no changing facilities or storage area and the musicians had to travel to work in uniform ready for parade, wearing a cape and forage cap, carrying their instruments, with their bearskins in bags and in some cases also carrying their boots to avoid them being trodden on while on the Underground. A few travelled in plain clothes carrying their uniforms; the larger instruments such as the tubas were left in the practice room.

Alongside the band room at this time was a piece of ground that Jiggs adopted as his 'barracks garden' where he cultivated roses. During the rehearsals in the lead-up to the ceremonial season there would frequently be horses in attendance to help familiarise them (and their riders) with the sound of the massed bands. Mick Moscrop, always known to Jiggs as 'Goosegog', shared a few chats with him about gardening and, as a result, he was appointed 'horse muck collector' which entailed him clearing up after the parades and redistributing the produce on the rose beds.

National Service was still compulsory and Geoff Broom recalls how this was looming for him in October 1958 while he was a part-time student at the

Guildhall. His trumpet professor was Bernard Brown who had served with the Irish Guards Band and he explained to Geoff the benefits of joining a Guards Band, in that they generally only worked in the mornings, which would give him plenty of opportunity to continue his studies as well as doing a bit of teaching and playing outside. After much persuasion he eventually convinced Geoff that this was the right move and contacted the band office to arrange an audition for him.

This was arranged for 12 o'clock and Geoff arrived at Chelsea Barracks in good time and was taken to the practice room, lined all around with empty instrument cases as the Band was out on Guard Mounting (an hour earlier in those days). Jiggs's orderly, Chick Webb, had put some cornet music out for Geoff to look at and he began warming up, soon to be interrupted by an invasion of musicians returning from Guard, packing their instruments into the cases and making a quick exit within a few minutes.

One of the cornet players came over to chat and asked what Chick Webb had put out for Geoff, suggesting that he should look at the solo part in *The Bamboula* by Coleridge Taylor, telling him that the boss liked that one. Geoff took the advice and began playing it, soon to be interrupted by a gentleman wearing a string vest and army trousers. *"That sounds very nice,"* said the gentleman and Geoff replied that he had been told that *"he likes this one"*. The gentleman queried, *"Who likes it?"* to which the reply was along the lines of *"the boss"*. *"You mean the Director of Music?"* and as Geoff mumbled something like *"probably"* he announced that *"I'm the Director of Music; my name is Major Jaeger – I assume you know yours?"*

So much for creating a good impression – but Jiggs went on to confirm that he did indeed like that piece and asked Geoff to play it again. After a few more pieces Jiggs said he had heard enough and told him to come in the office. Geoff followed him, somewhat dejected, assuming he had failed, only to hear the Band Secretary, Norman Madden, being told, *"I'm having him – take his details."* Not only that but Norman, the only man in the band at that time with a car, was told to give Geoff a lift back to Victoria station.

The Irish Guards had first became involved with the Annual Dinner of the Transport Golfing Society in 1953 when they began the tradition of playing fanfares to introduce the various guest speakers, most of whom were high-powered members from the transport industry. These were not just any old fanfares but were all specially composed by Jiggs, who researched the speakers' backgrounds and used melodies which could be readily associated with them, always ending with '*Why was he born so Beautiful*'!

These special fanfares caused a good deal of pre-dinner speculation, and loud laughter when they were played as the speakers and prize-winners stood up. In 1963 the dinner was presided over by Jimmie Lees of Leyland Motors, who managed to turn the tables, getting his own back by helping to write the fanfare sounded when a surprise presentation was made to none other than Jiggs himself! Jiggs became quite a good golfer and was made 'The Honourable Minstrel to the Transport Golfing Society'.

From 1959 the full orchestra of the Irish Guards became involved as well as the trumpeters, with the climax of the evening always being the *Post Horn Galop* played by Jiggs on a .303 rifle. In keeping with the nature of the function he gave an encore on a golf club that, needless to say, brought the house down.

This was an annual fixture for the band until 1967 after which the event moved with Jiggs to the Kneller Hall Band and was later taken on by the Welsh Guards. The tradition of writing special fanfares continued and in 2010, with the Welsh Guards unavailable, the Micks reclaimed it. The Director of Music of the day could not, however, be persuaded to resurrect the tradition of playing the 'Golf Club Galop' himself!

In 1970 the society presented the Jaeger Trophy in his memory, to be awarded annually for the best Company Band Concert during the winter season at Kneller Hall.

*The Band on stage in Birmingham Town Hall, October 1959.*

In 1959 Bandmaster Jimmy Howe was appointed Director of Music, Scots Guards, which meant moving the family home from Aberdeen, where Jimmy had been the Highland Brigade Bandmaster, to quarters in Caterham. This was made all the more difficult because the newly commissioned Lieutenant Howe was away on a six-week tour of Scotland, so his wife, Peggy, was very pleased when no sooner had the furniture van arrived than there was a knock on the door and she answered it to find Jiggs on the doorstep offering his help with settling in his new neighbours.

Back in 1954 when the band had visited the United States, it had played on the steps of the State House in Boston. Band members had been somewhat surprised when Mr Christian Herter, the Governor of Massachusetts, decided to take a break from his work and come out onto the steps to ask if he could conduct the band. Jiggs naturally had obliged and handed over the baton for the Governor, looking dapper in his bow tie and brown suit, to take the band through a rousing Sousa march.

*Mr Christian Herter, the Governor of Massachusetts, conducting the Band on the steps of the State House in Boston in 1954.*

Watching the scene was Mrs Ellice Endicott, a Scottish born artist who was to make a painting of the scene with Mr Herter conducting and Jiggs standing alongside. In 1960 the painting was brought across to London and put on exhibition at the National Gallery, and with Herter now the US Secretary of

State it created considerable interest. Eileen Jaeger received a telephone call from a journalist asking about the occasion but she was only able to tell him that she knew of it because Jiggs had told her about it. However, journalistic license being what it is, when the article appeared she was apparently "... *there watching my husband...*" and able to comment on how amusing it was at the time. The newspaper cutting held by the family is clearly marked 'fiction' at this point!

Eileen and Maureen had been invited to attend a high profile function in London with Jiggs and had, so they thought, time in hand to visit the Gallery to take a look at the painting. Jiggs met them at Victoria station and decided that Maureen needed a hat (she took her mother's and Eileen bought a new one), which delayed them somewhat but they hailed a taxi to the gallery. There was only time for a quick look at the picture before they had to dash to the evening's venue, and just made it to the side of the red carpet in time to be presented to the Queen Mother.

Eileen was incredibly shy and hated public attention. On one occasion, the family was attending an Irish Guards concert on her birthday, 3rd September. At one point Jiggs went into his *"we have a very special birthday today"* speech but by the time he got to asking Eileen to stand up for the band to play *Happy Birthday*, she had long gone, slipping out and hiding in the Ladies until she felt the danger had passed!

When President de Gaulle paid a State Visit to London in April 1960 one of the highlights was a Review of the Household Troops on Horse Guards Parade with the Micks included in the Massed Bands. During his visit the band also appeared at the Royal Opera House, Covent Garden, to play the British and French national anthems on the arrival of H.M. The Queen and the President, as well as joining the Welsh Guards Band to play the music for the fireworks display.

On 14th June, the band was again playing for the Queen, this time at Smith's Lawn in Windsor Great Park for a cocktail party hosted by 1st Battalion Irish Guards. Jiggs and several members of the band had to make a quick dash from there to Windsor Castle where they were due to provide an orchestra for a private dinner party for Her Majesty.

In around 1960 the band's principal cornet, Lance Corporal Colin Casson, announced his intention to buy himself out and Jiggs was rather at a loss to know whom to appoint as his replacement. Keith Oxley recalls how he solved the problem by way of auditions:*"On one rehearsal he got out the well-known cornet solo, Zelda, and required the whole cornet bench to play it one by one. There were some commendable performances but some dire ones. Sitting right at the bottom of the bench was Terry Camsey. Terry had managed for two years to keep a low profile thus avoiding jobs with the 'playing-out' band (normally just 25 strong) and allowing him more time to continue with his studies as a public health inspector.*

*Well, Terry played an absolute blinder. Jiggs immediately proclaimed, "What the xxxxxx are you doing down there?" and immediately instructed him to take the top spot where he remained for the last year of his service."* Terry later emigrated to the United States and went on to become a renowned soloist and composer with the Salvation Army right up to his death in 2011.

*Jiggs conducting a cornet solo from Musician Colin Casson on the steps of St Paul's Cathedral.*

On the 6th June 1961 the Massed Bands of the Brigade of Guards gave a concert in the Open Air Theatre in Regent's Park, promoted by Martini-Rossi International. The music selected was all composed specifically for military bands, with the first half comprising *HRH The Duke of Cambridge* (Malcolm Arnold), the two *Military Band Suites* by Gustav Holst and *A Lincolnshire Posy* by Percy Grainger, with the conducting shared between Lieutenant Colonel Douglas Pope (Senior Director of Music) and Jiggs.

The main work took up the whole of the second half of the concert – the *Symphonie Funèbre et Triomphale* (Funeral Symphony) by Berlioz. This was conducted by Colin Davis, then Principal Conductor of Sadler's Wells and one-time principal clarinet in the Band of The Life Guards during his National Service from 1946 to 1948, which meant the bands immediately accepted him as 'one of us'. He handled the bands fantastically and the concert was enthusiastically received by an audience of approximately 5,000.

On 28th August 1961 the band, together with the Pipes and Drums of the 1st Battalion Irish Guards, set out from Caterham at 4.30 am to fly to Italy for a Grand Military Band Festival, with the opening parade in Turin that very afternoon. The three hour flight took them high over Lake Geneva and the Alps to the sweltering heat of Turin, where coaches were waiting to take them to their quarters in brand-new ten-storey flats, all of them light, cool rooms with balconies.

The festival was part of ITALIA '61 and had been organised to celebrate the centenary of the unification of Italy in 1861. For the band, it was a great contrast to their previous visit to that country during the war years of 1943–44 when they had spent seven months giving around 300 concerts in 100 towns, villages and rest camps, at the end of which they had all been smothered in volcanic dust when Vesuvius erupted.

The place was crowded with bandsmen of all nations including the Garde Republicaine from Paris, the Carabinieri from Rome, the Belgian Guides from Brussels, the Swedish Life Guards from Stockholm, the German Central Army Band from Bonn and the Italian Air Force, all considerably larger in strength than the Irish Guards, in some cases numbering around two hundred.

*The Directors of Music at Italia '61*

On the first morning there Jiggs decided to have a rehearsal out on the green in front of the flats to run through their programme including *Trumpets Wild*, the comic trombone solo *The Joker* (with Mark Spendiff in fine form), *Begin the Beguine* and the wonderful overture to Emil von Rezni's comic opera, *Donna Diana*. It was the last piece that rather let them down, as the rehearsal did not go as well as it could have done, something quickly picked up by musicians from the other bands who had gathered to listen. As one from the Garde Republicaine put it when they finished at lunchtime: "*Donna Diana*, not good but we loved all the rest – we don't play this sort of thing." Clearly they all enjoyed hearing the lighter side of the repertoire.

The opening parade involved each band marching at intervals down the mile long Exhibition Avenue, the Corso Polonia, to great applause in temperatures exceeding 100 degrees but with suitable refreshments waiting for them at the end. The band's first concert was in Turin's dimly lit historic square, Piazza Castello, beneath walls dating back to the 12th century, with an audience of several thousands.

It seemed as though the entire population of Turin turned out for the next concert in Venaria, which was preceded by a short marching display in the town square with very little room to manoeuvre, with Drum Major Milligan having a real battle on his hands to get through the excited crowds. During the concert one of the musicians, later to join the BBC Concert Orchestra, was violently sick as a result of rather too much wine. Jiggs took no notice; but there was big trouble in store for the bass trombone player when he was spotted yawning!

On one of the free days the coaches took the musicians the 60 miles to the alpine ski resort of Sestriere, 6,000 feet above sea level, then a further 3,000 feet in cable cars to the top of the mountain and the chance to breathe some cool air, which came as a great relief after the stuffy heat of Turin. The Festival reached its conclusion with a mammoth concert in which all the bands played in turn; the Pipers played throughout the evening as the bands changed.

During 1961 the Band was, as usual, playing on the bandstand at Eastbourne and Jiggs happened to meet an old friend, Mrs Jean Thirtle, the divorced wife of Major 'Tommy' Thirtle who was Director of Music of the Royal Horse Guards (The Blues). She had recently been engaged as housekeeper at the Priory Court Hotel at Pevensey and Jiggs returned there with her one day for tea.

The hotel was run by Tim Lord and his recently widowed mother, Betty, and with their interest in music they soon developed a close friendship with Jiggs. They had an African grey parrot which Tim's brother-in-law had brought back from Nigeria and with which Jiggs used to have long conversations. One year it escaped from its cage and had been finally 'written off' after nothing was seen of it for four days, when Jiggs arrived. He was determined to find it and, since he had memorised its call, he spent two hours patrolling the field behind the hotel whistling it. Jiggs came back with the parrot on his shoulder – it had flown straight to him when it heard his voice, yet another example of his extraordinary musicality!

Jiggs regularly stayed at Priory Court, as did a number of the band. In the evenings, the dance band would often play at the bar, with Sid Hope-Childs leading on tenor saxophone, Peter Burgess on string bass and maybe Bill Eldridge playing trumpet. The piano would be manned by an old friend, Tony Spurgin. Jiggs would generally not attend these sessions and retire to bed but, on one occasion, with the party still swinging at 2.00 am, he suddenly appeared in his pyjamas, his thinning hair in curlers and a Victorian cornet in his hands. He played a rousing chorus of *Whispering* before leaving the party. He later remarked, *"I hope we don't get raided as I <u>shall</u> have some explaining to do."*

Jiggs proved a great inspiration to Tim and became his teacher and mentor, eventually coaching him to take the ARCM in military bandsmanship. There would be conducting lessons for him in the kitchen at midnight and Jiggs would sometimes conduct his Pevensey Village Band playing outside the local public house. Tim was also involved with Sussex Brass and, on one occasion, Jiggs had promised to make an appearance as guest conductor at the band's annual concert at the White Rock, Hastings. When Jiggs and Chris set out, *"we encountered some of the worst fog I can ever remember and turning back looked the safest option. Jiggs would have none of it and we struggled on, arriving after the interval. He snuck in at the back of the hall just to hear Tim Lord apologising to the audience that he had not made it. Whipping out of his pocket the miniature cornet which he always carried, to the complete delight of everybody present, he marched on to the stage playing 'Sussex by the Sea'."*

The Irish Guards Band went to the Isle of Man in July 1961 with the Pipes and Drums and Shaun, the wolfhound, to take part in the Tynwald Day Festival at Castletown. The bands appeared at various events across the island including the Kirk Bradden open air service on 2nd July. Jiggs had confirmed to the Tourist Board well in advance that one of the main items they would play would be Haydn Wood's tone poem *Mannin Veen* (Dear Isle of Man), which is a medley of Manx music that includes the *Manx Fisherman's Hymn* and the *Manx Fiddler*.

Another engagement during the tour was the Onchan Carnival, at which the band preceded a transporter with one of the brand new Mini cars on board, which created a good deal of interest. The band set off with Jiggs leading, after he had given instructions to the centre trombone players, Mark Spendiff and Mike Martin, to ensure that they kept in position so that he was in the centre.

There were tramlines along the left side of the road and Jiggs started to veer towards them so that the band followed him and they ended up marching over them. A policeman tried to direct them back off the tracks but Jiggs carried on and shouted back to him, *"I know what I'm doing."* He clearly didn't, as very soon a tram was seen in the distance, heading straight towards them in a scene which must have been reminiscent of the days of the silent comedy films. Harry Copnall had his view obscured by the bass drum and wondered what was happening when he suddenly found himself playing solo with musicians rapidly scattering left and right, unable to play for laughing!

Peter B. Smith was to become Bandmaster of The Queen's Royal Irish Hussars, an amalgamation of the 4th and 8th Hussars, and was to make a great name for himself as a composer and arranger. Some years earlier in his career he was sent as a flautist to play with the Irish Guards Band in a concert at Sandhurst. *"There was no rehearsal and after the opening march, The Stars and Stripes Forever (Sousa), came Rossini's William Tell overture. We had just reached that pastoral bit where the flute jumps about when I noticed Jiggs making signs to Paddy Donnelly, the bassoonist. Paddy came round just as I started the flute solo and he simply took away my pad, stand and all. Somehow I managed – but that was Jiggs!"*

Towards the end of September 1961 Jiggs was admitted to Queen Alexandra's Military Hospital, Millbank, to be treated for a dislocated knee (or hip?) with Eileen and Chris rather shamefully getting the giggles over his shouts of pain as he hobbled around after his discharge!

Twelfth January 1962 was a very sad day in the history of the band because of the death of its former Director of Music, Major George Willcocks. The whole band attended his funeral near Romford, Essex, and the Ford Motor Works Band played during the service.

Jiggs had an extensive knowledge of the classical repertoire and was a great lover of Brahms, Wagner and Elgar amongst others. However, he didn't listen to much music at home, never being one for sitting down doing nothing and, in the car, his family recall he generally listened to Radio 4 rather than Radio 3. He showed little interest in other types of music although, of course, everyone associated with military bands needs to have pretty eclectic tastes. The 1960s music revolution left him pretty cold although he did develop an admiration for the Beatles following the recording of the band's ground-breaking album 'Marching With The Beatles' in 1966.

Not surprisingly it was the 'big stuff' from the classics that Jiggs particularly liked to rehearse with the band, some of his favourites being *Scheherazade*, the *Original Suite, Toccata Marziale*, all the great overtures and the two *Suites for Military Band* by Gustav Holst. Band practice with Jiggs started at 10 o'clock on the dot but he would frequently not bother to say what they were to play but just make a comment like, *"Once upon a time there was a desert,"* bringing down the baton knowing the band would take the cue to play *Scheherazade*.

Most of the music for the bandstand programmes was not rehearsed, as it was considered to be the staple diet. He would never put too much in the programmes for bandstand concerts, leaving time for something from the extra pad. He had certain ideas of what he wanted from the band and really stamped his mark on them to make them what they were.

In 1962 Jiggs played host to the greatly respected band conductor, Frederick Fennell, who was visiting from the United States. He attended morning service at the Guards Chapel at Wellington Barracks, at that time still being held in a temporary Nissen hut, to hear the musicians. Only a small section of the band is used in the Chapel and on this particular day Geoff Broom was leading the cornet section and the programme included a solo item for him in Handel's *Song of Jupiter*, otherwise known as *Where e'er You Walk*. His playing clearly impressed Mr Fennell, who made a point of telling Jiggs so.

That afternoon the band began a week of concerts at the Victoria Embankment Gardens, close to Charing Cross Station, and Geoff took what was his normal position in the playing-out band as the second man down to Band Sergeant Jim Gladen. Jim was approaching retirement and Jiggs, having been giving much thought as to who should succeed him, walked round to him in a break between pieces and told him that Frederick Fennell thought that 'Broomy-Boy' was a good player. Jim replied, *"He is,"* and so Jiggs told them to swap places there and then with Geoff playing solo cornet for the remainder of the week's fourteen concerts. There is nothing quite like being pushed in at the deep end to concentrate the mind, but Jim proved a real friend to Geoff and would sit down with him before each of the concerts, to go through the parts and to point out what to watch out for.

Jiggs liked the sound produced by Geoff, who was to remain in the solo chair for the next eighteen years. He rather took him under his wing and would often mark the solo cornet parts with the phrasing he wanted, particularly for operatic selections when Jiggs generally knew the opera well. They struck up a great rapport and in Jiggs's last couple of years he would generally conduct programmes without a score, relying on Geoff to *tick-tack* him in selections to signal a change of time coming up or when there was a stinger at the end of a march.

Geoff's first solo in public was on the bandstand at Eastbourne, playing *O for the Wings of a Dove*. Jiggs, sensing some nerves, announced that it was to be played by Lance Corporal Geoff Broom, and for the young ladies in the audience, his telephone number is Chelsea 1234. The band laughed and this had the desired effect of relaxing Geoff and bringing forth a faultless rendition.

Jiggs was very possessive and would only very rarely let anyone else conduct the band. However, one day during rehearsals he announced that *"we have another conductor in our midst – Broomy-Boy"* and proceeded to inform the musicians that Geoff had been having some conducting lessons. Geoff was ordered to the rostrum, despite his protests, and given the opportunity to practise his skills.

At one point Jiggs grabbed hold of his arm in the middle of a piece and advised him to *"do it this way"*. He then threatened to charge Geoff five bob for the conducting lesson! One of Jiggs's pet hates was to see conductors bending their knees extravagantly and he was frequently heard to comment that they looked like *"a greyhound having a crap"*.

In those days, when a battalion stationed at Chelsea Barracks mounted or dismounted Queen's Guard, they would march to or from their barracks via Buckingham Palace Road led, of course, by the Band and normally a Corps of Drums. On one particular occasion in the early 1960s the band marched back to Chelsea with a frontage of nine trombones, and probably eight or nine deep. The road at that time carried two-way traffic and the band took up pretty well the full width of the road. The one mounted policeman accompanying them could do nothing to get cars past them with the result that traffic chaos descended on a substantial portion of central London. The next day a standing order was issued that in future the band was not to march any wider than six across.

Jiggs himself would not march in any particular place but had the habit of wandering around the band checking whether everyone had the correct music card in place. Anyone spotted erring would be quizzed as to whether they knew the march and, with the reply normally being, *"Yes Sir,"* the musician would be invited to come and play his part in Jiggs's office in the afternoon. This was one thing if it involved the melody but much more of an ordeal if it was one of the 'inside' parts involving lots of offbeats while trying to remember the melody!

On another Chelsea Guard Jiggs marched alongside 'Broomy Boy' at one stage and related that he was a happy man as he had just received a cheque for royalties amounting to a few hundred pounds, a substantial sum in the 1960s. The itemised list he showed him on his return included money for an arrangement of the National Anthem that Jiggs had made for the ABC Cinemas, who had filmed the Irish Guards playing it to be shown at the end of each evening in their cinemas.

1962 started with a 'bang', the Regimental Band being invited to appear in a television spectacular entitled 'The Big Parade', which was shown on 6th January. In addition to the Irish Guards, 80 trombone players, the Welwyn Garden City Male Voice Choir, Michael Friedeman's Ladies' Orchestra, and a number of speciality acts were engaged to complete the cast. The show culminated in a special arrangement of Tchaikowsky's *1812 Overture*, with intermittent graphic film flashes, resulting in a show which met with overwhelming success and a very high rating by the viewing public.

The result of this was that a second 'Big Parade' followed within three months and this time included the Luton Girls' Choir with 60 trumpeters playing the *Trumpet Voluntary* by Jeremiah Clarke, 60 post horn players in Koenig's *Post Horn Galop*, with the tone poem *Finlandia* by Sibelius as the finale. This programme was another outstanding success and on the strength of this HMV asked the Band to make a further long-playing record to be called 'The Big Parade' which was released in October 1962, with two songs from the baritone, Frederick Harvey:

## THE BIG PARADE

*Side 1:*

The Horse Guards Whitehall *(Wood arr. Duthoit)*
Trumpet Voluntary *(Clarke)*
(a) Hey, Look Me Over *(Coleman arr. Duthoit)*
(b) Funiculi, Funicula *(Denza arr. Jaeger)*
(c) Poppa Piccolino *(Mascheroni arr. Jaeger)*
When the Sergeant Major's on Parade *(Longstaffe arr. Denham)*
Seventy-Six Trombones *(Willson arr. Lang)*
Irish Salute (Galway Bay, With My Shillelagh Under My Arm, Dear Old Donegal) *(arr. Cofield)*
Maigret Theme *(Grainer arr. Jaeger)*

*Side 2:*

Commonwealth *(Jaeger)*
Mexican Serenade *(Coles arr. Murphy)*
A Trumpeter's Lullaby *(Anderson arr. Lang)*
When the Saints Go Marching In *(Trad arr. Walters)*
The Red Cloak *(Mansfield)*
The Yeomen of England *(Hood-German arr. Denham)*

Again, some of the tracks were issued on a 45rpm record: *Trumpet Voluntary, Seventy-Six Trombones, When the Saints Go Marching In* and *The Horse Guards Whitehall.*

As well as in the Big Parade, the band had appeared at many concerts with the Luton Girls Choir and so it was fitting that they should take part in the BBC television programme 'This is Your Life' when the choir's conductor, Arthur E. Davies MBE, was the subject of Eamonn Andrews's infamous red book. Jiggs spoke of the close association between them saying that, *"Our band and the choir are linked by Holy Wedlock."* Having flown specially from Toronto, in walked Mr and Mrs Bob Oades, ex-choirgirl and ex-bandsman, who had first met at a joint concert by the band and the choir.

*Appearing with Eamonn Andrews on* This is Your Life *for Arthur E. Davies.*

The previous year, 1961, had marked the choir's silver jubilee and the band had joined them for a celebratory concert which, as well as the individual items, brought them together in such numbers as *Britons Sing* (Purcell), *The Gypsy Chorus from Carmen* (Bizet) and selections from Sigmund Romberg's *Student Prince* and *The Desert Song*.

Another television appearance featured the band's principal flautist Bob Horton on the popular talent show *Opportunity Knocks* playing the piccolo solo *Picaroon,* accompanied by an orchestra out of view. Jiggs had telephoned Bob one day and asked if he would like to appear on television, waiting until he had agreed before telling him the show in question. The format of the show was that someone (Jiggs, of course) was interviewed by presenter Hughie Green to introduce the act. Bob was apparently very embarrassed by the whole thing, particularly as he had to follow a striptease type act, but Jiggs clearly enjoyed his own part of the show.

On 9th March 1962 Jiggs was invited to Deal to conduct at one of the series of Winter Concerts given in the Concert Hall by the Orchestra of the Royal Marines School of Music. His main work that evening was four movements from Handel's *Royal Fireworks Music* but before that he conducted a trumpet solo, played by

Junior Musician S.I. Misson. Aged just 18, Musician Misson had just won the Cassel Prize as the best soloist at the School and, as a result, had been invited to the Worshipful Company of Musicians to be presented with the medal. This was his first meeting with the Principal Director of Music, Lieutenant Colonel F. Vivian Dunn who was, for a Junior Musician, *"an unapproachable God-like person"* so it was with some surprise and much apprehension that Misson was informed that he would be performing at the concert. He played Purcell's *Trumpet Tune and Air* on what he later described as *"a strange D fanfare trumpet"*, an experience made all the more unnerving as the conductor was unknown to him. Jiggs must have helped put him at ease at the brief rehearsal in the morning as he recalls having taken it all in his stride with no mistakes.

Steve Misson went on to enjoy a very successful career with the Royal Marines as a bandmaster, ending his service as the Chief Librarian of their Central Music Library, where one of his responsibilities was looking after music donated to the band service, including the 'Colonel Jaeger Collection' which was presented to them after Jiggs's death. Following his retirement in 1984, Steve Misson moved into recording and publishing, having set up Cinque Port Music. Following the bombing at Deal in 1989 he was heavily involved with the Memorial Bandstand and the annual charity concert.

Towards the end of 1960 a request was received in London from 4th Guards Brigade, stationed in Germany, for the loan of a Director of Music to assist the preparations for their Queen's Birthday Parade the following May. Jiggs duly volunteered, but the request was rejected by the Major General who felt this was unnecessary, as Major Leslie Statham from the Welsh Guards had advised them recently and the details of the parade had not changed. The request was re-submitted the following year and this time permission was granted for Jiggs to fly to Dusseldorf on 21st May 1962 in time for the preliminary rehearsals by the massed bands but with a firm stipulation that he must be back in London by the afternoon of Friday 25th May. He was accommodated with 1st Battalion Irish Guards at Hubbelrath.

The parade itself was to be held at the Rhine Centre, Dusseldorf, on Saturday 2nd June 1962. The 4th Guards Brigade at that time comprised 1st Battalion Irish Guards and 1st Battalion Welsh Guards, who would find the 'Guards' for the parade, and 1st Battalion The Lancashire Regiment (Prince of Wales's Volunteers) who provided the ground-keepers and one of the bands, along with three cavalry bands to make up the Massed Bands: 5th Royal Inniskilling Dragoon Guards, 10th Royal Hussars (Prince of Wales's Own) and 15th/19th The King's Royal Hussars.

The Senior Bandmaster for the parade was Mr Gordon Turner, 15th/19th The King's Royal Hussars. Now Major (Retd) Turner MBE, a much respected elder statesman and historian of army music, he recalls that he gladly accepted the original offer of a sergeant from a Guards band to fly out to advise, so at the appointed time he set off to meet him at the airport, not knowing who was actually arriving. Imagine his surprise when the man who appeared was in fact Jiggs, wearing a civilian suit complete with sergeant stripes and insisting on being addressed as 'Sergeant Jaeger' throughout!

When Jiggs arrived for the start of the rehearsals the bands were lined up and he went along the ranks with Mr Turner telling the bandsmen that if any of them had worked with him before, please tell him as he could not necessarily remember everyone. A number of the bandsmen indeed made mention of previous encounters and he eventually reached Band Sergeant Major George Saville of the 15th/19th who snapped to attention, saluted and said, "*Number 27, Sir.*" Jiggs's expression suddenly turned to thunder and he shot off.

Later when the marching rehearsals were under way, Jiggs spoke to the Regimental Sergeant Major from the Guards who was in charge, pointing out Mr Saville and saying something along the lines of "*watch him, put his name in the book, I'm not happy about him at all*". The RSM, sensing potential problems, reported the conversation to Mr Turner and suggested that as Jiggs was clearly gunning for him, it might be an idea to send him home, which is what happened. It transpired that George Saville had been an orphan at school with Jiggs and they were then known by their number. Quite what triggered Jiggs's bad reaction is not known but it can only be surmised that he did not want too much of a reminder of those days.

On one of the evenings Jiggs arranged a dinner in the Sergeants' Mess for the Bandmasters, Band Sergeant Majors and Drum Majors. He arrived and was introduced to each of them. When he got to one of the bandmasters Jiggs really tore into him, seemingly as he had been given a Freemason's handshake. Jiggs had been Master of his Lodge, the Incorporated Society of Musicians, during 1956–57 but his involvement in Freemasonry lasted for a relatively short time and he soon gave it up. There were suggestions at the time that he took exception to some bandmasters apparently using their Freemasonry connections to pass the 'psm' examinations but this was, of course, very much conjecture.

These incidents aside, everything on the parade went very smoothly and it was a very happy period as Jiggs knew exactly the problems regimental bands and bandmasters would have, when working with the Brigade of Guards and his advice made life very easy for them. Despite the strict timescale the Major General had set for the visit, it seems that Jiggs was there for about a fortnight.

On his eventual return to London he wrote to each of the Bandmasters thanking them for their work, and passed on a very lucrative job to the 15th/19th which entailed the band touring Germany and Belgium with Sadler's Wells in a production of Gilbert and Sullivan's *Iolanthe*. The Band of the Irish Guards had been approached to work with the UK part of the tour. Jiggs also pointed out to

Mr Turner that a couple of his bandsmen had been asking for auditions to come to the Irish Guards but had been given short shrift and told to put it though the proper channels. Unfortunately, it would appear that the same degree of integrity was not exercised the following year, and the Director of Music sent out to assist was thought to be actively poaching some of the best musicians from the massed bands.

On Saturday 30th June 1962, Jiggs conducted the Massed Bands of the Brigade of Guards, together with Massed Corps of Drums, for the Annual Greyhound Derby at the White City Stadium. This proved to be an outstanding success with the final item being a special arrangement by Jiggs of the theme music from the BBC Television series *Maigret*.

The band, by this time, had moved out of Chelsea Barracks, which, apart from the Chapel, was completely demolished and rebuilt. They moved into temporary accommodation in a basement at Wellington Barracks with the new luxury of having lockers, thus ending the problem of having to travel to London in Guard Order. The practice room was a Nissen hut at the back of the barracks alongside Petty France, next to accommodation for the musicians who lived in the barracks, with a wooden hut for the library.

In October 1962 the band prepared to move into their 'sumptuous' quarters

*Jiggs rehearsing the band in their new purpose-built practice room*
*at Chelsea Barracks.*

in the newly rebuilt Chelsea Barracks. Anyone who served at the barracks, particularly in its latter years before being finally sold off, will doubtless be amused to read the account of the new accommodation which appeared in the regimental journal: *"The new quarters are really luxurious and for the first time in the history of the Band we have adequate room for practice, offices, changing rooms, etc. The practice room itself is large enough for a Band of 60 musicians to practise in comfort, is soundproofed and centrally heated. The new Barracks have 'all mod cons' including a heated swimming pool, squash court, excellent married quarters, and most comfortable lounges for the NCOs and Guardsmen for their 'NAAFI Break' and leisure hours."*

*Immediately below Jiggs's right hand is Sergeant Mike Millard, Jiggs's orderly for many years.*

Away from the band, Jiggs had a very busy November in 1962, being on the panel of adjudicators at the Croydon Music Festival which covered 7th to 17th November, with competitions for choirs, soloists, piano and various groups including orchestras and military/brass bands, and a prize-winners' concert at Fairfield Halls. On Saturday 24th November he was at the Civic Hall in Exeter, adjudicating the South West Brass Band Association's Sixteenth Annual Brass Band Contest (First Prize: Ten Guineas) followed the next day with conducting a Demonstration Band Rehearsal at a school in Pinhoe on 'Test Piece Music', which had been organised by the Association of Brass Band Conductors.

# CHAPTER 10

# SENIOR DIRECTOR OF MUSIC

Jiggs became Senior Director of Music of The Brigade of Guards in July 1963 following the retirement of Lieutenant Colonel Douglas Pope, OBE, of the Coldstream Guards. This brought a considerable increase to Jiggs's responsibilities, all of which were in addition to his already high workload with the Irish Guards, and entailed conducting the Massed Bands on such occasions as the Queen's Birthday Parade (Trooping the Colour), Cup Finals and various international football matches at Wembley Stadium.

*The seven Directors of Music of the Household Brigade pictured at the Duke of York's Headquarters, Chelsea; from the left of the picture: Captain Jimmy Howe, Scots Guards; Major 'Jacko' Jackson, The Life Guards; Captain Trevor Sharpe MBE, Coldstream Guards; Captain Ted Jeanes, Royal Horse Guards; Major Jiggs Jaeger, Irish Guards and Senior Director of Music; Captain Arthur Kenney, Welsh Guards and Captain Rodney Bashford, Grenadier Guards.*

As well as these high profile occasions, there is a great deal of work for the Senior Director of Music in planning these events and co-ordinating the five bands, overseeing the master diary which must ensure that bands are allocated to public duties and ceremonial occasions, not to mention acting on behalf of the bands for policy decisions.

However, the most moving part of the role of the Senior Director of Music must surely be to conduct the Massed Bands of the Brigade of Guards at the Cenotaph on Remembrance Sunday, a real test since the programme of music commences at 10.36 am and must be very carefully timed so as to finish at exactly 10.58 a.m. The first time Jiggs had this responsibility was on Remembrance Sunday 1963 and, although the musical aspects of the parade had changed little since they were standardised in 1931, he was aware of an anomaly with the trumpet and bugle calls. Perhaps as a former bugle major, he had taken a little more interest in these matters than his predecessors.

For many years the Trumpeters of Royal Air Force Halton had sounded the Infantry *Last Post* on their E flat trumpets following the two minutes silence, while Buglers of the Royal Marines sounded the Naval *Reveille* at the end of the service. This is the call which is generally known as the 'Charlie' *Reveille* due to the unofficial words of '*Charlie, Charlie, Get Up and Wash Yourself, Charlie, Charlie, Get Out of Bed*'. Jiggs wanted this changed and first secured the support of the Principal Director of Music, Royal Marines and the Organising Director of Music, RAF and then wrote to the Chief of Staff, London District, on 5th October 1963 pointing out that "*Last Post was composed essentially for the B flat bugle, and being of a different pitch it is a technical impossibility to perform this on the E flat trumpet unless certain modifications are made, which distorts the original melodic shape of the call*". Put another way, the call had to be played using the incorrect notes, something that had caused considerable comment and protest in the past as it sounded so wrong.

Jiggs went on to suggest that the roles should be reversed so that the Royal Marines Buglers sound *Last Post* and the RAF Trumpeters instead sound the call *Rouse*, which was an official RAF trumpet call and suitable for their instruments. The RAF requested that the matter be deferred until the following year but this eminently sensible suggestion was then taken up.

Jiggs never took part in the Edinburgh Military Tattoo but clearly had some influence in the early part of the 1960s. The Massed Bands for the 1963 Tattoo were found from 1st Battalion The Royal Highland Fusiliers (Princess Margaret's Own Glasgow and Ayrshire Regiment), 1st Battalion The Argyll and Sutherland Highlanders (Princess Louise's) and the Royal Army Medical Corps, all directed by Lieutenant Colonel Lewis Brown, RAMC. Their display included Jiggs's slow march arrangement of *Eileen Allanah, Mountains of Mourne* and *Wild Colonial Boy*, as well as the theme music for *Inspector Maigret*. The following year the Massed Bands were centred on the Band of the Royal Air Force Regiment under Pilot Officer Eric Banks, who included two Jiggs arrangements, *Old Pops* and *Dominique*.

The original Guards Chapel at Wellington Barracks had been destroyed by a flying bomb on 18th June 1944 with many fatalities including the Director of Music, Major Causley Windram, and five musicians from the Band of the Coldstream Guards. After many years with a makeshift chapel in the form of a Nissen hut, the present building was completed in 1963 with a service of dedication planned for the November.

The Band of the Scots Guards played on this occasion, as the Irish Guards were away on tour, but the responsibility fell on Jiggs, as the Senior Director of Music, to prepare the music. He liked to make new settings of some of the hymns that were to be sung, particularly with special arrangements of the last verse, sometimes rather upsetting Dr Henry Saunders, the organist at the chapel.

The band, choir and trumpeters assembled with Jiggs in the practice room one day to play the suggested music to an entourage including the Major General and Brigade Major, who then had to present the programme to Her Majesty for approval. After each of the hymns and other items, the response was along the lines of *"Yes, we like that one Jiggs"* and after about 40 to 50 minutes they said they had all they would need for the service. Jiggs protested that he had another one for the finish, a special arrangement of *He Who Would Valiant Be*. Despite the General's insistence that they had enough, Jiggs wouldn't let it go until the General eventually sighed, *"If you persist Jiggs, we'll hear it."* All the stops were metaphorically pulled out with a tremendous climax with choir, trumpets and band and as it finished Jiggs turned around, looked at The Major General and said, *"If God doesn't appear after that, no one else will."* It was included.

It was during the early 1960s that the Irish Guards Boxing Team reached the final of a competition held in Germany and the regiment chartered an aeroplane to fly out its supporters, along with some high ranking officers from Horse Guards and the Guards Depot.

Things had gone a little too quiet for Jiggs on the outward flight and he went to the back of the plane and managed to persuade a rather startled steward to lend him his tunic and cap. Thus attired, Jiggs marched jauntily up the aisle to the front gangway seat, occupied by the officer commanding the Household Brigade, Major General John Nelson, and demanded to see his passport. Jiggs would often tell this story and relate his delight at the way in which he was requested to depart!

The return flight to Gatwick became a somewhat different experience, as at three o'clock in the morning the airport was shrouded in thick fog and the plane spent some time circling and twice started to make descents but had to climb away. At the third attempt all the airport buildings flashed past the windows before the pilot again powered up and abandoned his attempt to land. In the tension that followed, Jiggs was heard quietly to remark, *"Well, anyway, if this lot goes up we should get a full page in the Brigade Magazine!"*

The flight was diverted to an ice-cold Southend Airport, with a long wait to get through the customs and, of course, no transport available for them. A number of the party, Jiggs included, were due to be on the Commandant's Parade at the Guards Depot at Pirbright later that morning. Fortunately Jiggs was able to hire a taxi back to Chelsea Barracks, along with Major Philipson, Scots Guards, who had arranged for a Guardsman to be waiting for them at Chelsea to drive them to Pirbright, where they arrived in good time for a very welcome breakfast.

The Commandant, meanwhile, had shown considerable initiative in hiring a double-decker bus (bearing in mind in was four o'clock in the morning) for the main party from the Guards Depot. The bus proved to be in bad order and after three punctures and a good deal of pushing, it was finally abandoned, leaving the Commandant hitchhiking in full mess kit on the Brighton Road. Nothing pleased Jiggs more than being on the one parade that the Commandant himself missed!

1963 was memorable for another major overseas tour for the band, this time to spend a month in South America, visiting Argentina, Uruguay and Chile along with the Pipes, Drums and Dancers of 1st Battalion The Royal Scots (The Royal Regiment). This was the oldest regiment in the British Army, the 1st of Foot who stood at the 'Right of the Line' as the senior infantry regiment, bearing the proud nickname of *Pontius Pilate's Bodyguard.*

The tour was thought to be the first time that the British Army had been to Argentina since The Queen's Own Cameron Highlanders attended an Exhibition in Buenos Aires in 1932. It was organised by two Frenchmen named André Guerbilsky and Jean Clairjois, whose last trip to South America had been to sponsor the Sadler's Wells Ballet.

The party left London Airport on Sunday 10th November 1963, Jiggs having joined them immediately after conducting the Massed Bands of The Brigade of Guards at the Cenotaph. Their destination was Buenos Aires and some 22 hours after leaving London they landed at Ezeiza Airport and were taken to the Richmond Hotel where they would be staying. The instruments and uniforms were secured in the Luna Park Stadium, a building not unlike Olympia, which was the venue for their displays for the forthcoming 2½ weeks.

The bands' first task was a wreath-laying ceremony at the statue of General de San Martin, the national hero of Argentina. The band marched down the Avenida Santa Fe in brilliant sunshine, led by Drum Major McMeekin of The Royal Scots, immediately followed by Jiggs, with the Pipes and Drums behind the band. The size of the crowd, estimated at 120,000, was such that

*The Irish Guards and The Royal Scots posing for a photograph on arrival at Buenos Aires to start their tour of South America in 1963*

*The bands marching through massive crowds to the statue of General de San Martin*

135

*Jiggs saluting at the conclusion of the display at the stadium in Santiago*

*The Band of the Irish Guards performing in Luna Park*

the bands had to struggle to get along the route, while the cheers rendered the music almost inaudible and clouds of confetti, carnival streamers, carnations, roses and sweet peas rained down on them. It was a wonderful reception but unfortunately meant that the ceremony had to be somewhat curtailed.

Jiggs had told the Band Sergeant, Jim Gladen, to choose some marches and suggested that *San Lorenzo* (Silva) could be included as it sounded a bit Spanish. The crowd was wildly enthusiastic right along the route but when the band struck up *San Lorenzo* the volume of the cheering reached fortissimo. The bands eventually reached the memorial, and wreaths were laid with Jim Gladen, as the solo cornet, stepping forward to play *Last Post* in Dougie Pope's setting of *Nightfall in Camp*. This was beautifully played, note perfect, and was followed by a Trumpeter from the Argentine Army playing their equivalent of the call. He was awful, with a host of split notes as the poor man clearly went to pieces and could be seen shaking. The band kept straight faces – but only just.

The performances in Luna Park took place daily at 10pm due to the heat (except on Mondays which were free days) and on Sundays at 6 pm, as well as matinees on Wednesdays and Saturdays.

*Music programme*

Without any knowledge of Spanish (the Argentines' language) it is still not too difficult to translate most of the titles and see that they began with the *River Kwai March, Leaving Port Askaig* and *Marching Sergeants*, moving on to *Light Cavalry, Irish Salute, The Three Jets* and ending the item with the *Maigret* theme. After the interval came a truncated version of Trooping the Colour including Bidgood's *St Patrick's March* and *Sons of the Brave*. The evening ended with *Nightfall in Camp* and the Regimental Marches, *Dumbarton's Drums* and *St Patrick's Day*.

For the first evening performance at Luna Park, Jiggs decided to include *San Lorenzo* in view of the reaction it had caused during the afternoon but he had not anticipated the audience's response when they all stood up and sang enthusiastically. He was soon to discover that the march, composed in 1901, commemorates the Battle of San Lorenzo in 1813 when the Spanish were defeated by General San Martin to give the country its independence. The lyrics were added in 1906 and it had become one of the country's national songs.

After the performance the Director of Music of the Argentine Army Band came down to see Jiggs and told him there were four bars missing in the version of the march published in Britain. He gave Jiggs the correct score and, by the next morning, he and Fred Wiles had written out the missing bars, stuck them on the cards and a quick rehearsal ensured that all was well for the remainder of the performances. Jiggs would cut the music at certain points and leave the audience to sing with just the basic accompaniment – he certainly knew how to sell the band.

He was later to re-score the march completely, adding a trombone counterpoint to the final section, and his arrangement became the standard version played by all the Foot Guards bands. (As an aside, the march was selected to be played for the Quick Troop at the Queen's Birthday Parade of 1982, which took place during the war to recapture the Falkland Islands. It was diplomatically changed; a pity really, as the British Army has a long tradition of stealing the enemy's tunes, from *Ça Ira* to *Lilli Marlene*.)

In each of the three countries visited, the band naturally played the host's National Anthem, each of which was of considerable length but the renditions clearly gave much pleasure to the spectators. A comment heard in Buenos Aires was, *"We always sing our anthem because we like it. But you play it so nicely we just listen."*

A local reporter wrote with great enthusiasm: *"The first half belonged mainly to the scarlet tunics of the Guards. After an introductory march past they form into a circle to play the sort of music that might go down very well at a Buckingham Palace Garden Party. From von Suppe's overture Light Cavalry they move on to swing, a samba and a beautifully executed number, The Joker, with a solo trombone. This is a band of maestros rather than soldiers. Their Director, Major C.H. Jaeger, conducts with vigour and bonhomie, looking more like a bearskinned Toscanini than a strict military officer.*

*The second half featured the two bands together for a representation of the famous Trooping the Colour ceremony. But for many of the Argentinians present, the high spot of the evening is the playing of their National Anthem by the Irish Guards. They certainly play it very beautifully."*

The bands received tremendous hospitality throughout the tour, particularly at La Plata, the seat of Government of the Province of Buenos Aires, where

Jiggs and the other officers were invited to an excellent lunch with the Military Garrison officers before being presented to the Governor of the Province.

The next leg of the tour found the bands flying to Santiago, the capital of Chile, where the dry heat was something of an improvement over the rather humid heat of Buenos Aires. The bands played at the stadium that was built for the World Cup football tournament and the two performances were enjoyed by a total of 130,000 spectators including the President of Chile. The musicians arrived at the stadium dressed in uniform and had to run the gauntlet while getting inside, as the enthusiastic audience were trying to pull bits off the uniforms. After five days in Santiago it was time to return to Buenos Aires, flying over the Andes with a perfect view of the mountains, for a final open-air performance in the Belgrano Athletic Club.

The last leg of the tour was in Uruguay with five days in the capital, Montevideo, flying across the River Plate on Thursday 5th December. This stage began with a wreath-laying ceremony at the statue of General Artigas in a similar form to that in Buenos Aires, although with a somewhat more orderly crowd. The bands gave four performances at the Estadio Centenario football stadium, a somewhat unfriendly structure built entirely of concrete, including the seating, with the nearest spectator at least twenty yards from the touchline and separated by a barbed wire barricade and deep concrete moat.

The bands took the opportunity of visiting the beaches on the final Saturday and Jiggs only got back for the matinee performance thanks to the Uruguayan Navy producing an aeroplane to fly him back from near Punta del Esta. On the final Sunday morning the bands gave their last performance in the stadium.

They left Carrasco Airport on the BOAC flight which landed at London Airport on 10th December, with the considerable drop in temperature and the impending Christmas celebrations being something of a jolt to their systems. The tour had been a great success and the friendship with The Royal Scots was continued with Captain Hay, Drum Major McMeekin and Pipe Major Burns being invited as guests at the annual reunion dinner in the Eccleston Hotel the following February.

*Telstar* was a big hit tune in 1962 for the pop group 'The Tornados' and rapidly achieved great popularity, so much so that Jiggs decided to arrange it as a march in a big bold flowing style, which the Band recorded in the early part of January 1963 for an E.P. 45 rpm record with EMI:

### TELEVISION AND RADIO THEME TUNES

*Side A*
Telstar March *(Meek arr. Jaeger)*
In Party Mood *(Strachey arr. Barsotti)*

*Side B*
Out of the Blue *(Bath)*
Dance in the Twilight *(Coates arr. Wright)*

The other titles may not be familiar but the melodies will be instantly recognisable to anyone of a certain age: *In a Party Mood* was the theme music from 'Housewives' Choice', *Dance in the Twilight* came from The Dales, while the BBC's Sports Report has been introduced by *Out of the Blue* since its very first episode in 1948.

The band made regular appearances at the Royal Albert Hall for the Burma Star Association Reunions and the Alamein Reunions, providing much of the music during the evening and accompanying several well-known artists, including Vera Lynn, Marlene Dietrich, Cardew Robinson, Clive Dunn, Ted Ray, Anne Shelton and Ted Durante. Rehearsals lasted all day and as well as the show itself the evenings were rounded off by the Dance Section, which played for dancing until midnight.

In fact, the musicians must have started to look on the Royal Albert Hall as a regular venue as they were there on 10th June 1963 for a concert given by the Massed Bands of the Brigade of Guards, along with the Pipes and Drums of the 1st Battalion Scots Guards and 1st Battalion Irish Guards in aid of the Freedom from Hunger Campaign. Each Director of Music took his turn with the baton, Jiggs conducting the Suite '*The Royal Fireworks Music*' by Handel, with the finale being the *1812 Overture* conducted by Sir Adrian Boult.

The concert was an enormous success and was repeated the following May, this time for the Outward Bound Trust with the addition of the Choir of the 1st Battalion Welsh Guards and the Corps of Drums of the Junior Guardsmen's Company, with Jiggs conducting the Overture from Wagner's *Tannhauser* as the finale.

At one televised concert in the Royal Albert Hall the band hired a huge concert bass drum to simulate the cannons in *1812* and Harry Copnall was duly assigned to it. A problem arose when he found that, although the required drum had been provided, the correct soft beater had not. He therefore had to improvise with the normal parade beater, which was a very compact hard tool so he tried not to hit the drum too hard to avoid damage. Jiggs became frustrated at the lack of volume during the rehearsal and shouted at Copnall to, *"Hit the bloody thing"*. This rather embarrassed Harry – so he did just that, resulting in the awful sound of ripping pigskin resounding through the Albert Hall! *"Jiggs looked at me and in my innocence I said, 'Well you did say hit it, sir.'"*

Come the actual performance, Jiggs capitalised on the situation and got them to tape up the ripped skin. He then had a word with the camera operators so that, at a given moment, they would swing the camera onto the bass drum and

Copnall was to 'hit the bloody thing' again and make it appear that it had just ripped – quite a production scoop!

The band's regular visits to Northern Ireland continued to prove popular. In August 1963 the tour took up three weeks in August, visiting eighteen towns accompanied by a drill squad of twenty men from the 1st Battalion with the wolfhound, Shaun. As well as parades in each of the towns there were a number of concerts including a performance outside the City Hall in Belfast which included the Waltz from *Swan Lake* by Tchaikowsky, an Irish medley *Hibernia*, *American Patrol* and a selection from *The Music Man*. A special round of applause greeted the band's rendition of *Waltzing Matilda*, played at the request of two Aussies who insisted on thanking Jiggs personally. One of the highlights was Beating Retreat in the grounds of Stormont Castle with around a thousand spectators including the Lord Mayor of Belfast.

*Jiggs with Lord Wakehurst, the Governor of Northern Ireland,*
*before a dedication ceremony*

141

Jiggs continued to attract very favourable reports from his commanding officer, his report for 1963 reading: *"Full of energy and resource he has done a great deal to enhance the reputation of the Regiment wherever the Regimental Band has performed. He maintains a very high standard within the band, not only from a musical point of view, but also as to their turnout and drill. He is an extremely well qualified and talented Director of Music."*

With the battalion in Germany, St Patrick's Day 1964 in England was celebrated at the Guards Depot with the Regimental Band providing the music for the Church Services and March Past as well as giving a very successful evening concert in the Army Kinema Corporation's Globe Cinema for recruits and staff of the Guards Depot, which included Jiggs playing *Post Horn Galop* on a rifle as well as the Dixieland Band under the direction of 'Big Sid' Hope-Childs.

One of the band's engagements in 1964 was to play at Twickenham rugby ground for the annual Army v Navy match. The Army team was led by Captain Mike Campbell-Lamerton of The Duke of Wellington's Regiment, who was also captain of the Scottish and British Lions teams. Amongst the other players in the team that day was Lieutenant Charles Guthrie, Welsh Guards, now Field Marshal The Lord Guthrie of Craigiebank, Colonel of The Life Guards and one-time Chief of the Defence Staff.

The band's customary appearance at Eastbourne during the Easter period attracted a good deal of attention in the press for the wrong reason when the musicians arrived to open the Easter Monday Bonnet Parade, only to find that the bass drum and cymbals had been stolen from the Bandstand. Jiggs reported the matter to Eastbourne Police and, fortunately, the Inspector also happened to be Secretary of the Eastbourne Silver Band and so was able to arrange the loan of replacements.

The missing items were soon discovered at the New Wilmington Hotel, 100 yards from the bandstand, when one of the owners noticed a bed was tilting at a strange angle and found them underneath. Members of a London rugby club had been staying at the hotel and appeared to be the likely culprits. The press rather enjoyed it all with headlines such as *"The Band that lost its Boom"*.

On Sunday the 19th April a concert was given in conjunction with the Luton Girls Choir to open the new Civic Hall in Dunstable, which was attended by the Mayor and several local dignitaries. The success of this concert was marked by the fact that a 'repeat performance' was immediately booked for November but in the meantime another joint concert was arranged at the Fairfield Halls, Croydon, in September. For the first time in its 28-year history, the girls arrived late, since even back in 1964 London's traffic was a huge problem which the choir clearly underestimated. The first of their two coaches arrived at the Hall half an hour after the start time, with the second arriving another half hour later.

The Band, of course, carried on regardless with their part of the programme,

*Jiggs leading the Band of the Irish Guards along the seafront at Eastbourne for an afternoon concert on the Bandstand*

impressing a local journalist who reported that they played in their usual impeccable style and that *"Major Jaeger, who might have been a popular light entertainer and compere if he had not been such a brilliant musician, dealt with the situation admirably during that first hour when most of the girls from Luton were conspicuous by their absence. His dry sense of humour kept the audience entertained in between the band numbers."*

The Band was a great favourite at the Shrewsbury Musical and Floral Fete and in August 1964 they were joined by the Bands of The Life Guards and Scots Guards. The show days ended with the three bands massed on the bandstand, joined by the Rolls Royce (Shrewsbury) Male Voice Choir. Jiggs conducted the final part of the concerts on the first evening with *Tannhauser Overture* (Wagner) and *Finlandia* (Sibelius), with *Welsh Rhapsody* (German) and *1812* (Tchaikowsky) on the second.

Radio broadcasts at this time were regular dates in the band's diary and, indeed, the diaries of all the top bands. Perhaps the most taxing for the band was the long-running series of 'Music While You Work' which was normally broadcast 'live' from the studio at Maida Vale and always started and finished with the familiar signature tune, *Calling All Workers* by Eric Coates. There were strict rules laid down for the musical content and the music had to be continuous with no breaks between items. This proved a great test for the Directors of Music when selecting the programme, to ensure that each piece was compatible with the next in terms of the key and that it was timed exactly to fit the 29 minutes or so available.

Here is an example of one of the band's many appearances on the programme, this one broadcast on Wednesday 2nd September 1964:

### MUSIC WHILE YOU WORK

| | |
|---|---|
| Calling All Workers | *Eric Coates* |
| Old Pops March | *arr. Jaeger* |
| Parade of the Tin Soldiers | *Leon Jessel* |
| Phil the Fluter's Ball | *Percy French* |
| Toy Trumpet | *Clement Scott arr. Jaeger* |
| Eileen Allanah | *Trad arr. Jaeger* |
| Swedish Polka | *Hugo Alfven* |
| American Patrol | *Gray* |
| Dominique | *Sourire arr. Jaeger* |
| Granada | *Lara* |
| Andalucia | *Ernesto Lecuona* |
| Jigger's Corn | *Jaeger* |
| Calling All Workers | *Eric Coates* |

The programme was, of course, quite a test of stamina and concentration for the musicians playing for almost half an hour without even time properly to change their music between pieces and, even with the country's finest, things didn't always go quite to plan.

Brian Reynolds, the acknowledged expert on the programme, recalls an incident which occurred as a result of the practice of writing out music in abbreviated form, using what are known as first and second time bars, in other words, instead of writing out a repeated section in full, just the part at the end which is different the second time is written. The band was playing its final march when Jiggs, noticing that they were running a bit late, signalled to the band to go straight to the 'second time bar'. Unfortunately, half the band had their music written out in full and therefore had no second time bar! The cacophony that followed necessitated Jiggs quickly stopping the march and going straight into the signature tune, 'Calling All Workers'.

On another occasion, Jiggs had timed the music in advance and found that it would overrun, so he made a number of cuts, leaving out some repeats and first time bars. They rehearsed the full programme in the studio prior to the broadcast but no one thought to time it. Come the actual live broadcast, the band finished the last item with 2½ minutes still to run so they went into the programme's signature tune, *Calling all Workers*, claiming the record for playing the short trio theme about ten times through as they hadn't got the parts for the full march!

As well as frequent appearances on the wireless, the band was to be heard regularly by large television audiences because in 1964 it recorded Arnold Steck's march *Drum Majorette,* to be used as the signature tune for 'Match of the Day' for the remainder of the 1960s.

Jiggs directed the Massed Bands of The Brigade of Guards as Senior Director of Music on five Queen's Birthday Parades, his first being held on 13th June 1964 with the Queen's Colour of 1st Battalion Coldstream Guards being trooped. He firmly stamped his identity on the music programme that year with a good sprinkling of his own arrangements including *Commonwealth on the March,* Von Blon's march *Under the Banner of Victory* and a slow march based on themes from Wagner's opera *Rienzi.* In addition, his *Tent Twelve* was played by the Massed Bands on the march back along The Mall. An innovation that year was the inclusion of a 'neutral' slow march after the regimental marches during the march past.

*Under the Banner of Victory* included a prominent role for the flutes of the Massed Corps of Drums and for the following two years Jiggs similarly adapted *Le Père La Victoire* and *Marche Lorraine*, both composed by Louis Ganne, with an additional enhancement of changing the key midway through the final reprise of the trio.

It was about this time that Jiggs invited Lieutenant Colonel Vivian Dunn and his wife 'Mike' to a Trooping the Colour parade, but they were unable to attend as the date clashed with a USA trip. Undeterred, Jiggs instead passed the invitation to their son, Paddy, and his younger sister Rosemary to take their place. Paddy recalls that they were *"hosted magnificently until well past closing time that evening. In fact I clearly remember having difficulty getting home that evening having drunk champagne almost continuously since lunch! Jiggs therefore has a special place in my heart for his kindness as an impeccable host that day; even now I still feel rather guilty that he allowed Rosemary and me to inflict major damage to his mess bill. A memorable occasion with an unforgettable character."*

Jiggs took up driving quite late in life when he was nearly fifty. He learnt his skills (?) in Sergeant Laurie Ward's car with no formal lessons and took an army test on the square at Chelsea Barracks in a three-ton army truck with an Irish Guards sergeant who wouldn't have dared to fail him! Maureen recalls that he was *"a terrible driver and he fell asleep at the wheel several times as he was so tired, fortunately with no real damage other than a few scratches on the car. I believe the phrase 'So I said to this judge' may well have emanated from this period."*

He had, in fact, acquired some earlier driving experience after the band arrived in Melbourne during the 1957 world tour when he was presented with a car to get around in. He informed the organisers that he couldn't drive but they simply took him somewhere outside of the city, gave him a few tips and he started driving. In Harry Copnall's judgement, *"I don't think he EVER improved following that quick lesson."* Another incident occurred outside the band office at Chelsea Barracks when Jiggs's car ran him over after he had tried to crank-start it while it was in gear. Jiggs spent a couple of days in hospital with injuries to his legs.

Jiggs was once caught speeding while at Eastbourne, a fact that became known to the band when Frank Wakefield brought in a cutting that his parents had sent him from the town's local paper. Nothing was said to Jiggs, of course, and discretion was exercised – until, that is, the following Easter when the band was playing on the bandstand.

The Easter Monday Bonnet Parade traditionally formed part of the afternoon concert and a number of dignitaries came onto the bandstand, including the Lady Mayoress, who also happened to be a local Justice of the Peace. As she left the stand after the presentations, Jiggs turned to the band and told them, *"That's the cow who did me for speeding."* Mark Spendiff quickly pointed upwards and hissed, *"Microphone, Sir!"* but it was too late!!

*Jiggs on the bandstand at Eastbourne with the 'intruding' microphone seen just above his head*

Jiggs's son Chris also learnt to drive on army property at the age of 14, taught by 'Pincher' Martin, the erstwhile Irish Guards euphonium player. On one occasion, for some unfathomable reason Jiggs decided to teach Eileen to drive. He set out across the nearby old Kenley aerodrome but, after two miles, clouds of smoke began to emerge from under the car – it later transpired they hadn't taken the handbrake off! Jiggs, in panic, shouted at her to get out and he drove off at high speed in search of water to put out what he thought was a fire. It was some time before he returned, by which time any appetite for learning to drive that Eileen might have possessed had long gone.

Fortunately Jiggs was not a great lover of driving and opted out whenever possible, his first and only car being a mini-traveller estate that he bought with the proceeds of a good win on the horses. However, he was not usually so lucky. Someone in the band office would be asked to put his bets on but as his horses rarely won, they would often just keep the stake money. One particular member came unstuck one day having 'forgotten' to put the bet on when Jiggs happened to have what should have been a good result.

Jiggs was a good tennis player, which was, of course, how he met Eileen. He taught Chris to play tennis in Caterham Barracks: *"On one occasion, he cycled there with me having borrowed my mother's bike and donned an extraordinarily baggy pair of shorts. On our way out, there was an Irish Guards corporal on the gate who smiled broadly as he cycled passed but failed to do anything else. It was one of the few times that I saw him stand on ceremony but he did it with typical Jiggs' panache – he u-turned, cycled back past and then turned again. As he came level, he shouted at the top of his voice, 'I might look a complete twat but I still hold the Queen's Commission. Get that ****ing sentry up!' (That was the first time I heard him use that word!)"*

Jiggs was a fanatical chess player who used to follow masters' games from books and always had a pocket-sized chess set with him. On long coach journeys he would invariably challenge 'Spud' Murphy to a game using this set. His favourite gamesmanship ploy was to try to intimidate his opponent by saying, *"A more experienced player would have resigned by now."*

He taught Chris to play and, if he was not playing enough, he would offer him a cash incentive if Chris could beat him over the best of five games. This invariably got Chris playing as he was always skint – they eventually became of approximately equal standard.

Maureen was a student when she celebrated her 21st birthday in 1963 and arranged for her father to bring her dress to her flat from home for her birthday bash. Oh dear – he turned up late, causing the rather predictable anguish!

Her wedding came in October the following year but it seems that Jiggs never quite 'got' wedding protocol. When the bridal car arrived at the house Jiggs insisted that he couldn't possibly accompany Maureen as he had to drive his own car so that it was there for him to get home afterwards. Rather reluctantly he was eventually persuaded otherwise. When they arrived at the church he got into conversation with someone at the far end of the car park and when the *Wedding March* began, Maureen had to yell for him to come so that she could take his arm!

Maureen also recalls with amusement a few months later, with her father raising his eyebrows quizzically when they were given the news that their first grandchild was due in August 1965 and Eileen, always good at her 'one-liners' said, *"What, THIS August?"* while all the time counting on her fingers behind

*The family at Maureen's Wedding on 10th October 1964*

her back to realise that Maureen was NOT guilty as charged!

The Jaegers had no real family holidays together other than, perhaps, when the band was playing on the bandstand at Eastbourne for the week, although Jiggs often took breaks in the Lake District to indulge in his passion for fishing. He was very keen at fly-fishing and they had a field at the back of the house in Caterham where he would spend many hours practising his casting.

He used to get many invitations to 'private waters', particularly when the band visited Northern Ireland on recruiting tours. Malcolm (Ollie) Ellingworth recalls a tour in the 1960s when Jiggs asked if he could come on one of their sea fishing trips organised by Todd Slaughter. *"The weather was foul as we boarded the boat. Jiggs and I used to play chess a lot and he asked 'Have you brought the board?' So there we were, Jiggs and I playing chess in the lee of the wheelhouse (the driest place on board). Rank does have its privileges you know.*

*On arriving at the fishing spot, Jiggs asked for a sea-rod as his fly-rod was not exactly suitable for hauling up fish. He got a hefty bite from a large fish which promptly swam under the boat with Jiggs hanging on for dear life. We had to cut his line!"*

In 1964 Jiggs was approached by the John Foster and Son Black Dyke Mills Band with a request for him to become what was known as their professional conductor, to take them to the National Brass Band Championship later in the year. Jiggs's predecessor with the Irish Guards, Major George Willcocks, had

*Gone fishing*

had considerable success with Black Dyke, which was, and still is, probably the best known and most successful of all brass bands. However, they needed to rebuild their reputation, since neither of the two professionals who followed Willcocks managed to maintain the momentum and they had failed even to reach the final the previous year.

The company director in charge of the band at the time was Peter Lambert, an ex-army captain, who always thought that a military man was right for the job, bearing in mind the enormous success of Major Willcocks.

The arrangement was that the professional took the band to the major contests and a few concerts each year, while the bandmaster did the rest, prepared the band for his visits, and shared the concerts with him. Jiggs was therefore kept very busy travelling to and from Bradford to rehearse, often flying up to

149

*Jiggs very much in party mood with some of the great names from the brass band world, Stanley Boddington, Harry Mortimer, Fred and Bert Felton*

Queensbury on a Sunday morning and returning after a three-hour practice session.

The North Eastern Area Qualifying Finals in 1964 took place at St George's Hall, Bradford, on Saturday 21st March with the test-piece being *Symphony of Marches* by one-time RAF Bandmaster Gilbert Vinter. Chris recalls, *"The final run-through of 'Symphony of Marches' remains one of the most exhilarating pieces of playing I have ever heard."* Black Dyke drew to play third and achieved first place with 187 points.

Gilbert Vinter again provided the test-piece for the final at the Royal Albert Hall on Saturday 23rd October; this time it was his *Variations on a Ninth*. Jiggs had suggested to a friend that he could get into the Royal Albert Hall free of charge to listen to the contest: *"Just tell them you have been asked to bring Major Jaeger his umbrella,"* he told him. It seems that he gave the same line to a number of others and it was estimated that about thirty umbrellas were brought to the hall for him that day!

Luck was very much against Jiggs on this occasion and Chris recalls that, *"I was stood with Dad when someone came to tell him that Dyke had been drawn No.1, the 'death' draw. It was only the second time I heard him use the four-letter word (he used it a lot, just not in front of me!)"* Black Dyke was placed second, three points behind the winners, the GUS Footwear Band under Stanley Boddington, with CWS Manchester under Alex Mortimer coming third. There was a genuine feeling that Black Dyke had been robbed and there was some booing when the result was announced, but this was a very creditable result given that Jiggs had been the professional conductor for less than a year.

During the rehearsals for this contest Jiggs had his first meeting with Roy Newsome. Soon to become one of the great doyens of the brass band world, Dr Newsome explained the impact that Jiggs made on him:

*"At the time I was studying for my Bachelor of Music as an external degree at Durham University. I'd sailed through the first exam, but on the very day of this rehearsal I'd received a letter to say I'd failed the second, and would have to re-sit. My friend Geoff Whitham asked if I'd heard from Durham. I told him the news and then he introduced me to Jiggs and gave him the news. Remember, this was the first time we'd met. He said that he'd done the very same exams, that he'd studied with Sir Edward Bairstow, and would I like to see his exercises with Bairstow's markings on them? Of course, I said yes.*

*"Come to the pub afterwards," he said. I did. He asked for my name and address and said he'd send these papers to me. I didn't think for one moment that he'd even remember meeting me, but sure enough, a few days later a pile of manuscript papers came in an envelope marked OHMS. I couldn't believe it, but it was true. I did eventually get my BMus, no small help from those papers of Jiggs's."*

In September 1964 Jiggs completed a week's engagement on the bandstand at Eastbourne with the Micks, and Tim Lord recalls that he came over to him and said, *"I'm going to Bradford tonight to conduct Black Dyke in the British Open competition. Come with me. Just be at Marylebone Station at midnight – I'll pay your sleeper fare"*. This was clearly too good an offer to refuse and they eventually arrived in the early morning and spent the best part of an hour in a taxi trying to find the public house where the band was due to rehearse. They eventually found it, a tiny pub in a back street, and had to climb over various instrument cases to get into the bar where the band had set up. *"Soon there was the glorious sound so unique to Dyke, playing the test-piece 'Lorenzo' by Thomas Keighley."*

They all travelled to Belle Vue in Manchester for the competition but this was a day when all four Dyke soloists 'pipped' their cadenzas and the band could only finish eighth. There followed a sombre coach journey back to Bradford and Tim was left wondering whether maybe Jiggs had started to realise that taking on Dyke might have been a mistake.

Black Dyke won the 1965 Qualifying Finals for the National at Leeds Town Hall, playing *Themes from Beethoven's First Symphony*, arranged by Eric Ball, but failed to reach the top three places in the finals.

Jack Emmott was the bandmaster when Jiggs first went to the band, and then Geoffrey Whitham took over and Jiggs shared the conducting with him on Dyke's first twelve-inch long-playing record, which was issued in 1964. The items conducted by Jiggs were *Poet and Peasant* (Suppé), *Can Can* (Offenbach) and *Thunder and Lightning* (Strauss).

Geoff Whitham was followed on 1st January 1966 by Roy Newsome who recalls; *"We had great fun, and he was always kind and very helpful to me as a young conductor, with no experience at the level of playing of Black Dyke. He was an inspirational conductor, not always well organised in rehearsal, which was his undoing eventually. He loved coming to Queensbury to get away from what he regarded as the snobs of Kneller Hall."* They became firm friends and Jiggs visited Roy and his wife, Muriel, at home many times, almost as one of the family.

However, contests aside, Jiggs managed a good deal of less stressful music-making with Black Dyke including a Sunday evening concert at George Lawton Hall, Mossley on 8th May 1966 where he shared the conducting with Roy Newsome. Jiggs conducted most of the second half of the concert, comprising:

|   |   |   |
|---|---|---|
| | Themes from Symphony No. 1 | *Beethoven arr. Eric Ball* |
| | Can Can (Orpheus in the Underworld) | *Offenbach* |
| March: | Tent 12 | *Jaeger* |
| Ballet Suite: | La Boutique Fantasqe | *Rossini-Respighi arr. A. Spurgin* |
| Polka: | Thunder and Lightening | *Strauss* |
| Overture: | Le Roi d'Ys | *Lalo arr. Frank Wright* |

Later in the year they combined with Colne Valley Male Voice Choir for a Christmas concert in Huddersfield Town Hall, with Jiggs leading them in the major works on the programme including *Crown Imperial* (Walton), *Le Carnaval Romain* (Berlioz) and Leroy Anderson's *Christmas Festival*.

At the Nationals on 15th October 1966 Jiggs was again beaten into second place by GUS with *Le Carnaval Romain* (Berlioz arr. Frank Wright) although, again, there was a general opinion that 'they wuz robbed!' with many believing they should have won.

It must have been a cause of great frustration to Jiggs that he twice came so very close to achieving the much coveted trophy. He was very unlucky at Dyke, having taken them to three Area Contests and won them all (the only one to do that in Yorkshire). Of his three appearances with them at the Royal Albert Hall he came second twice. Rather like football managers, professional conductors were rated in terms of contest results and one win would have made all the difference. For Dyke, coming second was no better than coming last although the band firmly believed that both seconds should have been wins (but don't they always?)

The band really loved and admired Jiggs but it seems that he probably became too familiar, with drinks all round in the pub after rehearsal and so on. Such familiarity, more so in the mid 1960s than today, can often make things difficult, with drink tending to loosen the tongues, and Jiggs rather got the idea that some of them were turning on him and began to consider finishing. Roy

Newsome recalled that, *"He tried to persuade me to finish along with him, thinking that the 'trouble makers' would then have been thrown out and a more happy state of things resumed. I wouldn't go."*

In January 1967 Jiggs and Roy Newsome shared the conducting at a Saturday evening concert in Wigan, built around the programme they were due to record for an LP record the following day. On the Friday evening Jiggs confided to Roy that he would definitely finish with the band after the recording. In the event, things did not go too well at the concert. He conducted with some very slow tempi, exaggerated rallentandos and long pauses, and after the concert he walked into the changing room, bade the band, *"Good Night Gentlemen,"* and left.

He didn't come to the recording session the next day. Perhaps his health problems and the strain of the long journeys to Yorkshire were beginning to take their toll and aggravated the tension he was feeling from some of the band members but it was a sad end to what had been, for the most part, a happy three years' association.

On 24th January 1965 the nation lost its great statesman and wartime leader, Sir Winston Churchill, and the whole country went into mourning. The state funeral had been planned over a number of years under the codename of 'Operation Hope Not' so it can reasonably be assumed that the initial planning for the musical aspects would have been undertaken by Lieutenant Colonel Sam Rhodes, MVO, MBE, Scots Guards, who was the Senior Director of Music until 1959. The plans were regularly updated and Jiggs took over this responsibility when he became the Senior Director of Music in 1963.

It was particularly appropriate that Jiggs should have charge of the musical arrangements, as Churchill had served in the 4th Hussars and had been Colonel of the Regiment since 1941. He retained the Colonelcy after the regiment amalgamated with the 8th Hussars in 1958 to become The Queen's Royal Irish Hussars and officers of the regiment marched in front of the gun carriage carrying Sir Winston's orders, decorations and the banners of the Cinque Ports and of Spencer-Churchill. Trumpet Major Basil Kidd from the QRIH had the honour of sounding *Reveille* during the service in St Paul's Cathedral (after Trumpet Major Peter Wilson of the Royal Horse Guards [The Blues] had sounded *Last Post*). On that very cold January morning, high up in the whispering gallery in the heart of such universal feelings of emotion, there can surely never have been such high-pressure moments for trumpeters.

The Micks' time-beater, Harry Copnall, along with Gerry Mansfield, his counterpart from the Scots Guards, had been attached to the Royal Naval Gun Carriage Crew for the week leading up to the procession, to assist with their rehearsals. They spent a great deal of time with Jiggs and Garrison Sergeant Major George Stone, Irish Guards, at all hours of the day and night pacing and timing the route, with rehearsals at 4.30 a.m. often followed by Guard

Mounting. They needed to beat a very rigid 97 paces to the minute, which was eventually settled on to accommodate the timings. A full rehearsal was held in the very early hours of the morning with the bands playing for part of the route but generally keeping the sound down out of consideration for those sleeping.

On the day itself the very long and difficult march in slow time moved the whole nation. It was a triumph of planning and organisation, for the mood of the day was so perfectly reflected in the music. The procession left Westminster Hall at 9.45am and marched in slow time to St Paul's Cathedral for the service. It included ten bands marching in pairs so that there was continuous music with the bands alternating, and the marches broadly mirrored those played at the funerals of King George VI and earlier sovereigns. Pride of place was given to the Bands of the Scots and Irish Guards, who marched immediately in front of the Earl Marshal's group which preceded the gun carriage, the Irish Guards marching in front of the Scots, since the order of procession on these occasions is for seniority nearest the gun carriage.

After the service the procession continued through the City towards the Tower of London. The Scots and Irish Guards Bands countermarched in Great Tower Street and continued playing as the gun carriage was taken down Tower Hill to halt opposite a Guard of Honour from the Royal Marines. The Massed Pipes and Drums then took over as the coffin was taken to the launch *Havengore* for the final part of the journey along the Thames.

The procession had arrived at Tower Hill after almost three hours' marching in slow time and a staff officer called to Jiggs ordering him to put the time-beaters 'in the report' for being 36 seconds late! Copnall *"couldn't believe what I was hearing as I stood there with blood pouring from my skinless hands"* but Jiggs sensibly answered that he would refuse to do as requested as he thought 36 seconds was quite an acceptable allowance. Perhaps a British Empire Medal would have been more appropriate since 'Big H' had one of the most difficult and responsible tasks of the whole day.

In November, Jiggs was invited to attend a dinner at Claridge's given by the Duke of Norfolk for all personnel who had been involved in the arrangements for the state funeral.

The Band's next recording, for EMI, was made on 1st April 1965 in the Guards Chapel, with Side 1 containing a selection from the music played each year by the Massed Bands of the Brigade of Guards at the Cenotaph on Remembrance Sunday, and Side 2 containing music from the British Legion Festival of Remembrance at the Royal Albert Hall. The record was due to be issued in October that year but owing to technical difficulties it was delayed until October 1966. The recording also included the Pipes and Drums of 1st Battalion Irish Guards under Pipe Major T.R. Ramsey, and the Guards Chapel Choir directed by the Chorus Master, Alan Barlow.

# MUSIC FROM THE CENOTAPH

*Side 1*
Rule Britannia *(Arne arr. Retford)*
Heart of Oak *(Boyce arr. Pope)*
The Minstrel Boy *(arr. Pope)*
Men of Harlech *(arr. Statham)*
Flowers of the Forest *(Pipes and Drums)*
Isle of Beauty *(Whitmore arr. Richardson)*
Skye Boat Song *(Pipes and Drums)*
Solemn Melody *(Davies)*
Last Post
Funeral March No. 1 *(Chopin arr. Hartmann)*
Reveille
O God Our Help in Ages Past *(with Choir and Organ) (Watts arr. Jaeger)*
It's a Long Way to Tipperary *(Douglas)*
Pack up your Troubles *(Powell arr. Ord Hume)*
There'll Always be an England *(Parker and Charles arr. Wright)*

*Side 2*
Heart of Oak *(Boyce arr. Barsotti)*
A Life on the Ocean Wave *(Russell arr. Alford)*
Red White and Blue *(arr. Winter)*
The Lass that loves a Sailor *(arr. Winter)*
The Great Little Army *(Alford)*
Royal Air Force March Past *(Davies/Dyson)*
Princess Royal's Red Cross March *(Davies)*
Boys of the Old Brigade *(Barri arr. Myddleton)*
Sunset *(Green)*
Eton Boating Song *(Kaps)*
Cornet Carillon *(Binge)*
The Church's One Foundation *(with Choir and Organ) (Stone – S.S. Wesley arr.
Jaeger)*
Now thank we all our God *(Rinkart trans. Winkworth)*
Coronation March (from Le Prophète) *(Meyerbeer arr. T. Conway Brown)*

The 1965 Birthday Parade was a very wet affair. Her Majesty inspected the parade to the music of Jiggs's arrangement of *The Green Leaves of Summer* and, at the end of the parade, led her Guards off Horse Guards Parade towards The Mall to his arrangement of the hit song *Dominique*. That evening on Horse Guards Parade there was a pageant of Massed Bands from all the United Kingdom

155

based regiments (less the Household Brigade) that had fought at Waterloo, to mark the 150th anniversary of the battle. The Queen was present for the final part of the evening having earlier attended a celebratory dinner across the road at the Banqueting House in Whitehall, serenaded by the String Orchestra of the Irish Guards under Jiggs. A long day for the Micks – and nothing French on the programme of music!

*Jiggs making a presentation on behalf of the massed bands to the retiring Garrison Sergeant Major George Stone MVO, MBE (centre of picture) during a rehearsal at Chelsea Barracks for the Queen's Birthday Parade in 1965, with the Band Sergeant Major of the Grenadier Guards in attendance.*

Concerts in London's Royal Parks had a regular place in the band's calendar. The programme from a performance in St James's Park on Friday 13th August 1965 has survived and is interesting in that the final item was a march entitled *Major Jiggs* composed by Perkins. This remains something of a mystery because the march could not be found in the band library and no-one seems to have any recollection of it.

*Conducting the band in Victoria Embankment Gardens*

At the end of August 1965 the band made its annual visit to Northern Ireland for a tattoo run by Northern Ireland District as part of the 'Keep the Army in the Public Eye' (KAPE) initiative. The full display was presented at the Royal Ulster Agricultural Society's Grounds at Balmoral, Belfast, on 28th and 30th August from 11.00am until 10.30pm.

The Massed Bands comprised 1st The Queen's Dragoon Guards, Irish Guards, 1st Battalion The King's Regiment (Manchester and Liverpool), 1st Battalion The Devonshire and Dorset Regiment and the Women's Royal Army Corps, with Jiggs, of course, as the Senior Director of Music.

The King's Regiment and The Devonshire and Dorset Regiment opened proceedings with a bugle fanfare and the Massed Bands marched into the arena playing *Old Pops* (arr. Jaeger), breaking into slow time with *Holy Ground*. The WRAC Staff Band then joined the bands, who broke into quick time with *Hey Look Me Over* and, after a display of wheeling and countermarching, advanced towards the royal stand for the set pieces: *Rienzi* (Wagner) and the *Londonderry Air*. They marched off playing another Jiggs arrangement, *Dominique*. The bands returned for the finale to *Sambre et Meuse* (Planquette), then played Dougie Pope's setting of *Nightfall in Camp*, finally marching off to *When the Saints Go Marching In*.

After the Belfast performance, various elements including the massed bands toured the Province visiting Newry, Banbridge, Moira, Lurgan, Larne, Armagh, Omagh, Ballymoney, Magherafelt and Cookstown. On the final day of the tour, Sunday 12th September, the band was at Cookstown where it provided the music for a Drumhead Service for the local branch of the British Legion.

The Band appeared in the 1965 film 'The Ipcress File', which has acquired something of a cult status, still being frequently shown on national television some 48 years later. Jiggs is seen in the film conducting the band in Kenneth Alford's march *The Thin Red Line* with Harry Palmer (played by Michael Caine) listening in the audience. The march finishes and Jiggs appears on screen to announce the next item, the Overture to *The Marriage of Figaro*.

The 1st Battalion Irish Guards received new Colours from Her Majesty The Queen on Friday 10th June 1966 on the lawns of Buckingham Palace. The Band led the Battalion into the grounds to *Paddy's Day*, a march in which Jiggs had elongated (his word) the theme of the regimental quick march, *St Patrick's Day*. The old Colours, presented shortly after Jiggs's appointment to the Micks, were marched off parade to the strains of *Auld Lang Syne*.

After the parade the band provided music in the other ranks' dining rooms for the guardsmen's guests, and in the afternoon played background music for the Regimental Garden Party in Ranelagh Gardens. All in all, a very busy day for everyone concerned, with no prospect of a rest as the following day the battalion was to troop its new Queen's Colour on the Birthday Parade.

The music for Trooping the Colour 1966 bore a strong Irish flavour, with Jiggs contributing *Eileen Allanah* to begin the slow march past. The march also incorporated two other much loved airs, *The Mountains of Mourne* and *The Wild Colonial Boy* and, unusually for that part of the parade, was written with a ¾ time signature which meant there was something of a musical jolt when the bands changed into the regimental slow march, *Let Erin Remember*. The Jaeger arrangement of *If You're Irish* was included for the march past in quick time, with his *Double X* being used for the march off.

Another of Jiggs's popular arrangements was a march called *Old Pops* which was based on three popular melodies with a very small snippet of the Beatles' hit song *She Loves You* included as the bridge passage in the trio. This nearly got Jiggs into trouble over infringement of copyright.

However, in 1966 the songs of the Beatles were firmly back on the band's agenda. Brian Culverhouse had been working as a producer for some orchestral records being made at the studio in Abbey Road and on one of these days the Beatles were recording in the next studio. The group's producer was George Martin, a good friend of Brian and the man who had produced a recording by the Irish Guards back in 1951. At one point Brian was obliged to ask him to keep the group quiet as they were disturbing his recording and he only had a limited time slot to complete the session.

This was the germ of Brian's idea to commission and record a series of military band arrangements of a dozen songs written by the Beatles, arranged in various styles of marches. The natural choice to make the arrangements was Arthur Wilkinson, who had begun composing and arranging while serving with the

Royal Air Force during the war, providing many numbers for the Squadronaires. He had produced a number of orchestral scores for Brian including the very successful *Beatle-Cracker Suite* in which he had taken melodies of John Lennon and Paul McCartney and arranged them in the style of a Tchaikowsky ballet.

Having been so impressed by the sound of the Irish Guards under Jiggs on previous LPs, Brian naturally chose to invite the band to record these arrangements, the result being *Marching with the Beatles*. The recording was completed in three sessions over a day and a half with the Beatles coming into the studio during one of the sessions to have a listen; George Martin apparently thought the arrangements were fantastic.

The record was to become one of the most successful military band records of its era. The December issue of *The Gramophone* magazine voted it the top military band record of the year and *Michelle* became particularly popular, being heard at least twice a week on various record programmes such as 'Housewives' Choice'.

## MARCHING WITH THE BEATLES

*Side 1*
She Loves You
Yesterday
I'll Keep You Satisfied
From Me to You
A Hard Day's Night
All My Loving

*Side 2*
Can't Buy Me Love
Things We Said Today
Michelle
It's For You
I Want to Hold Your Hand
Help

These broadcasts clearly attracted attention in high places. On one rather damp afternoon the band was setting up in the grounds of Buckingham Palace in preparation for playing for the guests at a garden party. Jiggs was there talking to Band Colour Sergeant Mark Spendiff and some of the band members, when a lady wearing a raincoat and headscarf, with some corgis in attendance, was seen walking towards the band. One of the musicians said to Jiggs something along the lines of, *"Excuse me Sir, I think that's Her Majesty."* Jiggs immediately told Mark to call the band to attention and he saluted.

He was greeted with, *"Hello Jiggs,"* and the Queen told him that she had heard a track from the record on the radio that morning and enquired whether she could have a copy to play that evening. He could hardly contain his excitement and spoke of the request several times to Mark in the breaks between items during their performance. Meanwhile, Jiggs's orderly, Chick Webb, had been hastily despatched to search the local record shops for a copy and returned a couple of hours later with the record, which Jiggs signed before it was handed over for passing to the Queen.

Another 45 rpm recording was issued on 10th June 1966, this time featuring Arthur Wilkinson's march *World Cup*, composed for the forthcoming football tournament with snippets included from tunes associated with each of the sixteen countries due to participate. England's victory for the first and (possibly?) last time ensured the record (with *Michelle* on the 'B' side) was a success, finding a place in the pop charts. The *World Cup* march was later re-named *International Scene*.

*The musicians raise their glasses during the annual Presentation of the Cheeses at the Royal Hospital, Chelsea. Standing behind Jiggs is his orderly, Lance Corporal (later Sergeant) Mike Millard. The ceremony dates back to 1692 when the first Pensioners were admitted and the Hospital approached a local cheesemonger to provide a cheese as a Christmas treat. The presentations are now made by the Dairy Council.*

As well as for these records, the Irish Guards had a great reputation at this time amongst the guardsmen for presenting them with 'modern' music during Guard Mounting. Denis Cleary, who went on to become the Academy Sergeant Major at Sandhurst, recalls how as a young guardsman his sergeant major would warn them to stand still when the band struck up the *Saint Louis Blues* in the forecourt, when the temptation was to swing to it. The first time the band played it marching back from the Palace, the time-beater Harry Copnall *"couldn't resist having a peek over my shoulder to witness the guardsmen with a new swing to their marching – to which Jiggs said to me, 'What are you looking at, you big egg?'"*

Jiggs was certainly not a man overly to stand on ceremony and Chris recalls that, *"He always used to wander around inside the Palace Forecourt on Guard Mounting and I often saw him walk up to the railings and pass barley sugars to tourists."*

*Playing in the forecourt during Guard Mounting and posing for the camera*
*(Photo: Vera Elvin)*

On 29th June 1966 the Band was invited to join forces with the students and pupils of Kneller Hall on the bandstand for one of the regular Wednesday evening Grand Concerts. Jiggs's love of the classics once again came to the fore with his choice of Berlioz' *Le Carnaval Romain* as the item for him to take the baton as guest conductor.

In June 1966, Jiggs conducted a Festival of Brass at Bishop Otter College at Chichester, which included bands from Warbington, Camberley and Southsea, organised by Tim Lord who was then studying at the college. The aim was to raise money for the Sussex Church Campaign which, amongst other things, aimed to fund repairs to the cathedral, and so was yet another example of Jiggs's selfless enthusiasm to work for good causes.

It was about this time that a friend of Maureen's, Philip Leach, was travelling

*Marching back to Wellington Barracks and, again, spotting the camera!*

regularly to the Faroe Islands (situated in the North Atlantic, about halfway between Scotland and Iceland) as a 'rep' and became aware of the Havnar Hornorkestur (Torshavn Town Band), a brass band made up from the best players on the islands.

*Jiggs with the Havnar Hornorkestur (Torshavn Town Band) in the Faroe Islands*

Somehow or other, the idea developed that the band could benefit from the guidance of a professional conductor and as a result Jiggs was approached and regularly used some of his leave periods to visit them. He was initially rather wavering about whether to accept the invitation but when they said that they would pay for Chris to go as well, he agreed. Chris recalls: *"We flew from Heathrow (the first time I had ever flown) and his ticket had been issued in the name of Major Jaeger. They asked who I was and Jiggs immediately said 'Minor' Jaeger. They duly issued the ticket and we boarded the plane as Major and Minor Jaeger."*

One of the concerts with the band took place on 17th April 1966 and opened with Jiggs's own march *Tent Twelve*. He took with him two of the world's finest soloists, Jim Shepherd (cornet) and John Clough (euphonium), both from Black Dyke. Jiggs's association with the band as its professional conductor was to continue up to his death.

Another of his brass band connections was serving as Patron of the Camberley and District Silver Band, having once conducted them at a concert at Chichester.

In August 1966 the Band of the Irish Guards found itself once again playing at the Shrewsbury Flower Show and this was to be Jiggs's first meeting with Martin Grant. Martin takes up the story: *"Before that we had been corresponding for some three years, starting when I was the precocious age of 14. I use the word 'precocious' advisedly as even then I was full of views on bands, Teike, Blankenburg and many other composers, and already aware of a wealth of obscure and rarely heard marches. I had started to assemble a substantial record collection of band music which in those days was biased towards 78s and 45s.*

*The letters started after I had seen my first Trooping the Colour on TV in 1964, the first year of Jiggs's tenure as Senior Director of Music, Brigade of Guards. I was much taken by his arrangement of von Blon's 'Under the Banner of Victory' used as the Quick Troop. I wrote a thoughtful letter to Major Jaeger and to my surprise and delight received a response by return. Subsequent letters covered Jiggs's compositions and arrangements and the band's hectic engagement diary. Every subject was dealt with meticulously, with enthusiasm and always by return.*

*In the July of 1966 I received a postcard from Jiggs suggesting we meet up at the Shrewsbury Flower Show. In those days before motorways it was not an easy journey and so I had a reluctant father to persuade to drive there. The great day came and we arrived at the show late morning, in time for me to rush to the bandstand to see and hear the combined bands of The Life Guards and Grenadier Guards conducted by Major Jackson.*

*Then came the search for Jiggs, which led me to a tent where, in those days, the Directors of Music changed. It was clearly the right tent as on its roof was a frock coat airing, with its owner, the then Captain Rodney Bashford, Grenadier Guards standing at the entrance. A lively encounter lasted the few minutes until Jiggs arrived. Rodney Bashford made the introductions and Jiggs looked surprised. "Surely you are Martin*

Grant's son," were his first words. I produced his latest postcard in an attempt to prove otherwise. Jiggs had clearly expected to meet someone a good deal older!

As there was a little time to spare before Jiggs was due to appear on the bandstand we left RB and went off for a drink and a chat. Amongst the many things we discussed was the famous, and unique, spin wheel executed by the Massed Foot Guards Bands at Trooping the Colour. To explain the process Jiggs tore two pages from my show programme to illustrate how the bands pivot around their centre point and so turn through 90 degrees within their own constrained space on Horse Guards Parade. He also talked about the turning point in his career, which he considered to be the introduction to, and subsequent tutoring by, Sir Edward Bairstow at Durham University which led to his music degree. He likened the introduction as being on a par with someone saying that "they knew God and could arrange a meeting with Him if you liked".

As we wandered around the stands he showed me a magnificent jewelled tie pin in the form of the Irish Guards Regimental Crest which the Queen had presented to him. Jiggs was looking for a friend of his, General Sir Oliver Leese, who was National President of the British Legion. The General had some floral exhibits at the show, dahlias and chrysanthemums, which we duly inspected when we arrived at his stand. There was much banter between Jiggs and Sir Oliver, coming to a head when I was asked what I was up to. I mentioned that I was in the midst of learning to fly with the RAF and this generated what I came to realise was a typical Jiggs riposte: "Just because the RAF had a good war it doesn't mean we have to be nice to them now," to be followed by much laughter.

The time came for some music from the Irish and so, via the changing tent, I accompanied Jiggs to the bandstand. The programme commenced with his arrangement of Louis Ganne's great 'Marche Lorraine' and was conducted with Jiggs's typical energy and ebullience and peppered with anecdotes as he introduced each item. One particular joke I recall, straight from the Directors of Music manual of corny jokes, involved a country parson who had been asked to give a parishioner's son a talk about the birds and bees. The parson, a sailing enthusiast, was a little hard of hearing and thought he had been asked to talk to the young man about sailing. The punch line was along the lines of … 'The first time I tore the sheet, the second time I got soaked and the third time my hat blew off.'

All too soon a memorable day came to a close and the exchange of letters continued."

On 3rd September 1966 the Micks band caught the midnight train to Edinburgh for a week's engagement on the Ross Bandstand in Princes Street Gardens. This coincided with the last week of the Edinburgh Military Tattoo, which in 1966 featured the Band of the Royal Scots Greys (2nd Dragoons) and the Massed Bands of the Royal Artillery, comprising the regiment's three bands, Woolwich, BAOR and the Mounted Band. The Tattoo finished on the Saturday, and it was then the custom for the massed bands to join the band playing in the Gardens for a concert on the Sunday.

The following morning the band departed at the crack of dawn for Liverpool and thence to Douglas, Isle of Man. Owing to a seamen's strike, the Isle of Man Tourist Board had extended their season by two weeks and engaged the Micks at the last minute after some juggling with the diary to swap various duties with the other bands. The band played on the bandstand every afternoon and accompanied various acts at the Villa Marina in the evening as well as playing for old time dancing.

*Jiggs escorting Miss World 1966 around London for publicity photographs. No one can quite remember how he became involved with this.*

Jiggs continued to find prestige concerts for his band at which they frequently rubbed shoulders with the great show business names of the day. On 2nd December 1966 the band was once again at the Royal Festival Hall at a concert in aid of the Timber Trades' Benevolent Society along with Tommy Cooper and Tom Jones, with the evening compered by Hope and Keen. The band's varied contribution to the proceedings started by combining with Trumpeters of The Life Guards in Meyerbeer's *Coronation March* and also included *American Patrol*, Bach's *Toccata and Fugue in D Minor* and one of Jiggs's own marches, *Double X*.

# CHAPTER 11

# LIEUTENANT COLONEL JAEGER

## Promotion to Lieutenant Colonel came on 1st September 1966

Towards the end of 1966 Jiggs and the band appeared at the Birmingham Town Hall with the Birmingham Police Choir for their annual concert. Martin Grant recalls: *"This was a few weeks after Jiggs had been promoted to Lieutenant Colonel. The concert started in fine style. The band assembled on stage and struck up 'St Patrick's Day,' which played Jiggs smartly to the rostrum with the tune ending perfectly in time with his arrival, followed by an immaculate salute and enthusiastic applause from the full house as the band stood to attention. It was a dramatic and highly effective start which set the tone for a great concert.*

*The next item was the overture 'Zampa' at the end of which an unfortunate couple made their steady way to their seats right on the front row almost immediately beneath Jiggs's eye line. "Sir, madam, I'm terribly sorry we started without you," was greeted with much laughter."*

On 15th December 1966 Jiggs was accorded the somewhat unusual honour of being invited to be the Inspecting Officer at the End of Term Parade and Concert at the Depot, Royal Marines, in Deal, Kent, the first occasion that a director of music had taken the parade. The 3/66 New Entry Squad comprised five junior buglers and nineteen junior musicians who had completed fourteen weeks initial training at the depot and were now to progress to the musical and educational elements of their training.

The day began in the drill shed in North Barracks with Jiggs inspecting the Juniors and, following a short drill display, presenting a shield to the best All-Round Junior, Junior Musician C.E. Crossman. Jiggs then took the salute for a march past and watched displays by the Junior Band and some PT before addressing the Squad, no doubt in the entertaining and inspirational manner that was his trademark. The day ended in the concert hall in Canada Road with performances by the orchestra, military band and choir.

The day was clearly a success, as Lieutenant Colonel Vivian Dunn subsequently wrote to say, *"It was nice to have you here and I thought you did everything perfectly."*

166

*Jiggs as Inspecting Officer at the Royal Marines School of Music, Deal*

In early January 1967 the band recorded two long-playing records for Luverne Records, an American music publishing company; they were to be used as demonstration records for the items in their catalogue. The fact that they chose the Band of the Irish Guards for this purpose, and not an American band, was testimony to the high standard and wide reputation the band had attained.

## FOUR CONCERTS BY THE BAND OF THE IRISH GUARDS

*LP One:*

Little League
When Jonny Comes Marching Home
Little French Overture
Folk Song Blues
Suite for Band
Swiss Walking Song
Song and Polka
Battle Hymn of the Republic

Junior Varsity
Little Town Band
Concerto Americano
Hymn of Thanks
March Mellow
Beginners' Cha Cha
Rudimental Rumpus
Good Night March
Snappy Snares
American March

*LP Two:*

| | |
|---|---|
| Aquanauts | Alouette March |
| Round for Band | America the Beautiful |
| Capriccio Italien | Moldau |
| Processional | All Through the Night |
| Beginners' Polka | Beginners' Stomp |
| Song and Prayer | Western Legend |
| Dixieland Blues | Valse Semplice |
| Quiet Song | Big Leagues |

As an example of the workload of the band at this time, it is interesting to study this extract from their diary for the summer of 1967:

## MAY

| | |
|---|---|
| 22nd | Guard Mounting; Massed Bands Rehearsal for Trooping the Colour |
| 23rd | BBC Recording 10.00 a.m. |
| 24th | Director of Music to Brussels |
| 25th | Massed Bands Rehearsal; Director of Music returns from Brussels |
| 26th | Music Rehearsal: Duke of York's Headquarters 10.00 a.m. |
| 27th | 1st Rehearsal – Trooping the Colour |
| 28th | Church Services: Wellington and Chelsea Barracks |
| 29th | Guard Mounting |
| 30th | Beating Retreat Rehearsal, Chelsea Barracks 2.00 p.m. |
| 31st | Beating Retreat on Horse Guards Parade 6.00 p.m. |

## JUNE

| | |
|---|---|
| 1st | Beating Retreat on Horse Guards Parade 6.00 p.m. |
| 2nd | Guard Mounting |
| 3rd | 2nd Rehearsal – Trooping the Colour |
| 4th | Guard Mounting; Concert in Morden Park 7.00 – 9.00 p.m. |
| 5th | Guard Mounting |
| 6th | *Quis Separabit* Dinner at Dorchester Hotel |
| 8th–9th | Guard Mounting |
| 10th | Queen's Birthday Parade – Trooping the Colour |
| 11th | Church Services: Wellington and Chelsea Barracks; DCM Parade at Chelsea Barracks p.m. |
| 12th | Film Premier – Odeon |
| 13th | Guard Mounting |
| 14th | Director of Music – Guest Conductor at Kneller Hall Concert |
| 15th | Guard Mounting |

| 16th | Service for the Order of St Michael and St George – St Paul's Cathedral; Retreat at Sandhurst |
|---|---|
| 17th | Guard Mounting; Concert at Burton's Court 3 p.m.; Depart for Northern Ireland |
| 18th–25th | Recruiting Tour of Northern Ireland |
| 26th | Orchestra at Royal Festival Hall |
| 27th–30th | Guard Mounting |

**JULY**

| 1st | Guard Mounting |
|---|---|
| 2nd–15th | Privilege Leave |
| 16th–19th | Guard Mounting |
| 20th | Guard Mounting; Buckingham Palace Garden Party |
| 21st | Guard Mounting |
| 22nd | Guards Depot Parade; Candover Park |
| 23rd | Church: Wellington and Chelsea Barracks; Afternoon/Evening concerts – Embankment Gardens |
| 24th–28th | Concerts at 12.30 p.m. and 7.30 p.m. at the Embankment Gardens |
| 29th | Guard Mounting; Concerts at 3.00 p.m. and 7.30 p.m. at the Embankment Gardens |
| 30th–31st | Guard Mounting |

**AUGUST**

| 1st | Guard Mounting; BBC Recording 2.00 – 5.00 pm |
|---|---|
| 2nd–5th | Guard Mounting |
| 6th–11th | Eastbourne Bandstand – concerts at 10.45 a.m. and 7.45 p.m. |
| 12th | Eastbourne Bandstand – concerts at 2.45 p.m. and 7.45 p.m.; Concert at Burton's Court 3.00 p.m. |
| 13th | Church Services: Wellington and Chelsea Barracks |
| 15th | Guard Mounting; Depart for Shrewsbury |
| 16th–17th | Shrewsbury Flower Show |
| 18th– 2nd Sept | Recruiting Tour of Northern Ireland |

At first glance, today's musicians would regard this as an incredibly busy schedule, but there were two major differences. Firstly, at that time the band's duties were all music, without the additional burden of courses, fitness training, weapons tests and endless administration (made worse by the dreaded computers), which now take up so much of the musicians' time. Secondly, with a band numbering around 65 musicians the duties and engagements could be rotated to enable all members of the band to have a reasonable amount of time off. This, of course, did not apply to Jiggs, who would have been present for almost all of them and, while he clearly revelled in his busy workload, the downside was that his family never got to see him as much as they would have liked.

In 1967 Jiggs was commissioned by the Incorporated Society of British Advertisers (ISBA) to compose a special 'Britain Must Market' bugle call which was to be used to open the ISBA's first ever National Conference at the Queen Elizabeth Hall on the South Bank. The Director of the Society, Commander D.C. Kinloch DSO OBE was quoted as saying, *We hope that this colourful call will be taken up by other organisations and used in British selling efforts wherever it is needed overseas.* On 7th April 1967 the call was sounded on Horse Guards Parade by Lance Sergeant Michael Wiggan, 2nd Battalion Coldstream Guards, as a publicity stunt, posing for photographers with Jiggs and Commander Kinloch. Lance Sergeant Wiggan, incidentally, was later to become Senior Drum Major of the Guards Division.

*Jiggs with Commander Kinloch on Horse Guards Parade as Lance Sergeant Wiggan sounds 'Britain Must Market'*

Beating Retreat on Horse Guards Parade by the Household Division is now very much an established tradition but, although there were London District Tattoos held in the early post-war years, the ceremony in its present form really dates from 1966 when just two bands, the Grenadier and Scots Guards, were on parade along with Massed Corps of Drums and Pipes. In 1967 the event expanded to include three Foot Guards bands and a mounted band, under Jiggs as the Senior Director of Music:

## BEATING RETREAT 1967

Taking part were:

Mounted Band of The Life Guards
Trumpeters of the Royal Horse Guards (The Blues)
Bands of the Coldstream Guards, Irish Guards, Welsh Guards
Corps of Drums of 1st Battalion Grenadier Guards,
1st Battalion Coldstream Guards,
2nd Battalion Coldstream Guards,
1st Battalion Welsh Guards,
Guards Depot

## Programme of Music

1. Fanfare by Trumpeters of the Royal Horse Guards (The Blues)
Fanfare:          **Dorchester**                          *Coote*

2. Drummers Call and Entry of the Massed Corps of Drums
March:          **For Flag and Empire**                  *Turpin*

3. Retreat March of the Corps of Drums:
Marches:          **The Longest Day; Green Berets**      *Arr. L. Mayhew*

4. Entry of the Mounted Band of The Life Guards
March:          **The Vedette**                          *Alford*

5. Static Item by the Band of The Life Guards and Trumpeters of the Royal Horse Guards (The Blues)
March:          **Fehrbelliner Reitermarsch**            *Henrion*

6. March off by the Band of The Life Guards and Trumpeters of the Royal Horse Guards (The Blues)
March:          **Punjab**                               *Payne*

7. Entry of the Massed Bands
March:          **Horse Guards, Whitehall**              *Wood*

8. Marching Display by the Massed Bands and Massed Corps of Drums
Slow March:          **Dominique**                       *Sourire arr. Jaeger*

171

| | | |
|---|---|---|
| Quick March: | **San Lorenzo** | *Silva* |
| 9. Finale | | |
| Fanfare: | **Dettingen** | *W. Jackson* |
| | **Introduction from Third Act, Lohengrin** | *Wagner* |
| | **Nightfall in Camp** | *Arr. Pope* |
| | **The National Anthem** | |
| 10. March off | | |
| Marches: | **Old Comrades** | *Teike* |
| | **The Thunderer** | *Sousa* |

*The Finale to Beating Retreat 1967*

On 12th June 1967 the band played at the World Premier of the James Bond film 'You Only Live Twice' at the Odeon Theatre, Leicester Square, attended by Her Majesty The Queen and sponsored by the Variety Club of Great Britain. Ten days later they were in Wellington Hall, Belfast, for a Grand Charity Concert for the Belfast Round Table. The Guest of Honour was Captain The Rt. Hon. Terence O'Neill, Prime Minister of Northern Ireland, who had served as an officer in the Irish Guards during the Second World War. The music programme included two of the items from 'Marching with the Beatles':

| March: | International Scene | Wilkinson |
|---|---|---|
| Overture: | A Night in Venice | Strauss |
| Clarinet Solo: | Clarinet Concertino | Weber |
| | *Soloist: Musician A. Sutherland* | |
| Selection: | Mary Poppins | Sherman |
| Selection: | Roman Holiday | arr. Kenny |
| Adagio from: | Farewell Symphony | Haydn |
| | INTERVAL | |
| March: | The Minstrel Boy | arr. Jaeger |
| French horn solo: | Horn Concerto | Mozart |
| | *Soloist: Musician F. Prosser* | |

Excepts from our Long-Playing Record 'Marching with the Beatles':

| | (a) Michelle | Lennon & McCartney |
|---|---|---|
| | (b) All My Loving | Lennon & McCartney |
| Trombone solo: | Selected | |
| | *Soloist: Band Sergeant M. Spendiff* | |
| | American Patrol | Meacham |
| Finale: | Hibernia | arr. Charrosin |
| | Regimental Marches | |
| | God Save the Queen | |

The next visit to the Province involved the band taking the train from Euston Station en route for the Belfast Boat Train and a period of recruiting in the form of a United Services Week in Bangor, County Down. They joined the Bands of the Royal Marines (Plymouth Group), 4th Battalion The Queen's Regiment and 1st Battalion The King's Regiment (Manchester and Liverpool), along with the Pipes and Drums of 1st Battalion The Royal Ulster Rifles for a most successful week, ending with a grand parade and fly-past and a massed bands concert in Ward Park Playing Fields.

The band again played for a week on the bandstand in Edinburgh during September, this time sharing the final massed bands concert with the Scots Guards and three Scottish Infantry bands. They returned to London and had just two days of hectic packing to prepare for their flight to Germany for the next engagement, the Berlin Tattoo. The Band had been detailed to take part, with Jiggs as its Musical Director, meaning that much of the administrative arrangements for the massed bands were made through the Irish Guards Band Office, causing a good deal of extra work for Sergeant Fred Wiles. Unfortunately, it also meant that Jiggs had to spend part of his leave period attending conferences in Berlin.

Fog in Berlin delayed the band's flight from RAF Lyneham, leaving them with no time to settle in before beginning rehearsals. The Tattoo took place on the 22nd and 23rd September 1967 in the vast Olympic Stadium built for the 1936 Olympic Games and still very much associated with a little man called Hitler. The producer was a young cavalry officer, Captain Michael Parker of The Queen's Own Hussars, later to become Major Sir Michael Parker KCVO, CBE, who was to produce the Royal Tournament from 1974 to its demise in 1999, as well as a host of other royal and national events including the parades to celebrate the Queen Mother's 90th and 100th Birthdays.

Jiggs was not at all well at this time, suffering from angina. Not being one for the conventional, his meetings and briefings were held in a helicopter hovering high over the Olympic Stadium away from prying ears and to give him a birds' eye view of the arena to help plan the displays.

A total of fourteen military bands took part, from regiments all but three of which have now been consigned to the history books:

The Life Guards
The Royal Dragoons (1st Dragoons)
The Royal Scots Greys (2nd Dragoons) *with Pipes and Drums*
14th/20th King's Hussars
15th/19th The King's Royal Hussars
17th/21st Lancers
Irish Guards *with Pipes and Drums of 1st Bn. Irish Guards*
1st Bn. The Royal Scots (The Royal Regiment) *with Pipes and Drums*
1st Bn. The Royal Anglian Regiment *with Corps of Drums*
1st Bn. The Duke of Wellington's Regiment (West Riding)
1st Bn. The Black Watch (Royal Highland Regiment) *with Pipes and Drums*
1st Bn. The Duke of Edinburgh's Royal Regiment (Berkshire and Wiltshire)
    *with Corps of Drums*
1st Bn. The King's Own Yorkshire Light Infantry *with Bugles*
1st Bn. Queen's Own Highlanders (Seaforth and Camerons) *with Pipes and Drums*

The Tattoo opened with a fanfare for cavalry trumpets, *Dettingen* by Major 'Jacko' Jackson of The Life Guards, and then came the Massed Bands with:

| | |
|---|---|
| Children of the Regiment | *Fucik* |
| Deutschmeister Regiments March | *Jurek* |
| Old Comrades | *Teike* |
| Rienzi | *Wagner* |
| River Kwai March | *Arnold* |
| Dominique | *Sourire arr. Jaeger* |
| Yellow Submarine | *Lennon and McCartney* |

*Jiggs conducting Massed Bands of over 500 musicians at the Berlin Tattoo 1967*

The rest of the Tattoo included the normal displays that would be expected: Gymnastics, Motorcycles from the Royal Corps of Signals, Massed Pipes and Drums with Highland Dancing under Pipe Major T.R. Ramsey, Irish Guards, a DKW (a German Jeep) Assembly Race, a Drill Display by the Queen's Colour Squadron of the Royal Air Force and a Musical Drive in Scout Cars by the 2nd Royal Tank Regiment. The house band was the Royal Air Force (Germany) under Pilot Officer Barrie Hingley, later to become Principal Director of Music as a Wing Commander.

Particularly familiar to Jiggs amongst the participants were the Band and Bugles of 1st Battalion The King's Own Yorkshire Light Infantry, with the buglers being required to play *Last Post* in Douglas Pope's setting of *Nightfall in Camp*, which combines the call with the hymn *Lead Kindly Light*. Having once been their Bugle Major rather compounded Jiggs's annoyance and embarrassment at the rehearsals as the buglers had not had time to learn the arrangement properly. Jiggs took a bugle and summoned the Senior Bandmaster, Mr Gordon Turner of 15th/19th The King's Royal Hussars, who was acting as his assistant.

He told Mr Turner to conduct the massed bands and that he would play the call himself. After a moment's reflection he changed his mind and said, *"I will play it – and I will conduct it,"* and he proceeded to do just that, note perfect and earning a round of applause from the bands at the end!

The Finale of the Tattoo was a performance of Tchaikowsky's great *1812 Overture,* which Jiggs had arranged in a shortened version for the massed bands. The overture, of course, tells the story in music of the advance into Russia by Napoleon's army and his subsequent retreat from a burning Moscow. Captain Parker's vision for the Tattoo was for the music to be accompanied by fireworks and gunfire, culminating with a representation of 'Moscow' on fire. A large three-dimensional structure was constructed by the local squadron of Royal Engineers comprising scaffolding and hardboard some seventy feet high, with hessian soaked in paraffin in the centre to provide the flames. Things did not go quite to plan as most of the structure blew down in a high wind on the morning of the first performance but fortunately was re-erected in time.

It should be remembered that this was at a time when Berlin was in the heart of Soviet-controlled East Germany and relations with the West were somewhat strained, to say the least. The Russians were clearly not comfortable with the idea of Moscow being depicted in flames and they raised objections. Thankfully an escalation of the Cold War was averted when it was explained to them that the French had really been the losers and they backed off, although perhaps not being entirely convinced.

The performance was a great success and as the smoke cleared from around the massed bands, Jiggs could be seen waving a white handkerchief from the end of his baton! However, it was decided to play safe at the next Tattoo, which was in 1969 with Major Rodney Bashford as Musical Director. He wrote in the LP notes that, to avoid causing offence, they used an imaginary battle between the English and the Scots with the result being a draw and with both sides taking part in the Victory Parade – honours even!

The 1967 Tattoo was sadly marred by a tragic accident at the opening of one of the performances. A giant Union Flag was suspended from a helicopter hovering over the arena. The flag had weights attached to the bottom and a sudden gust of wind blew it towards the crowd causing a number of injuries and killing a German spectator.

Two days after the Tattoo there was a reception in the Sergeants' Mess in Berlin where Jiggs met Charles Raison, his bandmaster and mentor with KOYLI to whom he owed so very much. This was the first time they had met for eleven years and it was quite a party!

During the first weekend in Berlin the Irish Guards gave two concerts, the first at Spandau and the second in the magnificent setting of the Kongresshalle, that latter concert featuring a trombone solo from Band Sergeant Mark Spendiff. As he finished, Jiggs presented him with two bottles of whiskey, having been 'tipped off' that it was his birthday.

After the Tattoo the band travelled to Belgium on the Military Train*, passing through communist East Germany. The senior members of the Band (remember in those days there were only 7 NCOs in a band of 65) along with the time-beater, Harry Copnall, were called into Jiggs's compartment for a glass of Scotch to celebrate the success of the Tattoo. Harry recalls how very honoured he felt to be included: *"I think that again was an example of his 'fatherliness' towards me."*

Their stay in Belgium lasted from 29th September to 7th October 1967 and Jiggs was the Senior Director of Music for various events to mark 'British Week in Brussels' which was organised by the Board of Trade to promote the sale of

*The band playing for British Week Brussels*

*The Military Train was the Berlin–Brunswick–Hannover train via Marienborn and Helmstedt which went through the corridor. There was a small British military guard force on each train. They dismounted at every stop, put out yellow flags to keep the driver aware that there were men patrolling, and then ensured that the train was neither robbed by East Germans, nor entered by would-be escapers.

British goods. This involved eight bands together with Pipes and Drums and Corps of Drums and included a massed bands display in the Heysel Stadium that featured another spectacular performance of the *1812 Overture*. A few bars from the end of the overture, all the lights in the stadium were extinguished and the only light visible was a small torch with which Jiggs conducted. He composed a march, *British Week Brussels,* for the occasion, based on two traditional Belgian tunes, which was well received by the audience.

Two days later, the massed bands were back at the Heysel Stadium for the opening ceremony of British Week, performed by Lord Snowdon in the absence of Her Royal Highness The Princess Margaret who unfortunately was confined to bed with a slight chill. During the week the various bands gave individual performances which included concerts outside large stores, in Galleries (the equivalent of our Arcades), playing at a table tennis match between England and Belgium and a marching display at an international soccer match between England and Belgium which resulted, rather fittingly, in a 2–2 draw.

The Irish Guards Orchestra provided 'drinking music' at one or two cocktail parties as well as background music for a reception given in honour of Princess Margaret and Lord Snowdon. The Finale for British Week was held in the Grand Place, in the heart of Brussels, and all musical combinations took part.

The tour was also memorable for the wrong reasons in that the bands were accommodated at a Belgian army barracks where the conditions and the food were not what were expected. Jiggs was clearly not at all well at this time and could be seen going blue with the angina. However, he got all the bands together and explained that there was little he had been able to do about the food but assured them that they would get some decent food that evening. Quite how he managed it, no-one was too sure but a proper hot meal was duly provided for everyone and Jiggs had managed to defuse a difficult situation and made the bands happy.

Later in the year Jiggs took off for the United States where he had been invited by the organisers to act as one of the adjudicators at the Tri-State Music Festival of Enid, Oklahoma. This festival dated from 1932 and initially featured about ten bands from Oklahoma, Kansas, and Texas but eventually expanded to include a whole range of musical combinations.

Although not a Salvationist, Jiggs loved Salvation Army people and always made a big fuss of them when they came into the bandstand area at Eastbourne after their open-air service at the pier. He gave much of his time to attending their festivals as the Chairman, to introduce and compere the event. One such occasion was the Festival of Music held on 18th November 1967 in the Central Hall, Westminster, which featured organist Dr William Lloyd Webber, whose sons were later to become household names in the music world, and the International Staff Band of the Salvation Army.

*Conducting the Eastbourne Citadel Salvation Army Band in 1961*

Continuing his willingness to work for youth organisations, Jiggs was an adjudicator for the Scout Association's Festival at the Royal Festival Hall on 25th November 1967, along with Anna Neagle, Norrie Paramor, Charles Proctor and Russ Conway, with the programme including the orchestra from the Irish Guards as well as the Alexandra Choir and participants from the Gang Show.

Early in 1968 it was announced that Jiggs was to be appointed as Chief Instructor at The Royal Military School of Music, Kneller Hall although there was, of course, still a busy schedule with the Irish Guards to be undertaken.

In April 1968 the Band was engaged by Richard Attenborough to take part in the film, *Oh! What a Lovely War*, set during the First World War. The scenes were shot with the band marching along the promenade at Brighton and the musicians, including Jiggs, all had to spend time in 'make-up' having false moustaches attached. As further gestures towards authenticity, Jiggs was obliged to appear improperly dressed without his Second World War medals and Richard Attenborough fortunately spotted that the Drum Major's sash bore a large royal cipher E II R which, within a couple of hours, had a piece of card fixed to obscure it.

In fact, the whole band was incorrectly dressed for the period, because up until 1939 they would have worn gold laced tunics similar to those still worn by the Guards Drum Majors, and musicians' short swords rather than bayonets designed for the self-loading rifle introduced in 1960. Further, the band did not have an officer as Director of Music until 1919 but, fortunately, no one seemed to mind. By coincidence, the Orchestra of the Corps of Royal Engineers (Aldershot) also appeared in the film, conducted by Captain Gerry Horabin, who was shortly to succeed Jiggs in the Irish Guards.

*Jiggs and the band posing with American song-writing brothers Richard and Robert Sherman at Wellington Barracks. This was probably at the time of the London Premiere of Walt Disney's 'The Happiest Millionaire' for which they wrote the songs, one of which, 'I'll Always Be Irish', was arranged for the band by Jiggs.*

In 1968 the regiments of the Brigade of Guards were granted the Freedom of the Royal Borough of New Windsor which *"confers the right, privilege, honour and distinction of parading or marching through the streets of Windsor on all ceremonial occasions with bayonets fixed, colours flying, drums beating and bands playing in recognition of the long and close association between the Royal Borough and the Regiments and of the Regiments' distinguished achievements in the cause of the Nation and the Commonwealth".*

The honour was conferred at a parade on 4th May 1968 in Home Park, attended by HM The Queen as Colonel-in-Chief, with detachments from all regiments of the Brigade. A composite band and corps of drums was formed from all five regiments and Jiggs composed a new slow march for the occasion, entitled *Freedom of Windsor*.

This march was also used for the Inspection of the Line at the Queen's Birthday Parade on 8th June 1968, a particularly proud day for Jiggs as it was announced in the Queen's Birthday Honours that he had been appointed as an Officer of the Most Excellent Order of the British Empire (OBE). He was gracious in recognising that the honour reflected the support he received from the band by insisting that OBE stood for "Our Band Earned-it".

He received the insignia from Her Majesty at an Investiture at Buckingham Palace on 29th October and it was fitting that the Orchestra of the Irish Guards, by then under Captain Gerry Horabin, was there to provide the music. Jiggs had earlier received a personal letter from the Lord Chamberlain's Office informing him that the Comptroller had reserved three seats for his family for the occasion.

Jiggs's second Beating Retreat on Horse Guards Parade took place on 28th and 30th May 1968. The number of bands on this parade steadily increased from two in 1966, three in 1967 and now four. The Band of the Scots Guards was absent (and also missed the Queen's Birthday Parade) due to its involvement with Public Duties in Scotland. However, with the remaining four bands parading at a greater than usual strength with a frontage of five, the overall size was little different.

The display opened with six mounted Trumpeters sounding Major 'Jacko' Jackson's *Fanfare Royale* and a Drummer beating *Drummer's Call*. The Massed Corps of Drums then marched on, playing Sousa's *Washington Post* after which *Retreat* was sounded. The Pipes and Drums then took over, followed by the Mounted Bands playing *On the Square* (Panella), *Fehrbelliner Reitermarsch* (Henrion) and *The Vedette* (Alford).

Finally, came the Massed Bands of the Brigade of Guards, a splendid title that was sadly to be replaced by the much less inspiring 'Guards Division' a few weeks later on 1st July 1968. They marched on from the Admiralty Passage to *The Ambassador* (Jansen – actually a pen name of Lieutenant Colonel Fred Harris OBE, Grenadier Guards), changed into slow time to *Coburg* and then into Julius Fucik's *Children of the Regiment* before halting in front of the dais.

Jiggs mounted the rostrum to conduct the Massed Bands in the Finale:

| | |
|---|---|
| Fanfare: Coronation | *Jackson* |
| Bridge on the River Kwai | *Arnold* |
| Strike up the Band | *Gershwin arr. Sharpe* |
| Light Cavalry Overture | *Suppe* |
| Lament *(played by Pipe Major T. Ramsey, Irish Guards)* | |
| Nightfall in Camp | *Pope* |
| *(During this item flags will be lowered)* | |
| National Anthem | |

The Bands, Drums and Pipes marched off to *My Home* and *Scotland the Brave* and returned towards the barracks with Rodney Bashford's *By the Left!*

Jiggs's final tour with the Irish Guards was a visit to Canada that included performances at the Calgary Exhibition and Stampede. Seventy-three Irish Guardsmen gathered at Gatwick Airport on 27th June to board a specially chartered Transglobe 'Britannia' and as it taxied along the runway the Regimental Journal records that: *"The Director of Music removed his shoes and socks, put on his slippers, extracted his feather pillow from his hand baggage, challenged the conducting officer to a game of chess and the Band of the Irish Guards together with the Pipes and Drums of the 1st Battalion were off on another tour."*

They arrived later in the day at Toronto Airport where two buses were waiting to take them the hundred or so miles to London, Ontario where they were to stay with the Canadian Army at Wolseley Barracks for the next six days. They soon met the Director of Music of the Royal Canadian Regiment Band, Captain Derek Stannard, a cornet player in the Irish Guards some 20 years before.

The first engagement was to give a preview performance at a large war veterans' hospital with the Band giving a concert in the forecourt, whilst the Pipes and Drums marched around the blocks for the benefit of those unable to leave their beds. Jiggs took the opportunity to look round some of the wards afterwards and was clearly impressed to see how well Canada looks after its veterans.

The next day was the official opening of the Festival Fortnight, which had the motto 'London, Canada, goes British', with all shops displaying British merchandise, double-decker buses, bobbies, beefeaters, Nell Gywn selling her wares, a pub, a tearoom and, of course, what could better set the scene than the Band and Pipes of the Irish Guards! The bands played at the opening ceremony in the main street and, in the afternoon, at the official opening of the British Exhibition.

The band gave three concerts in the main park, attracting the largest audience known, after which the President of the Festival Fortnight bade them farewell and Jiggs received a kiss from the Festival Princess – rarely had he more enjoyed being the personification of the band!

The next stage was to fly to Calgary, where they were hosted by the Band of the Lord Strathcona's Horse at Currie Barracks; there they met another former member of the band, Eric Whiteside, a bass player who had just retired from the Canadian Army and was teaching at the local university.

The bands were to play at two performances on 5th–6th July 1968 in the Stampede Corral, an indoor stadium seating 6,500 spectators. Once again Jiggs's great charisma came to the fore and on arrival he was presented with the VIP white stetson, the 'ten gallon' cowboy hat which he seemed to wear all the time they were there.

## The Band of the Irish Guards and Pipes and Drums of 1st Bn. Irish Guards

| | | |
|---|---|---|
| Fanfare: | **Dogsbod** | *Jaeger* |
| **MARCH ON:** | | |
| Band: | **San Lorenzo** | *Silva* |
| Pipes and Drums: | **St Patrick's Day** | |
| | **National Anthems** | |

**PIPES AND DRUMS:**

| | | |
|---|---|---|
| March: | **Captain Norman Orr Ewing** | |
| Strathspey: | **Loudon's Bonnie Woods and Braes** | |
| Reel: | **Piper of Drummond** | |
| March: | **Gary Owen & Dear Old Donegal** | |

**BAND:**

| | | |
|---|---|---|
| March: | **Canada on the March** | *Jaeger* |
| Cornet Trio: | **Trumpets Wild** | *Walters* |
| Patrol: | **Dominique** | *Sourire* |
| Trombone Solo: | **The Joker** | *Moss* |
| | **Congratulations** | *Martin & Coulter* |
| March: | **River Kwai** | *Arnold* |

Display of Traditional Irish Dancing

| | | |
|---|---|---|
| March off: | **Double X** | *Jaeger* |
| | *INTERVAL* | |
| March on: | **Marching Sergeants** | *Siebert* |

| | | |
|---|---|---|
| **RETREAT CEREMONY** | **Sunset** | *Green* |
| Pipes and Drums: | **Loch Maree** | |
| Slow Troop: | **My Home** | *arr. Jaeger* |
| Quick Troop: | **Slattery's Mounted Fut** | *French* |
| Pipes and Drums: | **Haughs o' Cromdale** | |
| | **Morag of Dunvegan** | |
| | **John D Burgess** | |

**BAND PROGRAMME**

| | | |
|---|---|---|
| March: | **If You're Irish** | *arr. Jaeger* |
| Overture: | **Light Cavalry** | *Suppe* |
| | **Michelle** | *Lennon & McCartney* |

*(continued overleaf)*

| | | |
|---|---|---|
| Tenor Saxophone Solo: | **Begin the Beguine** | *Porter* |
| | **American Patrol** | *Meacham* |
| Finale: | **Nightfall in Camp** | *Pope* |

| | |
|---|---|
| Pipe Major T. Ramsey | **Lament** |

**MARCH OFF:**

| | |
|---|---|
| Band Pipes and Drums | **St Patrick's Day** |

*The Band, Pipes and Drums at the Stampede Corral*

As the band marched off after each performance, Jiggs would place himself at the head, in front of the Drum Major, and immediately he was out of the arena would remove his bearskin and pass it to his waiting orderly, Mike Millard, in exchange for his white Stetson and his miniature trumpet, then march through the middle of the band back into the arena on his own and give his final salute in true Guards style and then play a quick blast on his little trumpet.

*Jiggs and Drum Major Milligan at Calgary with two former members of the
15th Light Horse Band who had entertained the Irish Guards Band over sixty years
earlier during its first visit to Canada in 1905: John Foss (cornet) and Vic Bihar*

On Monday 8th July the bands were accorded the honour of leading the
Stampede Parade of numerous bands, floats, film stars, chuckwagons, cowboys
and Indians over a route of almost five miles around the centre of Calgary, with
spectators estimated to number up to half a million. Immediately behind the
bands, flanked by four Mounties, rode the Duke and Duchess of Kent, named
the previous day by the Blackfoot Indians as Chief Running Rabbit and Pretty
Woman.

The bands gave performances on two occasions before a crowd of 25,000
in the grandstand as a prelude to the chuckwagon races, which were said to
have made the old Roman chariot races look pretty tame by comparison! The
musicians took time to watch the various rodeo events including bronco riding
contests, calf roping, steer wrestling, wild cow milking, brahma bull riding,
and wild horse racing. Needless to say, the bands joined in the efforts made by
everyone to enter into the spirit of the occasion, with the streets thronged with

sights from the past: cowboys mingling with Indians, square dancing, Indian dancing and all kinds of other entertainment.

There were a few free days at the end, which were put to good use to explore the foothills of the Rockies, which are only seventy miles from Calgary. The National Parks of Banff and Jasper were visited, whilst the more adventurous souls journeyed to British Columbia. On 19th July, the pipers departed by bus to join the rest of the battalion on training exercises at Camp Wainwright and the band began the journey home, suffering a fourteen-hour delay at the scheduled stop at Gander when it was realised that there was no navigator aboard! A nearby luxury hotel was made available for them to eat and rest whilst a navigator flew up from Toronto.

It must have been a rather sad day for Jiggs as they finally landed at Gatwick to conclude his last of many happy overseas tours with the band. On Monday 29th July 1968 the Brigade Major hosted a Farewell Dinner at the Connaught Rooms in London to mark Jiggs's forthcoming departure from the Guards Division.

The 'swan song' of Jiggs's long association with Eastbourne came on Saturday 10th August 1968 with the bandstand enclosure packed to capacity for his final concert, which had been specially advertised in the local press. The Mayor of Eastbourne, Councillor Clifford Scott, expressed the appreciation of the town and the thousands of visitors whom the band had entertained, and a tribute was also given by Reverend Bob Skillern, the religious adviser to the National Association of Boys' Clubs. The Mayor presented Jiggs with a travelling clock on behalf of Eastbourne, as well as a gift from a Mrs Jessie Hall, one of his 'fans', who was celebrating her 77th Birthday.

In his farewell speech, Jiggs paid tribute to the band: *"They have given me unstinting service. They are tremendous musicians with a great sense of fun."* He also spoke of his association with Eastbourne which went back to before the war and he recalled how he had been in the town when the Cavendish Hotel and Marks and Spencer had been bombed. After he had expressed his thanks to the Corporation, the concert ended with *Nightfall in Camp,* which included *Last Post* sounded from the balcony.

As Jiggs left the bandstand for the last time, Tim Lord with Tony Spurgin and some other brass-playing friends, had gathered in the corner of the auditorium with their instruments to lead the audience in a chorus of *For He's a Jolly Good Fellow.* Jiggs loved it.

## Grand Parade Bandstand

*TODAY,*
*SATURDAY, AUGUST 10th*

THE BAND OF THE

# IRISH GUARDS

*Special Farewell Performance*

*to*

# Lt.-Col. C. H. JAEGER

MUS.BAC., L.R.A.M., A.R.C.M., p.s.m.

at 7.45 p.m. TONIGHT

**NEXT WEEK — Sunday 11th - 17th August**

## THE 'RHINE' STAFF BAND OF THE ROYAL TANK REGIMENT

# CHAPTER 12

# SABBATICAL

After relinquishing the position of Director of Music, Irish Guards in August 1968, Jiggs was allowed a sabbatical period of four months prior to taking up his next appointment on 2nd December. This was granted to him by the Commandant at Kneller Hall, Colonel Charles Morris CBE but was almost certainly something that would have emanated from discussions with his old friend, soon to be knighted as Sir Vivian Dunn. Sir Vivian retired as Principal Director of Music of the Royal Marines at about the same time and used his many contacts in the civilian musical world to arrange a comprehensive sabbatical period of study and visits for his successor, Major Paul Neville MVO, prior to him taking over the mantle in October 1968.

The sabbaticals would no doubt have been of immense value to both officers, giving them the opportunity to establish valuable contact with their opposite numbers in the other services and to study teaching and organisation in other institutions.

The first part of Jiggs's sabbatical was spent in America, beginning with a visit to a summer camp clinic for about 500 students at Redland University on the far west coast, about 60 miles north of Los Angeles. Next came a visit to Disneyland for a few days as a guest of the American music publisher, Charles Hanson, and the President of the Walt Disney Music Company, Jimmy Johnson.

Jiggs then took a flight across the continent to New York, arriving at 6 o'clock on a bright Sunday morning to enjoy a sightseeing tour of what was, at that time of the morning, a deserted city. In the evening he was guest conductor of the 200-piece band at West Point at a concert in front of around 10,000 spectators. This was done without any rehearsal whatsoever and the experience for Jiggs was enjoyable and frightening in equal measure! He spent three days at the Academy, the American equivalent to Sandhurst, and gained something of an insight into both the establishment itself and its band.

His next stop was at Washington to spend a few days as a guest of the United States Army Band, the personal band of the Chief of Staff of the US Army at the Pentagon, and comprising the finest musicians available to the US Army.

*Jiggs with Colonel Samuel R. Loboda while visiting the United States Army Band
(Pershing's Own) (both photographs)*

*Jiggs conducting the United States Army Band on the steps of the Capitol*

This time Jiggs was able to spend some time rehearsing with them, leading up to his conducting the 250-strong band in a concert given on the Capitol steps in front of vast crowds enjoying their holidays.

As part of his visit to Washington, Jiggs visited Arlington Cemetery and was accorded the honour of laying a wreath on the Tomb of the Unknown Warrior, a distinction normally reserved for much higher ranking officers and dignitaries. The trip to the United States continued with visits to the Field Army Band in Fort George Meade and to Freedoms Foundation in Philadelphia. Commander Louis Kriebel of the United States Air Force Band at Stewart Air Base acted as his host for this part of the tour and Jiggs was able to visit and conduct his band.

Jiggs's next journey was to West Germany and had a dual purpose. At that time a considerable number of British bands, mostly from the cavalry and infantry, were stationed there as part of the British Army of the Rhine (BAOR) and Jiggs paid informal visits to a number of them to get a feel for the work they undertook and the problems encountered. He was also able to meet the bandmasters and get to know them, as the time was approaching when he was to have a degree of responsibility towards them.

The second purpose was to visit Colonel Fritz Masuhr at the musical services of the Bundeswehr. Jiggs came away impressed with the high standards he had witnessed but also with the feeling that perhaps some of the better players had been brought in from other bands to ensure that this was the case.

After returning home and taking some leave, the next item on his agenda was to visit the Royal College of Music, the Royal Academy of Music and the Royal School of Church Music at Addington Palace, spending a week at each of them. He already had a close relationship with the first two institutions through examining for them for the best part of twenty years but this gave him the great opportunity, not only to study their organisation and teaching methods, but also to establish valuable links with the principals and teaching staff, all of which helped to bring some fresh ideas to take forward to his new appointment.

The final part of the sabbatical was spent visiting the Royal Marines at Deal and Portsmouth, and the Royal Air Force at Uxbridge, Locking and Hereford, to study their band services and schools of music. On Thursday 7th November he was invited to be the guest conductor at one of the series of Winter Concerts by the orchestra of the Royal Marines School of Music in the concert hall at the barracks at Deal. Major Paul Neville, writing in *Blue Band*, the magazine of the Royal Marines Band Service, said:

> It gave us great pleasure to have Lt. Col. C.H. Jaeger, OBE, Chief Instructor at Kneller Hall, as our guest for two weeks in November. His visit was arranged in order that he could see and hear all we do in training musicians and NCOs for our bands. He had previously visited the RAF School of Music at Uxbridge and his stay with us came just prior to his taking up his new appointment at Kneller Hall after twenty years as Director of Music, Irish Guards. I was able to accompany him on a short tour of the Drafting, Pay and Records Office, Royal Marines, at Eastney and we took the opportunity whilst in Portsmouth to visit Bandmaster R.J.P. Kempston and the Band at HMS Daedalus.
>
> Colonel Jaeger was invited to conduct at one of our concerts during his stay and obtained excellent performances of the Meistersingers Overture and Elgar's Serenade in E Minor. The Orchestra particularly enjoyed working under his direction, and his charming personality and keen sense of humour were very much in evidence.

In the same edition, the editorial included:

> At the concert on Thursday 7th October a really gorgeous sound was obtained by all departments and particularly by the strings in the Larghetto from Elgar's Serenade for String Orchestra. This work was in the capable hands of our guest conductor, Lt. Col. C.H. Jaeger, OBE, who obviously shared the Orchestra's enjoyment of making music 'par excellence'.

On Monday 18th November 1968, Jiggs appeared as the 'Castaway' on the BBC's long-running radio programme 'Desert Island Discs', at which he was invited to choose eight gramophone records to take with him if he was to be marooned on a desert island. He told the presenter, Roy Plomley, that while he had little time to listen to records, being rather busy, most of his library consisted of 78s. He added that he would like the music to remind him of his musical career and so his choice of records therefore makes an interesting portrait of his musical life:

**Hear My Prayer (Mendelssohn)** – sung by boy soprano Ernest Lough in 1927 with the choir of the Temple Church, London; this was to remind him of his time as a choirboy.

**Air from the Orchestral Suite No. 3 in D (Bach)** – also known as the *Air on a G String*. This, he said, was chosen as a reminder of the days when he first got the feeling for music as an appreciative art. He described it as *"pure, relaxing, meditative music"* and this was his choice to take to his desert island if he was restricted to just the one record.

**I Was Glad (Parry)** – chosen to recall his participation in the 1937 Coronation Service with the Kneller Hall Trumpeters, who joined the Orchestra and Chorus in this great anthem.

**Symphony No. 3 (Brahms)** – this was one of the works that Jiggs conducted with the Vienna Symphony Orchestra in 1945. He was particularly pleased that the BBC had done its research and managed to use a recording for the programme by that very orchestra.

**Nimrod, from the Enigma Variations (Elgar)** – this was to recall the Remembrance Day services at the Cenotaph whilst he was Senior Director of Music, Brigade of Guards. Jiggs explained to the listeners that this particular variation was dedicated to Elgar's friend A.J. Jaeger (no relation) and that *Jaeger* is German for *Hunter*: the god of hunters was called *Nimrod*, hence the title.

**Gavotte from Symphony No. 1 (Classical) (Prokofiev)** – something that Jiggs said that he came across while running a musical appreciation class during the war; his comment was, *"It's so jolly."*

**Jigger's Corn** – one of his own marches, played by the Band of the Irish Guards.

**Michelle (Lennon and McCartney arr. Wilkinson)** – a track taken from Jiggs's final record with the Band of the Irish Guards, 'Marching with the Beatles'.

Asked about his interests, he gave his *"more philistine"* as fly-fishing and more academic, playing chess. Allowed to take one luxury he chose his pocket chess set and his compendium of games, which he said had been all over the world with him. For his book, he chose poems by Rupert Brooke or John Betjeman.

# CHAPTER 13

# DIRECTOR OF MUSIC, KNELLER HALL

Following his sabbatical, Jiggs became Chief Instructor and Director of Music, The Royal Military School of Music, Kneller Hall, taking up the appointment on 2nd December 1968, some fourteen years after he had been so highly recommended for the position. Shortly after he took over, Mr P.B. Smith was in Jiggs's office when the telephone rang and it was his sister on the line. She asked Jiggs just what his new job entailed and he replied, *"When one looks up the career ladder all one can see is my backside!"*

As explained in an earlier chapter, this appointment was regarded as the most senior in army music and to recognise this, the incumbent was paid as a regimental officer, rather than as a Quartermaster officer as was normal for Directors of Music.

The School was run by the Commandant, a full Colonel who at this time was Colonel Charles Morris CBE. The only other officer was the Adjutant, Major Frank Betts, Coldstream Guards. The School Bandmaster, Mr Derek Taylor of 16th/5th The Queen's Royal Lancers, had been appointed to the post in May that year and went on to have a distinguished career as Major Derek Taylor MBE, Director of Music, Welsh Guards. In addition, there was a Regimental Sergeant Major, always from the Foot Guards, and a team of civilian professors to teach the academic subjects and for instrumental lessons, with the remainder of the administration being in the hands of the fifty or so student bandmasters as a vital component of their training.

An important aspect of Jiggs's new appointment was his role as Assistant Inspector of Army Bands, which entailed him accompanying the Commandant (the Inspector of Army Bands) on visits to each of the army's bands every five years. This involved a good deal of foreign travel as at that time the bands were spread across the globe with many based in Germany as part of the British Army of the Rhine.

Someone once asked Jiggs if he thought that the Kneller Hall Inspections achieved anything. His response was: *"Yes, it makes the band put their instruments away and get polishing everything."* He added that, for a band to rehearse one piece for weeks is a bit like brass band contesting and that visiting the band on a parade or in concert, providing they are given a few days' warning, would be a more realistic way of assessing them. He was clearly way ahead of his time as it was not until fairly recently that this method began to be adopted.

The appointment also meant a move for the Jaeger family from Caterham to Whitton, with a married quarter in Duke of Cambridge Close, adjacent to the school's sports field and very close to Twickenham's rugby ground.

*Family photographs taken in 1969 on the sports field at Kneller Hall showing Jiggs with his daughter, Maureen, and her children Nicki and Mark*

Jiggs was soon faced with having to find replacements for his two clarinet professors, who were retiring. A few months earlier, the Irish Guards had broadcast on 'Friday Night is Music Night' along with the BBC Concert Orchestra, whose ranks then included one of his former musicians, Paul Harvey. Jiggs had been chatting with him and mentioned that he was shortly to take over at Kneller Hall to which Paul happened to remark that he was now living nearby in Twickenham. Remembering this conversation, Jiggs rang him to ask if he would like to pop over to do a bit of teaching. Twenty years later he was still there, by then having attained the position of Senior Professor.

Jiggs was clearly eager to get into the job, as Rodney Parker recalls that his first musical encounter with Jiggs came during his takeover period with Lieutenant Colonel Basil Brown: *"One of the elements of our course was called 'secondaries', the aim of which was to study every instrument of the military band. You were expected to gain a reasonable degree of proficiency on each instrument, culminating with a test before the Director of Music consisting of scales, sight-reading and a short prepared piece. The thinking behind this was that when you were eventually let loose to stand in front of a band and wave your baton around, at least you knew something about the instruments arrayed before you.*

*I had carefully planned my debut secondary on trombone, (tricky for a clarinettist), in front of Basil Brown who was then very near the end of his tenure and so, I hoped, would be more generous with his marks! As I stood outside of the Director's office waiting to amaze Basil with my trombone technique, along the corridor comes Jiggs! "Come in!," he generously invited me and to Basil, – "I'll take Student Parker – go and have a coffee." Whereupon I went through the longest twenty minutes of my life to date and decided that I would never see, hear or blow a trombone ever again! This sentiment was amplified by Jiggs who kindly mentioned at some stage during the test that I should stick with the clarinet! However, he gave me 7½ out of ten – exceedingly generous, for, if you got 7 or less, you had to be examined again on that instrument."*

Jiggs came to Kneller Hall with a wealth of experience and, to continue with Rodney Parker's words: *"He had also gained an intimate knowledge of world wind band repertoire, particularly the larger works, and this soon became apparent when he introduced some of these to the Kneller Hall bandstand. The musical forces at KH in those days were capable of taking on the largest of these works – the sort of music, of which those of us coming from regimental bands could only dream. This, I remember was the first of Jiggs's many positive moves to enrich our musical life, experience and exploration.*

*Two particular works which I remember him introducing were Shostakovich's Festive Overture and Rossini's Introduction, Theme & Variations for Clarinet, the arrangement being Jiggs's own and the soloist was Jack Brymer. During 1969 and 1970 Jiggs really put his stamp on the Kneller Hall sound. A recording engineer mentioned to me once at Maida Vale studios where we had been making a 'Listen to the Band' programme for*

*Radio 2 that we sounded just like the Irish Guards. Well, fancy that!"*

Another part of the student bandmasters' course comprised a series of competitions, the results of which determined their seniority in the class and thus the order in which they were offered appointments as bandmasters. One of these required them to compose an original quick march and Jiggs invited Mr Roger Barsotti to adjudicate for the 1969 competition. Mr Barsotti was Director of Music of the Metropolitan Police Band which at that time was made up of serving 'Bobbies' and played regularly in the London Parks, on the wireless and at many of the great occasions such as the State Opening of Parliament and Remembrance Sunday at the Cenotaph as well as taking their place in the State Funeral processions of King George VI and Sir Winston Churchill.

Jiggs explained this to the students as part of his briefing and added that the band was *"Not a brass band, not a silver band – but a Copper Band!"* In around 2005, a national newspaper that invites its readers to send in questions included a query asking the difference between a brass band and a silver band. A serious answer was duly published but a few days afterwards there was another letter, this time from a gentleman in Eastbourne repeating this quip as an explanation often given by Colonel Jaeger. His humour certainly stood the test of time.

The student bandmasters and pupils were divided into four companies and, when Jiggs took over at Kneller Hall, 'D' Company included three student bandmasters who went on to become Lieutenant Colonels: Frank Renton, Peter Hannam and Rodney Parker, as well as Pupil Malcolm Torrent, Royal Artillery, who was still *"very green around the ears and was quite impressionable"* but a promising and talented cornet player. Malcolm also eventually retired as a Lieutenant Colonel after 39½ years of service and looks back fondly at the way that Jiggs helped and encouraged him to mature as a musician during that year by making him believe in himself, and to nurture his talents in the best way he could.

There were few rising stars amongst the cornet section of the student bandmasters at the time and, as a result, Malcolm found himself increasingly used on Number 1 Band engagements such as 'Friday Night is Music Night' as well as a host of fanfare engagements in Westminster Abbey and St Paul's Cathedral. *"In the Company Concerts Jiggs encouraged me as a soloist and boosted my confidence on many performances with the assistance of Jack Mackintosh, a highly respected Professor at Kneller Hall. Subsequently I came on in leaps and bounds."* On a St Cecilia Concert at the Royal Festival Hall, Jiggs had Malcolm playing the *Golf Club Galop* in front of royalty with an extra encore of a solo on the club itself, played like an ocarina!

One particular coup for Malcolm came when he was absent from the final rehearsal for some prominent engagement, which resulted in a cry from Jiggs of *"Where's Pupil Torrent?" "He's on Guard Sir!"* replied the Band Sergeant Major, to which Jiggs responded, *"Well get him here now and he is to be taken off all guards for the remainder of the course."* However, he didn't escape being 'duty bugler' and this seemed to arise on more than his fair share of occasions!

Looking back at his experiences of Jiggs, Malcolm writes, *"I gathered Jiggs was quite a showman and always enjoyed taking the Students out after many an occasion in his old haunting grounds around Chelsea after visits to the Royal Hospital or the like. Naturally I was not party to any of those escapades!"*

A tale related by Nigel Borlase, one time Bandmaster of 1st Battalion The Duke of Edinburgh's Royal Regiment (Berkshire and Wiltshire), concerned his time as a student bandmaster and an occasion when Jiggs got carried away with a bit of playful teasing and his ear let him down:

*"There were a number of us in the Students' Mess at lunch time one day, having a quick pint. One of the company was Student Bandmaster Mick Schofield, who was reputed to have perfect pitch. Jiggs walked in, as he often did, and, as soon as he saw Mick he decided to put this to the test. There followed a session of banging on the bar rail, ringing the bell over the bar, beer bottles filled with different amounts of water, etc., and Mick naming all the notes produced by banging, tapping and blowing!*

*At the end of all this, Jiggs said, "This is all inconclusive. We'll go over to the piano and sort this out once and for all!" Off we all go, Jiggs at the piano and Mick with his back to the piano. We were all dutifully gathered around. Jiggs played a number of single notes and Mick said what he thought they were. After about 10 minutes, Jiggs said that his answers were all a semitone out, to which Schofield replied that the piano was wrong! Jiggs got a tuning fork and tested the piano, which turned out to have dropped about a semitone and needed re-tuning. Schofield was correct, the piano was wrong and Jiggs had been enjoying the fun so much that he had lost his concentration!"*

That piano seems to have been the subject of many a student's frustration, as Jiggs was in the habit of using it to test their aural perception without warning. One night a group of them, their thirst having been suitably quenched for most of the evening, decided they had had enough of it and managed to lift it about six feet off the ground – and then dropped it! After repeating the exercise a few times they satisfied themselves that this marked the end of these impromptu tests and left the piano, by now in pieces, for the Regimental Sergeant Major (who was rather fond of the instrument) to find next morning. His reaction was not known but he was given a wide berth for several days.

Norman Rogerson recalls driving Jiggs to one of his many speaking engagements where he would demonstrate his collection of brass instruments. To help pass the journey on one occasion, Jiggs decided to take out his post horn, poke it out of the car window and start playing it, rather reminiscent of its use on the back of the old mail coaches. No doubt the pedestrians they passed found it all very amusing but the long arm of the law saw what was happening, pulled them over and took rather a dim view of it. The driver was blamed!

Another tale recounted by P.B. Smith concerns a new Bandmaster who asked Jiggs how he should start conducting the French National Anthem, as it starts after the third beat. Jiggs promised to advise him but got him to drive around visiting various pubs and they ended up back at Kneller Hall rather late. The Bandmaster then asked again how to start the anthem. Jiggs said, *"Put your right hand over your left shoulder and swing it smartly back to the right – and that's all."* And of course it worked!

Jiggs's new appointment and responsibilities did not stop him from following his outside interests. Early in 1969 he was the speaker at the Portsmouth Command Golfing Society's Annual Dinner while a few weeks later he was the guest conductor at a concert by the British Legion Military Band at Norbury in South West London, taking the baton for the Overture to *The Merry Wives of Windsor* (Nicolai) and Gustav Holst's *Suite in E Flat*.

He was invited by the Yugoslavian Army to be a guest at their Armed Forces Day in Belgrade, with performances by their many outstanding orchestras, bands and choirs. This gave him the opportunity to meet a number of directors of music from around the world, including those from a number of communist countries. A final farewell party was quite deliberately arranged with no interpreters present, which rather ruled out any real conversations but, as Jiggs later wrote, *" … it proved conclusively to me that music (less politics), especially in the Services, is a great force of universal fraternity and not entirely dissimilar nation by nation, in gargantuan and bacchanalian characteristics."*

*Jiggs as a guest of the Yugoslavian Army for their Armed Forces Day in Belgrade*

The regular Wednesday evening concerts on the bandstand during the summer months continued to be a strong feature of the School's life just as they were when Jiggs had been an embryonic conductor in the late 1930s. While their main purpose remained that of giving the student bandmasters experience with the baton, one of the noticeable changes over the years had been the introduction of guest conductors. During Jiggs's two summer seasons these included the 'Man o' Brass' Harry Mortimer, Gordon Reynolds (organist at Hampton Court), the recently knighted Sir Vivian Dunn, and Colonel Fritz Masuhr, the Senior Director of Music of the German Army, as well as most of the army's more senior directors of music, who took their turn taking the band through some of the more substantial works.

Another guest conductor who appeared on the Kneller Hall bandstand (affectionately known as 'The Rock') on 19th August 1970 was the prolific American composer and arranger, Doctor Harold L. Walters, who conducted his concert march *Kneller Hall* which was "Composed for this occasion and dedicated to Lieutenant Colonel C.H. Jaeger and Kneller Hall". By way of an encore he followed it with his *Instant Concert*, a musical switch with snippets of thirty (or perhaps more?) tunes in about three minutes. Incidentally, this concert opened with Jiggs's march *Double X* conducted by a future Senior Director of Music of the Household Division, Student Bandmaster David Price, 2nd Battalion The Royal Green Jackets.

During the rehearsals for one of the concerts the pupils planted a uniformed dummy behind the xylophone. Jiggs didn't realise what was going on until he 'queued' the xylophone to come in. He took it in good part and gave the band the rest of the afternoon off.

*Leading the Kneller Hall Band for publicity photographs*

One particularly interesting, and probably unique, summer concert was held on 9th July 1969, with Jiggs conducting an entire programme of music by Hector Berlioz: the *Trojan March*, the overtures *Roman Carnival* and *Benvenuto Cellini*, and the Hungarian March from the *Damnation of Faust* making up the first half of the concert. The *Symphonie Funebre et Triomphale* (Funeral Symphony) made up the second half, a major work which the Guards bands had performed in Regent's Park back in 1961. The middle movement includes an extended trombone solo, on this occasion played by Pupil Chris Dean of The Life Guards, now one of the great names of the Big Band world as leader of the Syd Lawrence Orchestra. Unfortunately, on this occasion, the weather was unkind which meant that the concert had to be performed indoors.

Each of the four Companies had a Student Bandmaster as Company Commander and they competed with each other during the winter months with each giving its own concert. As well as the Company Concerts, there were three others in the winter series of 1968/69, one of which gathered string players from various bands of the Household Division, Royal Artillery and Corps to produce an orchestral concert on Wednesday 26th February 1969. Jiggs conducted the entire programme, which comprised:

| | |
|---|---|
| Symphony No. 4 (The Italian) | *Mendelssohn* |
| Excerpts from the Suite No. 3 | *Bach* |
| Scherzo from Concerto Symphonique No. 4 | *Litolff* |
| Serenade for Strings | *Elgar* |
| Le Tombeau Debussy | *Cumper* |
| Prelude to Act 1, La Traviata | *Verdi* |
| Dance of the Tumblers | *Rimsky-Korsakov* |
| Symphony No. 8 (The Unfinished) | *Schubert* |

A second orchestral concert was given the following year with Jiggs conducting the *Overture to The Meistersingers* (Wagner), Mozart's *Symphony Number 40*, Brahms's *Variations on a Theme of Haydn* and Dvorak's *Symphony Number 9, 'From the New World'*.

On 21st June 1969 Jiggs was the Director of Music for the first of the great Military Musical Pageants held at Wembley Stadium with massed bands of around 1,000 strong. This gave a new twist on the established pattern of Tattoos: no Musical Rides, dogs, motorcycles, PT, battle scenes and the like – just purely massed bands throughout the evening. The half-time massed bands performances at Wembley football matches were always popular so why not dispense with the footballers and expand on the music?

The producer in 1969 was Captain Michael Parker whom Jiggs had worked with at the Berlin Tattoo in 1967, and the bands taking part were:

Mounted Band of The Life Guards
5th Royal Inniskilling Dragoon Guards
Grenadier Guards
Coldstream Guards
Scots Guards
Welsh Guards
1st Bn. The Royal Regiment of Fusiliers
2nd Bn. The Royal Regiment of Fusiliers
1st Bn. The King's Regiment
2nd Bn. The Royal Anglian Regiment
1st Bn. The Light Infantry
3rd Bn. The Light Infantry
1st Bn. The Loyal Regiment
1st Bn. The Royal Green Jackets
Staff Band of the Royal Army Medical Corps
Staff Band of the Women's Royal Army Corps
Band and Trumpeters of The Royal Military School of Music, Kneller Hall

The Pageant opened with fanfares and routine trumpet and bugle calls, after which came massed bands drawn from Cavalry, Infantry and Corps bands, plus the Kneller Hall Band, with most of the marches having 'soldier' connections: *Soldiers in the Park, Soldiers' Chorus, Something About a Soldier* and so on, as well as *Boom Bang a Bang,* which had been a success for Lulu in the Eurovision Song Contest three months earlier.

After this the Massed Bands and Bugles of the Light Division raced in with all their usual style and panache, stealing the show as always. Eight Corps of Drums came next, joined by the Pipes and Drums of 1st Battalion Scots Guards and 1st Battalion Irish Guards and the first half concluded with a display by the Mounted Band of The Life Guards, joined by Cavalry Trumpeters of the 5th Royal Inniskilling Dragoon Guards for Richard Henrion's *Fehrbelliner Reitermarsch.*

The glorious sight and sound of the Massed Bands, Drums and Pipes from the Guards Division opened the second half, followed by Community Singing in the style that was at that time a regular pre-match feature at the F.A. Cup Finals. *Congratulations, Roll out the Barrel, Yellow Submarine, John Brown's Body, When the Saints, We'll Meet Again* and *Little Bit of Luck* were sung by the Choir of the 1st Battalion Welsh Guards under their young conductor, Miss Anita Sutcliffe, accompanied by the Bands of the Royal Army Medical Corps and the Women's Royal Army Corps. Jiggs led the singing as compere with his usual humour: *"My name is Jaeger; I expect you know yours,"* was his introduction. At one point he turned to Earl Mountbatten who was taking the salute in the Royal Box and invited him to *"Sing up Sir, please!"*

To end the evening, the various groups of massed bands entered the arena to appropriate marches: *Sambre et Meuse* representing the French army and

*Cavalry of the Steppes* the Russians, and joined together under Jiggs's baton to play Tchaikowsky's *1812 Overture*, enhanced by the voice of the Guns of The King's Troop, Royal Horse Artillery. Finally, Douglas Pope's *Nightfall in Camp* brought the evening to a close. The Pageant was a great success and, although the following year's event had to be cancelled as a result of the pitch being re-turfed, it was to continue in alternate years until 1985.

*Conducting massed bands of around a thousand musicians in the 1812 Overture at a rehearsal for the Military Musical Pageant at Wembley Stadium in 1969*

The following month Jiggs conducted three teams of Kneller Hall Trumpeters at the Investiture of H.R.H. The Prince of Wales, held at Caernarvon Castle on 1st July 1969. Each of the teams comprised eight trumpeters with a side drummer, and they were positioned on towers around the outer walls of the castle to play a sequence of magnificent antiphonal fanfares, especially composed for the occasion by Sir Arthur Bliss, Master of the Queen's Musick.

In the planning stages, Sir Arthur had attended rehearsals in the practice room at Kneller Hall and Jiggs was heavily involved in a good deal of liaison with the Constable of Caernarvon Castle (Lord Snowdon) and the Earl Marshal (The Duke of Norfolk) over the arrangements.

Jiggs directed the music from a lofty perch on one of the towers in the centre of the Castle, conducting each group in turn as the music passed from one team to the next and with what must have been a magnificent view of the ceremony.

Most of the trumpeters were student bandmasters but amongst them was Pupil Malcolm Torrent, albeit dressed as a Student, who recalls that Jiggs *"directed the antiphonal trumpet teams and bands and choirs with a well-practised style which delivered the goods and upheld his perfectionism to the end. Combined with the BBC Welsh Orchestra, the whole spectacle was something I will always remember and I still talk about the occasion on my regular lectures to local societies and clubs."*

*The Investiture of HRH The Prince of Wales at Caernarvon Castle in 1969 with Jiggs high up on the battlements. One of the three groups of Kneller Hall Trumpeters can be seen behind him, in the very top right of the picture.*

The fanfares were interspersed with processional music played by the Band of 1st Battalion The Royal Welch Fusiliers (augmented by a number of Kneller Hall Students) under the baton of the Bandmaster, Mr Ben Bentley, later to become Director of Music of The Brigade of Gurkhas. This was a huge honour for a regimental band to be taking centre stage in this way but the Castle was very much their home territory so it was quite right and proper that they should be there.

Student Bandmaster (later Lieutenant Colonel) Rodney Parker was present playing clarinet and recalls: "*It was here that Jiggs's experience of State events was comfortingly obvious. We sailed through the week with hardly a hitch, got back on the bus after the event, travelled back to Twickenham overnight and were on the bandstand the following morning in rehearsal for a Summer Concert that evening. This was a brief but interesting interlude in Wales. For many of us this was the first taste of being part of State Ceremonial at a very high level – an excellent experience for Student Bandmasters under Jiggs's experienced and inspired direction.*"

The Kneller Hall contingent had moved to Wales on a special train from Euston station, having arrived there in army four-ton trucks. The equipment was shunted to the relevant platform in a series of trailers but those responsible for the movements were not allowed to travel on this 'caravan', much to the annoyance of Student Bandmaster Bryan Briggs-Watson who was ultimately responsible for its safe passage.

Rodney Parker continues: "*When we eventually arrived at our tented camp near Caernarvon we discovered that four fanfare trumpets were missing. These instruments were required for an early morning rehearsal the following day and I imagine that Jiggs would not have been too impressed about their absence! We rang the Euston baggage handlers, "Yes, we've got them. They are safe, must have fallen off the trailers somewhere!" "OK, when's the next train up here?" "We can put them on the Irish Mail which arrives at Holyhead at midnight."*

*Consequently, Bryan and I 'borrowed' a Land Rover from the Mechanical Transport section and headed off across the Menai Bridge and Anglesey to meet that night's Irish Mail. Sure enough, the instruments had been safely stowed in the Guard's van. We heaved a sigh of relief! I sometimes wonder if Jiggs knew about this little adventure. He probably did.*"

By the time of the investiture, Jiggs had become quite ill with angina and was being treated at Millbank Military Hospital although he didn't really cooperate and wouldn't let on about his problems. The Medical Officer looking after him was greatly concerned as to how Jiggs would stand up to the huge logistical exercise in getting all the troops from London to Caernarvon and, more to the point, the effect on his heart of having to climb the difficult steps of the towers many times each day during the rehearsals.

Despite his reluctance, he eventually consented to Jiggs taking part on the condition that he would follow him up and down the tower to keep a firm eye on him and to ensure that if he did have a bad turn he would not fall off the battlements while conducting. There was also a very strict understanding that Jiggs would go into Millbank Hospital as soon as he got back. This he did and while he was there a large bunch of flowers arrived from the Duke of Norfolk, the man who had masterminded the ceremony. Jiggs was eventually sent to spend some time at the convalescent home for officers at Osborne House on the Isle of Wight.

By the beginning of November, Jiggs was back at work but doing *"as much as he feels like"* although he was said to be looking very fit and had had no symptoms for some time but was taking a number of pills. In March the following year he replied to some concerned friends saying, *"I have recovered pretty well though I still could say that I am not exactly out of the woods yet."*

Jiggs continued to charm his audiences at concerts with the Kneller Hall Band as he had done with the Irish Guards. On Saturday 14th February, St Valentine's Day, they played at Hayes Grammar School with the virtuoso horn player Alan Civil as the guest soloist. An item in the local newspaper reported: *"Lieut-Colonel Jaeger joked, winked and charmed his way through a dazzling programme of musical items that held a capacity audience enraptured … They brought the house down with an encore 'Circus Galop' that had all the stops out. Whistles blew, trombones blared, bandsmen shook hands and midway through the work the conductor strolled off to chat with his bass players."*

On Friday 22nd May 1970 the Kneller Hall Band and Trumpeters, 200 strong, were at the Royal Festival Hall for a Gala Concert in aid of the Army Benevolent Fund, which included the first performance of a new arrangement by Jiggs of Rossini's *Theme and Variations for Clarinet* with the School's clarinet professor, Jack Brymer, as the soloist.

| | | |
|---|---|---|
| Fanfare: | **Jubilant** | *Bliss* |
| March: | **Marche Militaire** | *Gounod* |
| Overture: | **Tannhauser** | *Wagner* |
| | **Theme and Variations for Clarinet** | *Rossini arr. Jaeger* |
| | *Soloist: Jack Brymer* | |
| Fantasy: | **Hello Mr Kaempfert** | *Arr. Shearn* |
| Finale from: | **Fourth Symphony** | *Tchaikowsky* |
| | **INTERVAL** | |
| Fanfare: | **Richmond** | *Arnold* |
| | **English Suite** | *Grundman* |
| | **Concerto for Trombone** | *Rimsky-Korsakov* |
| | *Soloist: Pupil Henry Hardy, Royal Artillery* | |
| Extravaganza | **Heykens' Serenade** | *Arr. Mitchell* |
| Finale: | **Music for the Investiture of** | *Bliss* |
| | **HRH The Prince of Wales** | |
| | **Lament** | |
| | *Pipe Major J. Roe MBE BEM, Scots Guards* | |
| | **Nightfall in Camp** | *Pope* |
| | **The School March** | *Arr. Roberts* |
| | **Fanfare and the National Anthem** | *Arr. Jaeger* |

Also that month, Jiggs took the Kneller Hall Band to the Portsmouth Guildhall for a concert with the Portsmouth Glee Club, opening with Vaughan Williams's magnificent setting of *Old Hundredth*. The programme included the *Slavonic Rhapsody No. 2* by Carl Friedmann, *The Late Twenties*, *Hampshire Suite* by Noel Gay and *Carnival in Paris* (Svendsen). Each half ended with the band and choir combined, the first with the *Easter Hymn* from *Cavalleria Rusticana* (Mascagni) and the second with *Hail, Bright Abode*, from Wagner's *Tannhauser*.

The concert had been staged to celebrate the Choir's 40th anniversary and at the end Jiggs invited the audience to join the band in a chorus of *Happy Birthday*. A press report commented on how the 'Birthday Party Atmosphere' owed a good deal to the genial, humorous personality of Colonel Jaeger, who *"had a seemingly endless fund of jokes, puns and anecdotes with which to entertain the audience"*.

On 12th June the Band was at the Fairfield Halls in Croydon. William Relton was a guest conductor for the Finale from Tchaikowsky's *4th Symphony* and the concert ended with Svendsen's great tone poem, *Carnival in Paris*.

In 1970 BBC television began a short weekly series of broadcasts that featured military band displays under the title 'Music on Command'. It was produced by former Coldstream Guards musician Ken Griffin, and Jiggs composed the winning entry in the BBC Title Music Competition held on 29th May 1970, with a fanfare which provided a stirring introduction to the programme each week. One of the events covered was the Aldershot Army Display where, although Major George Hurst of the RAMC was the Senior Director of Music, Jiggs appeared as a guest conductor to take the bands through *Finlandia* (Sibelius).

Major Roger Swift recalls another occasion at Aldershot when he was a young musician in the Band of the Corps of Royal Engineers (Aldershot) and Jiggs conducted the massed bands in one of the finale pieces. He conducted the rehearsal at some quite bizarre tempos and with many exaggerated pauses. However, on the day itself he took everything as it should be but knowing that every single pair of eyes in the massed bands was watching his baton extra carefully!

'The Marches of the Vanishing Regiments' was the title of an LP on BBC Records which was issued in 1970 by the Kneller Hall Band under Jiggs. This was based on a series of that name, broadcast on BBC Radio 4 in 1968 and 1969, which featured the regimental marches of those regiments that had been recently disbanded or amalgamated. The LP included the marches of Jiggs's early regiments, including the 4th Hussars, which had amalgamated with the 8th Hussars in 1958 to become The Queen's Royal Irish Hussars. They were represented on the record by both the slow march, *Litany of Lorretto*, and the quick march *Berkeley's Dragoons* which had been composed for them by Jiggs in the 1940s.

The march of The King's Own Yorkshire Light Infantry was also on the record, the regiment having amalgamated in 1966 into The Light Infantry, with the KOYLI effectively becoming the 2nd Battalion. It was therefore something of a nostalgic and special day for Jiggs when he travelled to Colchester with Colonel Morris to visit the Band of 2nd Battalion The Light Infantry for its quinquennial Kneller Hall Inspection. At the end of the Inspection Jiggs presented the band with a post horn inscribed:

"Presented to the 2nd Battalion The Light Infantry by Boy C.H. Jaeger (1927) on his appointment as Director of Music, Kneller Hall (1968)"

*Jiggs playing the Post Horn that he had presented to the Band of 2nd Battalion The Light Infantry during their Kneller Hall Inspection*

In 1970 Colonel Morris retired as Commandant and was replaced by Colonel Francis Jefferson, formerly of the Grenadier Guards. Colonel Jefferson would no doubt have been well known to Jiggs from his time as the Lieutenant Colonel Commanding Grenadier Guards and particularly from his role as the Chief Marshal at the State Funeral of Sir Winston Churchill in 1965.

Martin Grant's correspondence with Jiggs continued and *"on Jiggs's move to Kneller Hall I received and accepted several invitations to attend the Grand Concerts. They were always great events with excellent and varied music and a wide range of guest conductors.*

*My last meeting with him was at a Grand Concert on 22ⁿᵈ July 1970. As always there were some fascinating guests from the world of military music and brass bands. Major Alf Young (retired Director of Music of the Royal Engineers and also known by his nom-de-plume, Earl Brigham) guest conducted his 'Spanish Fiesta' and amongst the guests was Wing Commander A.E. Sims, retired Organising Director of Music of the Royal Air Force; his presence gave the lie to Jiggs's joke years before against the junior service.*

*Jiggs conducted the Finale, 'Music for an Investiture' complete with fireworks, which he had conducted for the Prince of Wales's Investiture at Caernavon Castle in1969.*

*I left the post concert reception quite late and Jiggs saw me to the front door of Kneller Hall to say goodbye. I knew he had not been too well, although there had been no signs of that that evening; in fact, quite the reverse. However, with all the gravity and naivety of a freshly graduated 21 year old I looked him in the eye and asked him to take care of himself. He responded with a similarly intense stare, a 'Well, well' and a pat on the shoulder."*

One of the BBC's long-running radio shows, 'Down Your Way', visited Kneller Hall in 1970 and a number of personalities were interviewed by Franklin Engelmann and allowed to select a piece of music to be played. The programme was broadcast on 15th August 1970, just a few weeks before Jiggs's untimely death.

Jiggs was naturally among those interviewed and was very quick to put the presenter firmly in his place when he referred to his first regiment as "Koylis" saying we must call them KOYLI. Jiggs set out the path that his career had taken since he joined up at, as he put it, the age of *"14 years and ten minutes"*. He spoke of his preference for orchestral music in his own private life and his choice of music was the overture, *'Merry Wives of Windsor'*, which he had been rehearsing on the bandstand that week with the Kneller Hall Band. The rendition that was broadcast was played by the Band of the Coldstream Guards. Not, frankly, a particularly good choice as this particular version was heavily cut, presumably in order to fit it into the available space on the record.

Amongst the others interviewed were the Commandant, Colonel Jefferson, who chose Elgar's *Nimrod*, and the School Bandmaster, Mr Tom Griffiths (later Major Griffiths, Director of Music of the Royal Army Ordnance Corps) who chose *Spanish Flea* played by Herb Alpert. The School Band Sergeant Major, Gerry McColl represented the Student Bandmasters and Andrew Morris of The Life Guards, the Pupils. They went on to become Major McColl and Band Corporal Major Morris, serving together with the Band of The Life Guards.

Paul Harvey represented the Professors and chose *Dance of the Tumblers* in a recording by the Irish Guards made when he had been a clarinet player in the band. One of the most respected gentlemen at Kneller Hall for many years was the librarian, Reg Sanders, a one-time clarinet player in the Band of the

1st King's Dragoon Guards whose knowledge of military music was second to none. He couldn't resist a dig at the BBC's unwillingness to celebrate anything English on St George's Day, by choosing *English Rose* from Edward German's operetta *Merrie England*.

Jiggs's health continued to be a major cause for concern. He was suffering regular angina attacks and was beginning to have great difficulty walking the short distance from his home, across the grass to Kneller Hall. He still refused to admit to his problems and seemed pretty determined not to let them get in the way of his very energetic and frenetic life style. When Chris broached the subject with his father of *"taking it easy"* the response was that, whatever the consequences, there was only one way he could live his life, and he would do little to reduce his workload and commitments.

Undeterred, he was a speaker at the 25th Conference of the Standing Conference of Amateur Music (SCAM), which was held at the University College of North Wales on 18th September 1970. He spoke about his experiences in America where he had attended a festival at which 15,000 young musicians had taken part, and went on to cover the range of studies undertaken at Kneller Hall.

However, there were further signs that his health was not all it should be as a few minutes before the lecture he had asked the organiser whether he should stand or sit while speaking. Standing was suggested but Jiggs replied that he did not feel so good so it was suggested he took breaks and sat down from time to time. In the event, once he started he was his usual irrepressible self, blowing top notes on the old style cornet he took along to demonstrate.

Jiggs went to Wimbledon Golf Club on Wednesday 23rd September 1970 for a meeting and lunch with members of the Transport Golfing Society and one of its members later wrote, *"Although I thought he looked very tired he was in high spirits."* On the Friday Jiggs travelled with Brigadier Robert Stott, Director of Appeals for SSAFA, to Salisbury Cathedral where they were planning to stage a Festival of Music on 4th December. Jiggs wrote up his notes on the return train journey to Waterloo and all seemed well.

The following day, Saturday 26th September 1970, a large marching band from Kneller Hall under the baton of the School Bandmaster, Mr Tom Griffiths, provided pre-match entertainment at Twickenham Rugby Ground. Later that afternoon the trumpeters led by the School Band Sergeant Major, Gerry McColl, left to join Jiggs at Windsor.

Jiggs had produced a 'Military Spectacular' to be held that evening under floodlights in the Lower Ward of Windsor Castle in front of the Guardroom as part of the Windsor Festival; it was to be repeated on the following Saturday. The display commenced at 10 pm and featured music and marching from the Bands of the Grenadier Guards and the Welsh Guards, along with the Pipes and

Drums of 2nd Battalion Scots Guards, including some Highland Dancing, with Trumpeters from The Royal Military School of Music, Kneller Hall positioned up on the battlements.

*Jiggs conducting the Bands of the Grenadier and Welsh Guards in the Lower Ward of Windsor Castle, about four hours before he died*

Jiggs conducted the finale, which combined the bands and antiphonal trumpeters in the fanfares and music that Sir Arthur Bliss had composed for the Investiture of the Prince of Wales. The show came to a conclusion with *Last Post* followed by *My Home* played by a piper on the ramparts of the Round Tower.

At the end of the evening, Jiggs returned to his home in Duke of Cambridge Close, adjacent to Kneller Hall. He had, as usual, given his all to his conducting and he arrived home feeling exhausted and complaining of chest pains. He felt that he couldn't breathe and went around the house opening windows and drinking water.

Eileen wanted to fetch a doctor who lived nearby but Jiggs retorted, *"Don't be silly, he is a gynaecologist – I'm not having a baby."* His condition deteriorated fast. He was in awful pain and eventually lost consciousness. Chris got him onto the floor and tried to give him resuscitation but he had had two massive coronaries.

He had died by the time that the ambulance arrived. The official causes of death were recorded as Myocardial Infarction and Coronary Disease.

# CHAPTER 14

# IN MEMORIAM

T he news spread fast. Student Bandmaster Rodney Parker had a knock at his door at 6 o'clock that morning to find the Duty Student Bandmaster, Jim Dott (later to become Bandmaster of the 1st Battalion, The Royal Regiment of Fusiliers). The message at that ungodly hour on a Sunday morning was quite blunt – *"Jiggs has died!"* The student had known that he had been having problems but had no idea that the end was that close.

Jiggs's funeral took place at the South West Middlesex Crematorium at Whitton on 2nd October. His coffin was carried by a Bearer Party of six student bandmasters including Nigel Borlase, Gerry McColl and Gerry Laverty.

A memorial service was held in the Guards Chapel, Wellington Barracks, on 12th October 1970 with standing room only. The Address was given by the very popular chaplain, Rev. 'Gus' Claxton:

"For me it is incredibly hard – as I stand in this pulpit – to realise that Jiggs is not physically present among the musicians in the band gallery. We have heard some of his music – some of it for the first time and none of it (I dare to think) for the last time. He will live on in these arrangements of his – characteristic as they are of the man, expressing the qualities of his personality and character. For what he has done is to take something familiar and pedestrian – and sometimes dull – and with a flamboyant gesture touched it with magic and made it live.

I well remember the day I first came to live in Wellington Barracks – very new, strange and frightened. I don't think I had ever spoken to a Guardsman in my life. When I'd been here a few days – reduced to what seemed like a permanent state of apprehension – I saw a small figure (wearing a bowler hat) walking briskly across the yard. He stood to attention.

"My name's Jaeger, Irish Guards for 17 years – Senior Director of Music. Always known as Jiggs."

He then took his hat off and put it on the wrong way round. At that moment my daughter came up behind.

"Tell me dear," he said, "why do bees hum?" … well, you know the answer to that! But from that moment onwards I knew I was among friends. He had

**MEMORIAL SERVICE**
**THE GUARDS CHAPEL, WELLINGTON BARRACKS**
Monday 12th October 1970 at 12.30pm

**ORDER OF SERVICE**

Music played by the Band of the Irish Guards:

| | |
|---|---|
| Pavane pour une Infante Defunte | Ravel |
| Sursum Corda | Elgar |
| Jesu, Joy of Man's Desiring | Bach |
| Nimrod | Elgar |

The Sentences

Fanfare for Band and Trumpets; Hymn: Praise, My Soul, the King of Heaven

The Bidding
Psalm 121
The Lesson: The First Epistle of Paul to the Corinthians, Chapter 13

Anthem: by the Band, Choir, Trumpets and Organ: Glory      Setting by Jaeger

Address by The Reverend L.E.M. Claxton, MC, MA, ARCM

Fanfare for Band and Trumpets; Hymn: All People that on Earth Do Dwell
The Prayers
The Regimental Collect

Hymn: Now Thank We All Our God

The Commendation
Nunc Dimittis
The Blessing
Sevenfold Amen

Voluntaries while the congregation leaves:

| | |
|---|---|
| Let Erin Remember | Trad |
| Crown Imperial | Walton |

an incredible gift for breaking down barriers – or (more accurately) behaving as if they weren't there. It was the supreme art of communication. Jiggs was a showman. We have heard that said of him many times – and I say it now without any hesitation. He himself never pretended not to be. After the Carol Service in the Chapel three years ago Jiggs came up to me and said: "We've already had one telegram." As so often, I fell for it. "Really?" I said. "Yes," he said. "It was from God. It said 'watch it'!"

His life's work needed a touch of showmanship. That great British pianist Cyril Smith in his autobiography *Duet for Three Hands* says that when he was a student at the Royal College of Music there were many student pianists better than he was, both technically and musically. But he knew they would never achieve the status of concert pianists. When Jiggs took up the baton – it was not only the scholarship and knowledge that went into the score reading, nor the accuracy of timing and the care of interpretation – it was a certain flair – the fact that he could get it across. And this gave to his performance an excitement and a quality that was electrifying.

But he knew when to turn off the showmanship. He knew when to be quiet. I always loved the way the choir came out after a church service when he was conducting. It was a verse or two of a well known hymn tune – played quietly and reverently but with subtle differences of harmony and arrangement which added a thrilling beauty and meaning to it.

Jiggs had innumerable friends all over the world and a wonderful way of keeping in touch with them. He could never help doing a kindness. Those who knew him well will never forget his love for his fellow man. He would go out of his way; he would think of little things; he would take the most immense trouble to help people. I think it must be very rare for him to have left anybody without their feeling better for having been in his company – more cheerful, more light-hearted, less pompous. Yes – and younger. His great appreciation for youth – and the tremendous practical help he gave them in various ways – was rewarded by the appeal he had for them and the response he was always able to get from them. He was large in heart and young in heart, and there was a childlike delight and enthusiasm about him when his own music was performed or when he demonstrated some new idea he had just had.

I have known him angry – very angry indeed. I have known him difficult – very difficult. I have said to him: "I don't know what I have done to deserve having to cope with you wretched musicians." But I have never known him able to harbour a grudge – or to be anything but magnanimous or charitable in his judgements. Most of you in this Chapel realise better than I do what a tremendous loss to music in the Army his going from us has been.

It has been an equal loss to gaiety and to laughter and friendship. When – to crown his brilliant career – he was appointed Director of Music at Kneller Hall, he outlined to me the plans he had for church music there. I don't know if he had time to put many – or any – of his ideas into action. They were, as you would expect, forward looking and alive – and I only hope the day will come when some of his ideas are realised.

Our thoughts and affections today are with Jiggs. Our sympathies and affections are with Eileen, Maureen and Christopher. I would like to say one last thing. Jiggs lived in the only way he could. He had been ill and he knew how serious it was. One is bound to wonder that – if he had taken more care and lived more quietly – whether he might have prolonged his life. But he was not one who could take that kind of care of himself. He was one who had to put everything that was in him into what he did. He was one whose nature was to burn himself out. That was one of the secrets of his personality. I don't believe we should wish to take it from him."

By an extraordinary coincidence, a memorial service was held in the same chapel exactly forty years later, on 12th October 2010, this time for another great Director of Music in the Foot Guards and at Kneller Hall, Lieutenant Colonel Trevor Sharpe LVO, OBE, Coldstream Guards.

Jiggs's death was to deny him realising a lifetime ambition, as he was due to adjudicate at the National Brass Band Championships which took place two weeks later.

On Saturday 28th November 1970 the weekly 'Listen to the Band' programme on BBC Radio 2 was set aside as 'A Tribute to the late Lt-Col C.H. Jaeger OBE' with a programme of music by the Band of the Royal Military School of Music under the new Director of Music, Lieutenant Colonel Rodney Bashford and the School Bandmaster, Mr Tom Griffiths.

A Memorial Plaque was positioned in the Chapel at Kneller Hall and Jiggs's ashes were placed behind it, following a Service of Dedication which took place on Friday 21st May 1971. The Service was taken by the Assistant Chaplain General, P. Malins, the man who had baptised Chris in the Guards Chapel in 1953.

The class of Student Bandmasters graduating in 1971 named themselves 'The Jaeger Class' in his memory. The top student was Student Bandmaster P.R. Evans, 3rd Battalion The Light Infantry, who ended his career as Lieutenant Colonel Evans with the Band of the Corps of Royal Engineers. Also in the class was Norman Rogerson, who was to have a highly successful career as Bandmaster of 1st Battalion The Black Watch (Royal Highland Regiment) and as the producer for a number of large-scale events including the Birmingham

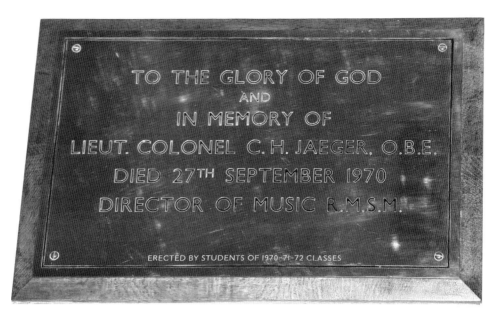

*The Memorial Plaque in the Chapel at Kneller Hall*

*Part of the Memorial Window in the Chapel at Kneller Hall with the names of past Directors of Music*

Tattoo and a series of 'East Meets West' tours.

The numerous tributes received included one sent on behalf of the Major General, passing on the words from a letter from the Queen's Private Secretary asking for Her Majesty's expression of sincere sympathy to be passed to Mrs Jaeger and the family.

Arthur E. Davies, Conductor of the Luton Girls Choir, wrote to say, "He was not only a meticulous and painstaking musician but had accomplished artistically (and often humorously) the presentation of his music in addition to being a trainer and conductor of high order."

Major Alf Young wrote: "I have always kept close to the School and have been keenly interested in its progress since it returned to Kneller Hall in 1946 and nobody was more aware than I of the reforms of the last two years, from which the School and its reputation has certainly benefitted. It is so sad to think that Jiggs was not to be allowed to see the final results of all his endeavours and aspirations. I am sure it will be a great consolation to you (Eileen) to know that he had the affection and respect of all who worked with him and under him and although we were never close, I include myself."

The Bandmaster of the Queen's Royal Irish Hussars, Mr P.B. Smith, wrote to Eileen to express his pride at being Bandmaster of Jiggs's old band (following amalgamation) and how more than twenty years after Jiggs left the regiment he continued to be mentioned in the Mess as well as on a recent tour of Northern Ireland when a great number of people had asked after him. Mr Smith added: "... to be so widely known and admired takes a rather special person."

He was later to write: "As for Jiggs the man, I find it very difficult to describe him and what I, and many others, feel about him. He was a musician's musician and he certainly looked after his musicians. He had some very temperamental guys in his Band who, had they served under anyone else, would certainly not have survived. He was a strict and fair boss; he often said that he could be very annoyed at people who mistook kindness for weakness.

I must say that the Irish Guards Band under Jiggs was in my mind the greatest band the British Army has ever had. There has been a lot of talk regarding Directors referring to them as great men. There was only one great man and that was Jiggs. I remember trying to tune my radio in to hear the Irish Guards Band broadcast and all I could get was this b***** orchestra playing the Marriage of Figaro Overture. Of course, that orchestra was the band – I have never forgotten that moment."

A tribute in the Guards Magazine started with a comment, "Whenever one met 'Jiggs' it would be revealed, sooner or later that he was the original 'imp' in impudence."

Harry Copnall's impressions of Jiggs were that, "He was VERY much in charge and although a somewhat pompous chap, he was very charismatic, a showman who leapt onto any chance to show himself and the band off. He would defend the band and gave praise where it was deserved to the extent that when he promoted me to Senior Time-beater of the massed bands, he used to present me with a bottle of whisky following *the Troop (one of his attributes which he passed onto me!!!).*

*As a youngster, my rank was BOY and right up to the day Jiggs left us he always called me 'Boy Copnall'. He had some wonderful nicknames for we younger ones. Later in my career I felt that really the old boy had a bit of a soft spot for me, maybe because he had studied at Durham University not far from my home and I think he appreciated the fact that I was not in the same class musically as my colleagues but trying like stink to get there. We had a long chat one day whereby he was explaining to me that – if you wanted anything in life then go for it and don't be afraid of upsetting anyone and if they get in the way – walk over them. As he said, That's what I have done."*

Martin Grant wrote: *"He was gone, and we had all lost a great character, a fine musician and a good friend. I knew him for a very short time but he made an impression which has lasted my lifetime. I continue to enjoy his music on record and still smile with pleasure at my memories of him."*

Many people have spoken of Jiggs's different personalities. Lieutenant Colonel Rodney Bashford was one of army music's finest wordsmiths, with a gift for being able to sum up a person or situation in a wonderfully amusing manner while making a serious point. He summed Jiggs up so perfectly:

*".... so I said to the judge ....*

*Shall we really* never *hear those words again? Is that seemingly indestructible and ageless ball of energy known as Jiggs never again to hold us enthralled with tales of his hectic and hilarious past? Jiggs: urchin, joker, cornet player, rifle-barrel player, raconteur, chess player, bon viveur, punter, fisherman, golfer sans [sic] excellence, Yorkshire Light Infantryman, bespectacled student, 4th Hussar, Bachelor of Music, Irish Guardsman, pillar of the National Association of Boys' Clubs, Our Man at Kneller Hall, Past Master of his Lodge, Lieutenant-Colonel, and Officer of the Most Excellent Order of the British Empire.*

*Was all this just one man? He did more in one short lifetime than most of us could fit into three, knowing, especially of late, that no human frame could support such demands as were made by an untiring and quicksilver brain.*

*Jiggs in the Adjutant's pear tree – the Adjutant below;*
*Lieutenant Colonel Jaeger controlling the solemnities at the Cenotaph;*
*Jiggs regaling all and sundry in the Corporals' Mess;*
*Lieutenant Colonel Jaeger on the Queen's Birthday Parade;*
*Jiggs teaching a raw subaltern the artful dodges of backgammon;*
*Lieutenant Colonel Jaeger amid the smoke and fireworks of '1812';*
*Jiggs rattling off the Post Horn Galop on the A flat golf club;*
*Lieutenant Colonel Jaeger endlessly up and down those deadly steps of Caernarvon Castle conducting Sir Arthur Bliss's Music for an Investiture, a work he was to conduct again – four hours before he died.*

*Yet Jiggs was not left behind on Royal Occasions. Lieutenant Colonel Jaeger rather liked him and I know Jiggs had a soft spot for Lieutenant Colonel Jaeger. It had to be, for the one existed not without the other. Each was each, and the whole man was, as the death notices so properly put it, Lieutenant Colonel Jiggs Jaeger. Victorian obituaries had it that "a light has gone out". It has, indeed, and what a dull world it is going to be for we dullards who are left behind. I would give the last few years of my life to know what Jiggs said on meeting* THE *Judge."*

Perhaps the last words should be those of Lieutenant Colonel Sir Vivian Dunn, writing an appreciation in *Fanfare 1971* and referring to Jiggs as "*... a man of deep personal integrity who combined the quality of a dedicated professional with a mercurial character, an engaging personality and an irrepressible sense of humour*".

CHAPTER 15

# CODA

Jiggs had collected a large and comprehensive library of music scores and text-books and it was Eileen's wish that this collection should be presented to the Royal Marines School of Music for use by its students. 'The Colonel Jaeger Collection' as it became known, included 192 scores by Bach, Mendelssohn, Mozart, Elgar, Handel and Tchaikowsky with works including concerti, symphonies, quartets, overtures and choral compositions, all of which reflected Jiggs's great musical taste and interest. The textbooks comprised some 47 volumes by such renowned music teachers as Tovey, Kitson, Forsyth, Buck, MacPherson and many others. The *Blue Band Magazine* in December 1971 recorded that *"The Royal Marines School of Music is indebted to Mrs Eileen Jaeger for this magnificent music library which we are proud to accept as a tribute to his memory."*

This, of course, rather begs the question as to why Eileen chose to pass it to the Royal Marines and not to Kneller Hall. It appears that the Army showed no real willingness to take it whereas Sir Vivian Dunn, although by now retired, had been somewhat more sympathetic towards helping her.

A number of awards were set up in Jiggs's memory:

**The Jaeger Trophy** – presented by the Transport Golf Society, to be awarded to the Company Band giving the best concert in the winter season at Kneller Hall.

**The Jaeger Memorial Fund** – established by the National Association of Boys' Clubs

**The Colonel Jaeger Trophy** – Crawley Youth Band

**The Jaeger Memorial Cup** – Junior Musicians' Wing, Guards Depot

**Memorial Book** – Musicians' Chapel – The Church of the Holy Sepulchre, Holborn

On a practical note, Jiggs and Eileen had always lived in Army married quarters, which Eileen was now obliged to vacate. They had never bought a place of their own and there was insufficient savings, so Eileen lived for a while with Maureen. She was offered a place in a SSAFA officers' home in Wimbledon,

219

Queen Alexandra's Court and lived there until she became ill, living her last two years in a nursing home and flat near Maureen. Following Eileen's death in 2002, Jiggs's ashes were removed from the Chapel and, with those of Eileen, were scattered in the grounds of Kneller Hall between the main building and the Morris Hall, marked by a new plaque.

*The Memorial Garden at Kneller Hall. The plaque for Jiggs and Eileen is on the left of the picture*

More than forty years on, Jiggs is still fondly remembered and oft talked about with everyone having a particular tale to tell. Indeed at a concert on the bandstand at Eastbourne in the 1990s the very mention of his name by the conductor brought an immediate round of applause. Many people have recalled the great kindness he showed to them but it was his sense of fun for which he is specially remembered.

Colin Casson had been principal cornet with the Irish Guards and, since leaving them, had a long career as one of the country's leading trumpet players. In his memoirs, *Blowing My Own Trumpet* he recalled the day in June 1978 when the Queen officially opened the Welsh College of Music at Roath Park in Cardiff. Colin was then responsible for the college's brass ensemble, which was to play a fanfare to announce the Queen's arrival. Afterwards, he was in the line-up to be presented to Her Majesty, proudly wearing his Brigade of Guards tie. As the Queen approached, the Principal of the College introduced Colin as *"an ex-member of your Guards, Ma'am"*.

*"Really! Which one?"* asked the Queen.

*"Irish Ma'am – with Major Jaeger"*

*"Ah! Dear Jiggs,"* replied the Queen, moving on to the next in line

On 13th June 2009 the 1st Battalion Irish Guards had the honour to troop its Queen's Colour at the Queen's Birthday Parade. The music for the parade was selected by the Major General Commanding the Household Division based on suggestions made by the Director of Music of the Irish Guards, Major Philip Shannon MBE (who in turn had received a little prompting from his Band Secretary!). The marches chosen included two from Jiggs's pen, *Freedom of Windsor* and *Blue Plume*.

A few days after the parade the Band Secretary took a telephone call from a lady asking if she could speak to someone about the music played on the parade as she thought that she recognised one of the marches as being composed by her father. When asked her father's identity she replied something along the lines of, *"Oh, I don't suppose anyone there now will have heard of him but he was your Director of Music in the 1950s and 60s."* The response was something like, *"Oh, you must be Maureen,"* and she was clearly somewhat taken aback to find that her father was far from forgotten: quite the opposite.

The result was an invitation for Maureen to come to the barracks to renew her acquaintance with the band, backed up the following day by a telephone call from Major Shannon more or less insisting that she paid the band a visit, something that was soon arranged.

Maureen trained as a Chartered Physiotherapist at King's College Hospital in Denmark Hill during the early 1960s and after a few years working for the NHS started a private practice in Hertford. Now retired, she can devote her time to pursue her hobbies, which include classical music, making fancy scarves to sell at craft fairs, cryptic crosswords and reading poetry. She has three children: Nicola (Nicki) was born in 1965, Mark in 1967 and Caroline in 1973.

The band has since hosted several visits including one in 2010 when Maureen, Nicki and her sons Taylor (now 16) and Keaton (12) came to see the Band and watch the form-up for Guard Mounting. All the music played that day was composed or arranged by Jiggs and clearly a good time was had as Maureen returned a few weeks later for a repeat performance, this time in the company of her brother Chris and his wife, Liz.

Chris spent 6 months at Pirbright with the Brigade Squad, the potential officer squad from all the Guards regiments, doing basic training and was rather amused that, *"Dad came down for my passing out parade, but got waylaid having drinks with old friends, and missed it."* However, Chris chose not to pursue an army career and completed a degree in History and Education at Reading University,

*Maureen with her daughter, Nicki, and grandsons Taylor (left) and Keaton (front)
visiting the Band of the Irish Guards*

*Maureen (left) Chris and Liz*

teaching for 18 years and also working as a freelance actor and professional drummer. However, his big success has been in the world of the theatre, clearly inheriting his father's skills for knowing what attracts an audience.

He is now the Chief Executive of Worcester Live, which runs Huntingdon Hall and the Swan Theatre. In 2002 he started the Worcester Festival, which has been highly successful with 650 events in August 2011. In addition, Chris started a two-week annual outdoor Shakespeare Festival in 2007, now coming up to its sixth year. He wrote the Historic Ghost Walk of Worcester in 2008, now an award-winning tourist attraction, and in September 2012 he opened the Swan Theatre School for would-be professional performers, preparing them for auditions and drama school. He was commissioned to write the lyrics for a Worcestershire Song Cycle by the Three Choirs Festival, which was premiered in 2011.

Jiggs's mother married 'Uncle Ern' in 1927 to become Mrs Mina Broadhurst; she died in 1940.

His brother, George, had a very varied life, living in Australia from 1930–1945 and again from 1962–1969, and in Canada from 1954–1962. He was to spend about twenty years as a minister, including the war years as a chaplain in the Australian Army, and another fifteen years as a teacher, as well as in various other occupations including the civil service. He died on 24th September 1991 in the Royal Free Hospital.

His sister Irene's first marriage brought two daughters, Rita and Sheila (who had seven children between them) and a handicapped son who had to be brought up in a home. Irene's marriage broke up during the war but she was happily remarried a few years later to one of George's work mates. She died in Clatterbridge Hospital, Bebington, Wirral from breast cancer in April 1969, aged 59, and her son died a few months later.

Mina's son with 'Uncle Ern', Bob, (Jiggs's half brother) had been a bomber pilot with the Royal Air Force during the war and afterwards qualified as a commercial pilot working for British Overseas Airways Corporation (BOAC).

# APPENDIX

# JIGGS'S MUSIC

Jiggs composed a considerable number of marches and other compositions which retain a firm place in the repertoire of the Band of the Irish Guards today, including an arrangement of *If You're Irish* and *Begorrah* which graces so many great parades. He once made a tongue-in-cheek arrangement of the *Wedding March* for an officer's wedding, with all sorts of tunes coming into it, such as *Post Horn Galop*, ending with a trumpeter sounding the *Mount*!

Chris recalls his composing: *"He did it everywhere – on coaches, trains, planes, etc. He had a fantastic 'ear' – everything in his head, didn't need to hear it. He composed a lot at Caterham on the odd day off which was normally during the winter (following a rained-off Guard etc.). He used to put the whole day aside, sharpen about six 4B pencils, put on both bars of the electric fire, and just work. He sometimes wanted to play it to me but was frustrated that he was a very poor pianist."*

His marches include:

**Berkeley's Dragoons** – the regimental quick march of the 4th Hussars

**Blue Plume** – written, of course, for the Irish Guards and taking its title from the plume of St Patrick's blue, worn by all ranks in their bearskins.

**Tent Twelve** – as far as can be ascertained, Tent Twelve was effectively a club formed by officers in the 2nd Battalion Coldstream Guards while they were stationed in Kenya for two years in the early 1960s. The club had a reputation for enjoying a 'convivial atmosphere', not to put it too mildly, and despite being an Irish Guardsman, Jiggs, also partial to a good party, was engaged or involved to the extent that he was asked to write a march for the club; it includes a quotation from *Figaro* in the trio.

**Double X** – the Band of the Irish Guards made regular visits to Northern Ireland where the Mayor would always present them with a case of Double X beer. The first section of the march rather gives the impression of someone being a little unsteady as a result.

*'Genius at Work'. His office door was adorned with a large sign 'Jaeger' taken from the clothing manufacturers.*

**Paddy's Day** – a full length march in which he "elongated" (his word) the theme of the regimental march, St Patrick's Day

**Jigger's Ajaunt**

**Jigger's Corn** – Jiggs was commissioned to write these as a play-out for cinema-goers. *Jigger* was, of course, Jaeger, and Corn? – he said it was corny music!

**Canada on the March** – written for a tour of Canada, originally with the title *Toronto City*. The march cleverly uses *Alouette* as the counterpoint to the repeat of the first section with *The Maple Leaf Forever* as the bass section and *O Canada* as the counterpoint in the Grandioso. In 2006 the Canadian Branch of the International Military Music Society was asked to nominate a march to represent their nation on a compact disc of marches from around the world and selected this march in preference to anything from Canadian composers.

**Commonwealth on the March** – based on melodies from the Commonwealth including *Sarie Marais, The Maple Leaf Forever, Waltzing Matilda* and *Now is the Hour.*

**Old Pops** – based on *California Here I Come, If You Knew Suzie* and *The World is Waiting for the Sunrise* with a short snippet from *She Loves You* as the bridge passage, something that was to cause him copyright problems.

**Dominique** – the song made popular by the Belgian 'Singing Nun' *Sœur Sourire* in the 1960s. Jiggs arranged the song as a quick march to be played at the Queen's Birthday Parade 1965 and also in the form of a patrol.

**If You're Irish and Begorrah!** An arrangement that has virtually become the signature tune of the Band of the Irish Guards

**Freedom of Windsor** – a slow march composed for the occasion when the Foot Guards were granted the Freedom of Windsor in 1968. The march fell into disuse for many years but was revived for the Queen's Birthday Parade of 2009.

**British Week Brussels (BWB)** – based on two traditional Belgian tunes and composed for the British Week in Brussels in 1967 at which Jiggs was the Senior Director of Music

**Whitehall March**

**Rienzi** – slow march based on themes from Wagner's opera

**Eileen Allanah** – a slow march in ¾ time of the lovely Irish air and also including Mountains of Mourne and Wild Colonial Boy.

**Green Leaves of Summer** (Tiomkin) – arranged as a slow march for the Inspection of the Line at the Queen's Birthday Parade 1965.

**ACF March** – for drums and bugles, written for the Army Cadet Force

**Music on Command** – the signature tune to the BBC series of that name, also used for a number of years to introduce the BBC television coverage of the Queen's Birthday Parade

**Harvest Recessional** (Recessional Extemporisations on the Harvest Hymns) – played at a Harvest Thanksgiving Service in Liverpool Cathedral.


**Further Jaeger Arrangements held in the Irish Guards Band Library:**

Brigadier Wellington-Bull (Stanford)
Costa Brava
Crest of the Wave (Reader)
Darby O'Gill
Easter Parade (Berlin)
Fantasy Overture (Bush)
Forty Years On
Funiculi Funicula (Denza)
Glory (Rimsky-Korsakov)
The Happy Land (Reader)
Hello Dolly (Herman)
Heroic March (Montgomery)
The Holy Ground
I Was Glad (Parry)
I'll Always Be Irish (Sherman) – from the musical 'The Happiest Millionaire'
Kathleen Mary (Whiteley)
Maigret Theme (Grainer)
The Minstrel Boy

Mortify Us By Thy Grace (Bach)
News Scoop (Lewis)
Picaroon (Green)
Praise My Soul (Goss)
Precision (Dumont)
Si Beag Si Mor (O'Carolan)/Let Erin Remember
Sonata Pathetique (Beethoven)
Telstar (Meek)
Toy Grenadier (Ewing)
The Toy Trumpet (Scott)
Trumpet Voluntary (Clarke)
Waltzing Matilda (Cowan)
A Walk in the Black Forest
Wedding March (Furwood)
Yellow Submarine (Lennon and McCartney)

# SUBSCRIBERS

**Richard Balmforth**

**Brian Bennett**

**John Bladon**

**Günther Blödorn** – son of half-sister Irene

**George Boote** – Irish Guards Band January 1988 – April 2006

**Mrs Pearl Bradford** – neighbour at Guards quarters in Caterham 1955–1959

**Gordon Brown**

**Musn. Tony Brownlow** – Irish Guards Band 1961–1966, formerly Gordon Highlanders

**E. Bury** – I have known Colonel Jaeger's son, Chris, for many years and have always enjoyed following army bands.

**Colin Casson** – principal cornet soloist 1953–1960

**David Cawdell** – Irish Guards Band 1956–1959, the best years of my whole life

**Jim Clow**, Irish Guards Band 1965–1978

**Harry Copnall** – Jiggs's bass drummer at 16 years old. His endearing term for me was "you big egg".

**John Cox**

**Jim Davies** – IMMS UK Secretary

**Bruce Douglas** – Irish Guards Band

**A. C. Easdown** – Complimented by him to my B/M (5th Dragoon Guards) which led to my promotion.

**Nigel P. Ellis**, IMMS UK (Founder) Branch

**Peter Elsdon** – memories of a post-concert chat (1956) after playing my request for 'Pineapple Poll'

**Malcolm Ellingworth** – I was Jiggs's chess partner and co-driver in his Mini estate car 1962–1969

**John P. Evans** – Irish Guards Band 1961–1964; RAMC 1952–1954 (bass 'G' trombone)

**J. A. C. Fleming**

**Clive Folkard** – Jiggs's number one fan

**Patrick Fox**

**N. R. Frost** – ex 4th Hussars Band. Joined at Tidworth on their return from Malaya; the new BM was W.A. Lloyd. I played flute and alto sax

**John Gale** – Arts Committee member, National Association of Boys' Clubs

**N. R. R. Gravett**

**Paul Harvey** – Irish Guards Band 1953–1956, Kneller Hall professor 1969–1995

**Charles Healey** – Irish Guards Band 1959–1966 – clarinet player

**WO1 (BM) R. Hibbs**, The Duke of Edinburgh's Royal Regiment (Berkshire and Wiltshire) 1959–1971

**Mr Patrick Higgins**

**Brian Hill** – IMMS Committee Member

**Mr Victor Hillsdon** – IMMS member

**Terry Hissey**

**Carl** and **Karen Hughes** – grand-nephew and wife

**Carla Hughes** – great-grand-niece

**Gemma Hughe**s – great-grand-niece

**Julia Hughes** – great-grand-niece

**Sheila** and **John Hughes** – niece and husband

**Dr Mark** and **Patricia Hughes** – grand-nephew and wife

**Matthew Hughes** – great-grand-nephew

**Mr Rodney Illsley**

**Frank Isaac**

**Anja Jäger** – daughter of half-brother Hans

**Ernst Jäger** – half-brother

**Hans Jäger** – half-brother

**Han Jürgen Jäger** – son of half-brother Hans

**Musn Michael Jeans**, oboist, Irish Guards Band 1957–1960

**Kenji Kawashima** – Japanese researcher in worldwide military music and bands

**John Kroes** – Vice Chairman NL Branch IMMS

**Edgar Liddle** – IMMS UK Treasurer

**D. R. McAndrew**

**John McGarry** – he auditioned me with Captain Gerry Horabin (RE) at my school in Belfast

**David McLellan** – Irish Guards Band 1964–1973

**Hilary Marsh** – my memories of Jiggs are from a period in the early sixties when his daughter Maureen and I were training to be physiotherapists. His generosity enabled us to go to the Festival of Remembrance at the Royal Albert Hall where he was conducting the massed bands, and also to a G&S show at Sadler's Wells in which the Irish Guards played a fanfare. My friendship with Mo continues to this day.

**Michael William Martin** – friend of the family

**Mike Martin** – served in the Irish Guards Band 1954–1981; Band Sergeant Major 1971–1981

William Martin
Michael Masani – close friend of the family
Philip Mather
D. E. Messer
Miss Martina Millard
Keith Moss MBE
Major John Mott
Sgt Matt Newberry – Irish Guards Band 1961–1976
Lance Sergeant J. G. Odell – Coldstream Guards 1961–1964
Musn Keith Oxley – Irish Guards Band 1958–1961
Keith Perry
Frank Prosser – joined the band as principal horn in 1962; retired 1984.
Alan Purdie
Valerie Pusey – niece: he was my Uncle Jiggs!
WO2 (ABSM) Bob Rawson, Band Secretary, Irish Guards Band 1974–1996
Brian Reynolds – light music aficionado/composer
Colin Ridgers
Musn Roger Rostron – Irish Guards Band 1956–1959
Les Scriver MBE
Duncan K. Sedgwick
Graham Sheldon – Irish Guards Band 1978–2000 (BSM). Listening to many of the 'old and bold' when I joined the band they all referred to Jiggs as a legend.
Geoffrey Shepheard – Member IMMS
Rita and Edward Shillito – niece and husband
Steven, Bernard, Peter, Paul and Rosemary Shillito – grand nephews/nieces
Ron Shooter, IMMS
Averil and George Skinner – band fans with many great memories
Peter B. Smith MBE – an admirer and friend
R. A. Spencer
John Stone – ex Welsh Guards RHQ. As a member of the Guards Chapel Choir in 1953 I recall Jiggs's superb accompaniment for services.
Helga Teichler – daughter of half-sister Irene
Bernard Tupman
Frank Tyler – Jiggs well remembered from concerts on Plymouth Hoe in the 50s; I was 10!
Mike Webster – nephew of Jiggs, son of Vic Webster MBE, ARCM - remember an overseas trip to UK where Jiggs arranged seats for Trooping the Colour.
John Weeks – Irish Guards Band 1953–1956; clarinettist and occasional pianist
Barry S. Willis
W. S. Wolfe
Rev'd. D. J. Woodward
Robert Young – a great respecter of Major Jaeger, as he was when I was in the band.

# Some Portraits of Jiggs

# INDEX